World Market Transformation

To the surprise of many, regionally embedded clusters of small to medium-sized businesses have continued to exist in spite of industrialisation and mass production. While scholars have discovered that the advantages of embeddedness in terms of industrialisation were situated in interfirm cooperation and conflict-resolving mechanisms, it is far less clear how changing historical circumstances on the world market, i.e. globalisation, affected such systems.

Taking a look inside Leipzig, a capital of the global fur industry between 1870 and 1939 with its numerous highly specialised businesses, both in production as well as trade, *World Market Transformation* examines the robustness of district firms within the highly volatile international fur business. This book examines how firm embeddedness not only served to overcome challenges related to industrialisation, but also strengthened the abilities of cluster firms to deal with changing world market circumstances.

World Market Transformation integrates the "interior-biased" research tradition on local business systems and industrial districts into the "exterior" fields of global and transnational history. It is demonstrated that the local business district not only emerged because of the expansion of international trade, but that district processes of interfirm cooperation also gave shape to the spatial distribution, conventions, and structures of the very same world market. The analysis of embedded communities thus offers an important instrument to examine phenomena of economic globalisation, but also how such macroeconomic developments have been shaped and actively constructed by local actors.

Robrecht Declercq is Postdoctoral Researcher connected to the research group Communities, Connections, and Comparisons (CCC) and the History Department of the Ghent University, Belgium.

Routledge International Studies in Business History

Series Editors:
Jeffrey Fear and Christina Lubinski

For a full list of titles in this series, please visit www.routledge.com

World Market Transformation

Inside the German Fur Capital
Leipzig 1870–1939

Robrecht Declercq

Routledge
Taylor & Francis Group

LONDON AND NEW YORK

First published 2017 by Routledge

2 Park Square, Milton Park, Abingdon, Oxfordshire OX14 4RN
52 Vanderbilt Avenue, New York, NY 10017

Routledge is an imprint of the Taylor & Francis Group, an informa business

First issued in paperback 2019

Copyright © 2017 Taylor & Francis

Library of Congress Cataloging-in-Publication Data
A catalog record for this book has been requested

ISBN: 978-1-138-66725-9 (hbk)
ISBN: 978-0-367-24300-5 (pbk)

Typeset in Sabon
by Apex CoVantage, LLC

Contents

Tables, Figures and Photographs

Tables

Figures

Photographs

Acknowledgments

Even though writing and researching can at times be a solitary experience, this book would not have been possible without the cooperation and support of numerous people. It was Frank Caestecker who first encouraged me many years ago to develop a PhD project that would ultimately lead to this book. I also want to express special thanks to Eric Vanhaute, the co-supervisor of my PhD, for allowing me the opportunity to spend a few semesters working and writing at the Ghent University and also for his continuing support of this book project.

This book is primarily the result of this research project that was kindly funded by the European University Institute. In a first stage, it primarily centered on migration and immigrant entrepreneurship linked to the fur capital. Over the course of time, the focus rapidly shifted onto both the local and global business networks of this business cluster. At the EUI, I was fortunate to enjoy the support of incisive and open-minded research promotors. I would like to thank in particular Heinz-Gerhard Haupt, who supervised the entire project from beginning to end, and Youssef Cassis, who assumed a role well beyond that of "a second reader" when this work increasingly ventured into the turf of business history. His ideas and suggestions for approaching both the complexity and richness of the Leipzig fur businesses have been invaluable. The support of my former colleagues at the Institute James White, Daniel Knegt and Moritz von Brescius, and his wife Meike, is similarly appreciated. They rank amongst the "unhappy few" who had the honour to comment on my first messy drafts and papers, allowing me to polish and refine my thoughts. My good friend Julia Heydorn from Hamburg/Amsterdam helped me on the administrative front, especially with German translations and drafting letters.

Retracing the global networks of the Leipzig fur industry has brought me to various places across Europe and the world, to archives and libraries large and small inside Germany, but also to London and as far as Canada. My appreciation goes particularly to the staff of both the Leipzig city and state archives of Saxony in Leipzig, where I spent most of my research time. Having to live on modest travel grants, I am grateful to Susanne Schramm (Leipzig) and Jan-Hendrik Schulz (Berlin) for their very kind hospitality.

I should also credit Alexander von Schwerin, who initiated me to the archival sources on fur farming in the beginning stage of my research. The contact with my Ghent colleagues of the Communities, Connections and Comparisons research group and the Ghent Centre for Global Studies was tremendously helpful in giving shape to the global framework of this book. Special thanks also to the series editors of the Routledge Series on International Business, Christina Lubinski and Jeff Fear, for supporting this book project. The same goes for the former editor of the series, Ray Stokes, whom I met at the very first conference I did as a young scholar and who has always been supportive to my work.

The most important words of thanks however come last. These are devoted to my family. My wife Griet had to share me with a bunch of businessmen in Leipzig during the last six years. I am unbelievably fortunate with her kind patience, love and support. This book is dedicated to her.

Abbreviations

BArch   Bundesarchiv
HStA   Haupstaatsarchiv Dresden
IPA   Internationale Pelzfachausstellung
RM   Reichsmark
StA-L   Staatsarchiv Leipzig

Part I

Local Business Systems and Global Trade

1 The Leipzig Fur Capital as a Local Business System

Industrial Districts as a Capitalist and Industrial Alternative

While it has been commonly held that both industrialisation and the emergence of modern capitalism favoured the rise of big business, regionally entrenched and decentralised modes of production have nonetheless persisted. The concept of the industrial district, which describes the spatial concentration of small to medium-sized firms and highly specialised businesses in a single sector, is one of the most well-known examples of such an alternative to big business and corporate development. The robustness of such business clusters has been traditionally explained by a number of advantages that were generated through the proximity of firms: a predisposition towards cooperation, interfirm networks, and the sharing of innovations or technological modifications. These factors mitigate the costs of decentralisation. A large number of historical studies have used the concept of the industrial district in order to revive 'alternative' worlds of industrialisation, to nuance the spread of corporate development, and to modify teleological accounts of modern capitalism. Most importantly, the emphasis on geographically defined industrial districts has revealed regional dynamism and economic variety beneath the level of national statistics.

Many bookshelves can be filled with examinations of the industrial district and regional economics. Why is another study about the industrial district necessary? This book is an answer to a remarkable lacuna in historical research, namely the link between the industrial district and the 'outside world' that remains largely understudied. Historical studies have predominantly portrayed industrial districts as self-contained entities.[1] This tunnel vision stands in sharp contrast to the recent interest in contemporary globalisation and its impact upon regional economic entities. While many predicted the final decline of such alternative structures because of imminent global competition, this did not happen. Moreover, despite threats from globalisation, the idea that regions (rather than nation-states) are the dynamic units of economic development is surfacing ever more strongly.[2] Currently the capacity to adapt to global competition is seen as constitutive of modern industrial districts and business clusters or, for that matter, of regional economies in general. However, industrial districts' ability to engage in global networks is anything but a recent phenomenon. Therefore, this book examines historical patterns of the adaptation of the industrial district to global competition and the framework in which industrial districts engaged in patterns of internationalisation.

The choice to study one such industrial district, the Leipzig fur industry concentrated in the region of Saxony, is almost self-evident. Saxony historically harboured many industrial districts and clusters that were governed by moderate-sized and highly specialised businesses. Saxon businesses were, on average, much smaller than in the Reich and the family firm was an important institution. Equally, the region's economy was surprisingly well oriented towards the world market. The small businesses in Saxony typically produced consumer goods and depended upon foreign imports and the export of finished products. The fur industry concentrated in and around Leipzig formed an archetypal Saxon industrial district, but it was also exceptionally well orientated towards the world market. The district's many small to medium-sized firms were specialised in an aspect of the production process, ranging from trade (wholesalers and brokers) to manufacture (dressing and dyeing). The fur industry of Leipzig was arguably one of the most agile business clusters in Saxony and perhaps even Germany. Over the course of several decades, they turned the city into a leading German and even international fur capital, and managed to retain this position even after World War I. These firms constructed the fur capital as part of one of the most well integrated historical world markets. Like for so many business clusters, the capacity of firms in the region to engage in global networks remains largely un-investigated. This book is about more than the fur industry itself. It is about the abilities of embedded business to deal with capricious globalisation tendencies and processes of world market transformation. How did industrial districts and decentralised business structures manage being part of an economy oriented towards the world market? Taking a look inside the Leipzig fur capital and its global networks, this book hopes to shed light on this blind spot in business history.

The Industrial District and Regional Business Clusters: A Short History

The economist Alfred Marshall was one of the first to wonder about the persistence of small firms in a world where the growth of big business seemed unstoppable. In 1922, he described the cost-saving benefits for firms located near external factors such as available labour, related industries, relevant knowledge, and exploitable resources. Marshall argued that these factors prevented the growth of "internal economies," by which he meant the growth of a firm. In other words, he asserted that large-scale production could also be achieved by groups of small-sized and specialised firms that were concentrated in a given geographical area.[3] A high number of specialised firms contributed to various stages of the production process and thereby prevented its concentration in a single corporate firm. Marshall called these localised production structures "the industrial district."[4]

The concept of the Marshallian industrial district (and by extension the link between location and firm behaviour) remained rather obscure for several decades because of the success of Chandlerian-inspired management literature. It re-appeared much later in post-war Italian economic sociology, where scholars put industrial districts at the centre of a post-Fordist economic growth model (the so-called "third Italy").[5] In the 1980s, Giacomo Becattini and others claimed that the post-war Italian economy saw the emergence of 60 to 100 industrial districts, which became leading economic entities in a period when major Italian firms were declining.[6] This new research trend introduced a few novel elements into industrial district theory, such as the importance of artisans and a shared 'attitude' to work.[7] Based on the Italian district, this research formed the canonical neo-Marshallian definition of the industrial district, which stressed the importance of external economies arising from the concentration of small to medium-sized business with characteristics derived specifically from Italian cases, such as the presence of artisans and an 'industrial culture' that gave a common identity to members of the district.[8]

Researchers who were dissatisfied with the conflation of the industrial district and the Italian context presented several new cases outside Italy. This expanded the research field and led to the development of new concepts to describe variations of business concentration, such as decentralised production systems and non-industrial districts. The variety exhibited in different regional case studies and dissatisfaction with the Italian-based neo-Marshallian research obviously put the consensus regarding the definition of the concept under pressure. In this book, I adhere to the definition advanced by Jonathan Zeitlin, who has returned elasticity to the notion and ousted some of the highly specific and context-bound elements of the concept. Zeitlin defined an industrial district as a "geographically localized productive system based on an extended division of labor between small and medium-sized firms specialized in distinct phases or complementary activities within a common industrial sector."[9] Importantly, Zeitlin stresses that essential elements are variable (the degree of localization, the extent of interfirm networks, etc.), which means that diversity is inherent to his definition of the concept.

An important advantage is that Zeitlin's definition brings the concept of the industrial district again closer to another popular concept that also deals with the phenomenon of business concentration, the 'cluster' as coined by Michael Porter. Michael Porter has defined clusters as "a geographically proximate group of interconnected companies and associated institutions in a particular field, linked by commonalities and complementarities."[10] Both concepts stress the importance of interfirm relations and tendencies to cooperate as part of the business structure.[11] The concept of the industrial district remains however more compelling in terms of the interfirm relations. The concept involves the presence of coordination mechanisms and fluid cooperation that checks opportunistic behaviour.[12] Social relations in the district actively direct economic behaviour and include tacit agreements, a sense of local belonging, the coordination of actions, joint investment, and cooperation.[13] In addition, the 'cluster' encompasses a wider economic structure and stresses externalities that are much broader in scope to those typically considered in industrial district theory. Porter's concept also involves configurations other than those existing uniquely of SMEs. While both concepts share many similarities and an intellectual pedigree, the size distribution of the firm, embeddedness and decentralisation differentiate both concepts. Therefore, industrial districts can be seen as a specific type of business cluster, characterised by multitudes and highly specialised SMEs.[14]

Contributions and Shortcomings

The concept of the industrial district has played a fundamental role in economic and business history. Firstly, industrial districts have been used to point to decentralised forms of production, like the varieties of capitalism that manifest in regional spaces. In this sense, the discussion about industrial districts is often merged with the debate surrounding the importance of economic regions.[15] Franscesca Carnevali stated that this extensive literature has the common goal of "seeking to provide an alternative tale of industrialisation than that found in the broad sweep of national statistics."[16] She argued that regionalised and localised economic structures often contributed to national economic growth in ways that are often overlooked in aggregate studies. As such, the contribution of the industrial district lies in the scale of analysis used. The discovery of industrial districts and regionalised economic structures has led to their deployment in a variety of national economic contexts.[17] With regard to industrialisation in England, John Wilson and Andrew Popp have established the importance of industrial districts and business clusters in processes of industrialisation and economic growth by assembling a variety of case studies ranging from the Lancashire textile industry to the Manchester industrial district. In doing so, they illustrated that industrialisation in Britain was a highly regionalised affair.[18]

Secondly, the industrial district concept has been used to illustrate the continued persistence of small business and the alternative forms of production associated with them, despite corporate development and the expansion of mass production. The work of Charles Sabel and Jonathan Zeitlin is highly prominent in this research field. They have argued that moderate-sized firms and specialised business communities were often very innovative when it came to the alteration of production processes or the development and exploitation of new technologies.[19] They called their methodology the "historical alternative approach."[20] Sabel and Zeitlin argued that mechanisation and industrialisation occurred much more incrementally than is commonly assumed and that business entities like industrial districts were often creative in finding hybrid forms of production.[21] Geographical clustering and collective action were key in developing flexible methods of industrial production. Similarly, Philip Scranton pointed to the importance of "specialty" production in the US' second industrial revolution. He looked at manufacturing units that focused on the production of custom-made nonstandard goods. Scranton argued that there was "no better location [for specialty production] than an urban industrial district."[22] Due to this extensive literature, the view that industrial districts determined regionalised economic growth and that they formed alternatives to the realms of big business and mass production is now widely accepted.

However, this book is devoted to an entirely different dimension of industrial districts. Whilst historical research on the industrial district has affected mainstream economic and business historiography, a considerable caesura continues to exist, one that has surfaced strongly the recent years. Overwhelmingly, industrial districts have been studied as closed internal circuits, supposedly based on local vitality alone and propelled solely by internal dynamism. Jonathan Zeitlin noted that "the self-contained character of the districts has been overstated even for earlier periods" and acknowledged that a research deficit exists in regards to "the district and the wider world." He added that "indeed it would . . . no doubt prove illuminating to investigate more closely . . . local firms' own attempts at internationalisation."[23] In particular, transborder activities, the impact of globalisation and de-globalisation, and, more generally, the reactions and strategies triggered by these macroeconomic developments have been ignored. Business historian Jean-Claude Daumas came to a similar conclusion in that there was a deficit "in connecting the local dynamics of the district to the global context."[24] He stated that it would be better to cease studying districts in terms of industrialisation so as to "confront the history of the district with challenges coming from the outside," by which he meant external market forces and global competition.[25] Patrick Fridenson noted that it is necessary "to get the ID out of the enclave" and "to question the relationship between the interior and the exterior dimension of the industrial district."[26]

In contrast, the relationship between internationalisation and the dynamics of contemporary industrial districts constitutes a growing body of literature. Becattini noted that "the nature, intensity and scale of the increasingly global networks that IDs have to engage with for knowledge, goods/services and labour exchanges . . . underlies their capacity to reproduce themselves."[27] In the light of contemporary economic globalisation, some have suggested the existence of a paradox: the local clustering of firms continues to be a defining feature of the modern world economy despite the spread of commercial activity due to economic globalisation.[28] Others have stressed that contemporary industrial districts can survive precisely by engaging in international activities. Such analysts warn about "over-embeddedness" or the danger of being "locked in." In order to survive global competition, local production systems need "to tap into external markets and engage in translocal interaction."[29] While the globalization of the last decades has attracted much attention, there is no reason to reject the premise that transborder activities and connections to the outside world have always been an integral dimension of industrial districts.[30] Decentralised economic structures and small businesses have continued to exist not only when industrialisation and mass production transformed the economy but also whilst they endured dramatic shifts in the world market and suffered from exogenous shocks.

The lack of interest in the nexus between the industrial district and the outside world is quite surprising given that the role of businesses in worldwide economic integration today forms a growing research field in historical sciences. Geoffrey Jones in particular has called for a more systematic understanding of businesses as agents in shaping the globalised world economy since 1850. Jones noted that "firms drove globalisation by creating trade flows, constructing marketing channels, building infrastructure and creating markets."[31] The obvious problem, however, is that such research tends to focus on the actions of big business in the form of multinational corporations. Without denying that the spread of multinational enterprises qualitatively changed the structure of the world economy, the attempts of smaller firms at internationalisation both existed and contributed extensively to processes of international economic entanglement.[32] In addition, the multinational enterprise does not own the monopoly on transborder business activity. There is thus, again, no reason to assume that small district firms remained on the sidelines.

I believe that this statement will be clarified by introducing the case study of the Leipzig fur industry when considered as part of the open Saxon economy. Most of the industries in Saxony harboured characteristics that correspond to those of decentralised production systems, as is evinced by the high number of small to medium-sized businesses and highly specialised enterprises. Simultaneously, the economy of the region was strongly oriented to the world market. A description of Saxony's economic landscape will exemplify the lacuna in the research regarding industrial districts and the outside world in a more concrete fashion.

Business in Saxony as World Market Players

Anyone who studies German history will acknowledge that the region of Saxony is an almost inevitable example for those who point to regional developments that ran counter to social, economic, and political developments on the national level.[33] Many socio-economic developments made Saxony unique. First of all, Saxony was the most densely populated territory in Germany. The population increased from 1,178,802 inhabitants in 1815 to 2,556,244 in 1871. Secondly, Saxony was already an industrialised territory with the majority of the population working in industry or craft manufacture. Saxony was thus one of the first regions to industrialise, in contrast to Germany's belated industrialisation.[34] Kiesewetter argued that Saxony industrialised relatively early because it became dependent upon agricultural imports after the loss of territory to Prussia as a consequence of the Napoleonic wars.[35] Others have stressed that early industrialisation was related to what could be called forms of proto-industrialisation, based on dexterous artisans or labourers working in Saxon towns.[36]

However, in his seminal book called *Industrial Constructions*, Gary Herrigel was one of the first to place emphasis on business structure rather than early industrialisation to define Saxony as an exceptional regional economy in Germany. Herrigel claimed that there were many vibrant worlds of moderate-sized business in Germany when mass production was increasingly becoming the norm. Herrigel characterised a number of German regions as "decentralized industrial orders," which he described as being "composed of multitudes of highly specialised small- and medium-sized producers and a host of extra-firm supporting institutions. Together, these actors have created (and in part were created by) a system of governance mechanisms that stimulate innovation, socialize risk, and foster adjustment, at both local and national levels, in ways that do not resemble the governing principles of either markets or hierarchies."[37] Herrigel advances a definition of the decentralised production order redolent of the industrial district. He portrayed the kingdom of Saxony as a "primary location of this pattern of productive organisation."[38]

Herrigel rightly pointed to the fact that the firms in Saxony were on average much smaller in terms of the number of employees than in the Reich. Middle-sized firms (with between 6 and 50 workers) "were present in percentages much above the Reich average."[39] The decentralised business structure encompassed many sectors domiciled in the region, both in the heavy and light industries. Family-owned small businesses produced textiles, instruments, brushes, textiles, furs, books, toys, and garments, but the model also encompassed heavy industries like machine construction.[40] Whereas this decentralised form of production was to be found in sectors across the entire region, many of the entrepreneurs decided to settle in urban industrial districts. Even the textile industry, the largest industry sector in Saxony, tended to be geographically clustered on a subregional level, like the textile garnishing industry in Annaberg-Buchholz.[41] The book-printing industry and the fur industry in Leipzig are also well-known examples of industrial districts in Saxony.[42]

The fact that Saxony was strongly oriented towards the outside world, in spite of its decentralised business structure, added an extra dimension to its regional particularism. The Saxon economy was mainly composed of "consumer goods industries . . . that basically imported raw materials from abroad and exported manufactured goods to other regions in Germany and the whole world."[43] Werner Bramke wrote that "industries based on consumer goods offered great opportunities on the world market" and claimed that "Saxony remained the number one German export region until the eve of the Second World War."[44] Many world-famous products, from

Rudolf Sack's universal plough to the coffee filter, were launched from businesses domiciled in the triangle between Leipzig, Dresden, and Chemnitz.[45] Industrial districts in Saxony, the fur industry foremost among them, were international players. Internationalisation occurred not despite the omnipresence of small firms but apparently because of it: "the Saxon entrepreneur was typically an owner or a partner in a textile, machine constructing, or any other small export-oriented manufacturing company that was not very large."[46] However, the openness of the decentralised production order had a downside too: arguably, crises raged more intensively and had a deep impact upon economic stability.[47] Due to Saxony's dependence on world trade, the region was often labelled with the rather unflattering description, "the storm centre of the trade cycle" (*Wetterwinkel der Konjunktur*).[48] Indeed, the negative consequences of economic crises and the First World War affected Saxony's consumer and world market–oriented economy much more deeply than it did other German regions.[49]

The lacuna concerning the industrial district and the outside world is thus replicated here in the description of the Saxon economy. Saxony was characterised as a decentralised mode of production but it was by no means locked in. Nonetheless, the historical structure of the Saxon economy in relation to its openness remains surprisingly understudied. It is precisely the interplay between decentralised production and the region's status as the storm centre of the trade cycle that will be questioned in this book. Why was one of the most decentralised regions (from a business point of view) also a leading actor on the world market? This main question can be split in two main subquestions. Firstly, how did firms in the region participate in processes of internationalisation? Secondly, how did the vibrant communities of small businesses persist despite being part of the "storm centre of the trade cycle"? In other words, I question how businesses in structures like the industrial district dealt with exogenous pressures. While one of Saxony's business clusters is advanced as a case study, the question is highly relevant and transplantable for historical business clusters as well. Another good example outside Saxony is the textile and linen industries in northern France. Considered strongly concentrated regional business clusters, most studies devoted little attention to the interesting links this cluster produced abroad—for instance, the many outward business investments from Lille and Roubaix in Poland.[50] This book is therefore as universal as possible in the questions and answers it seeks, and a study that is much more than a historical analysis of Leipzig as a fur capital. It is meant to give an impulse to business history by proposing historical research into districts and the outside world.

In the few paragraphs set out above, regional business decentralisation and world market orientation give rise to an intuitive assumption of incompatibility. However, this assumption might be the wrong way of looking at the problem. As suggested above, the decentralised business structure was perhaps not inimical to an orientation to the world market. Would it not make sense to ask the question in another way: how did the integration of the region in the global economy shape business structures in Saxony? Given that industries depended upon import and export trade, it makes sense to claim that firms in Saxony were proficient organisers of transborder trade. So why should the regional decentralised business structure not dovetail with its relative openness? Reversing the question means we see how district firms organised and constructed governance mechanisms in order to deal with being part of an open economy. In other words, the hypothesis is that linkages between the industrial district and the outside world have to be studied in the very characteristics of the industrial district itself. To put it differently, the external economic context is not external *per se* but constitutes one of the variables that determined processes and features typical of a district.

Indeed, the integration of the industrial district in the wider context entails a different reading of firm behaviour in local networks and collective actions, like patterns of local collaboration, appropriation of new technologies, and the sharing of innovations. In what ways could these aspects be advantageous in an open economy, if indeed they were? There are certain indications that support my hypothesis. Michael Schäfer argued that the strong family ties woven into the management of the smaller Saxon business were decisive in their willingness to protect the firm in times of crisis. Traditionally, such ties are seen as a handicap to organisational development.[51] In addition, Stephen Gross has stressed the importance of regional associations and umbrella institutions, like the Leipzig trade fairs, that coordinated the interests of small business operating in an international context.[52] But also other historical clusters, like the flower producers in the Westland region of Holland during the twentieth century have shown the ability to "constantly re-invent themselves."[53] Indeed, this is part of the hypothesis that I will employ here: local coordination mechanisms and institutions, which account for the industrial districts' productive competitiveness, also gave district firms the ability to deal with challenges abroad and to participate in processes of internationalisation. I claim that this also encompassed other elements of the industrial district, like sharing and local collaboration.

Having established this claim, it is necessary to establish a framework in order to examine collaboration at the local level (i.e. the industrial district) in interaction with the global level. As mentioned above, given the internal focus, industrial district literature offers no ready-made framework to study the linkages between the industrial district and the outside world. In the next section, I will construct a framework by placing commodity chain analysis into the theory of industrial districts.

Squaring the Circle: Collective Action and a Commodity Perspective

The Industrial District in the Commodity Chain

One problem in creating a framework that enables me to study the industrial district and the outside world is that external relations in industrial district theory remain relatively under-theorised: it has little to say about external relations, global networks, and the overarching market in which the local system is embedded. Since industrial districts are usually formed at the sectoral level (in our case the fur trade), it makes sense to suggest the commodity chain as the appropriate scale for examining the external relationships of the industrial district. There are three main concepts that apply the 'chain' metaphor to the organisation of global production. All of them are concerned with the organisational dynamics of international trade. Wallerstein and Hopkins first coined the concept of the "commodity chain" and defined it as "a network of labor and production processes whose end result is a finished commodity."[54] In 1994, Gereffi constructed a nuanced, expanded, and more 'workable' version of Wallerstein's commodity chain. Gereffi defined global commodity chains (GCC) as "inter-organisational networks clustered around one commodity or product, linking households, enterprises, and states to one another within the world economy. . . ."[55] Although Gereffi acknowledges the importance of social embeddedness of economic organisation in the chain, in practice the GCC focussed on contemporary large firms to set the terms of trade in a chain. A third variant are the so-called global value chains (GVC), an extension of Porter's concept of the value chain that usually applies to the internal organisation of firms. The GVC draws on transaction cost theory and describes activities that are "transactional linkages connecting firms in a global chain."[56] As such, GVC theory emphasises interfirm networks as the defining feature of global production. Differences in chains are explained by transactional variations in interfirm networks that can range on a continuum from arm's length transactions to hierarchies.[57] The nature of the networks between these firms determined the type of chain.

Two problems arise from linking industrial district theory to any of the chains mentioned above. The first is that firm behaviour seems overdetermined by chain structures, foremost interfirm hierarchies, and that agency is lacking in understanding commodity chains. As Ian Hunter has thoughtfully noted: "the commodity chain is not separate from the actors that constitute the chain, and these actors retain agency to determine the shape and characteristics of the chain."[58] The second is of an epistemological nature, since both theories seem difficult to reconcile in terms of networks. Jennifer Bair was the first to diagnose the tension between the "embedded network approach . . . and the network-based analysis of economic organization in . . . the global chains literature."[59] In essence, commodity chain concepts have claimed that global networks mattered in the organisation of the world economy but at the same time rendered local production systems like the industrial district abstract, despite Geriffi's claims regarding "social embeddedness of economic organisation."[60] Proponents of industrial district theory or regional business entrenchment have done the opposite, based on the Granovetterian notion that economic activity is embedded in social networks that are bound to place. As such, the external relations of such district structures have scarcely been theorised. Both concepts are therefore difficult to reconcile. In global value chains, for instance, economic organisation is synonymous with the networks between firms across geographic space. However, it says little about processes of local collaboration in terms of global networks. This means that we can only examine separate firms of the district and not its collective action.

Attempts to combine commodity chain analysis with embedded forms of business largely fail to resolve the aforementioned problems. An interesting solution is offered by economic geographers who suggested examining the district's "lead firms." In this perspective, it is argued that several district firms emerge as "lead firms" in the district, heading processes of transformation and organising transborder activities in times of increased competition. Lead firms in the district are thereby considered as mediators or "gatekeepers" of changes in the global value chain. Lead firms in the district were seen as gate-openers to foreign markets and as pioneers in adjusting the district to global competition. However, this approach remains highly problematic for my claims because "the district as a system" is reduced to the "individual strategies of a few firms through which the local system can open its structure."[61] Local lead firms are undoubtedly important but such a perspective does not give us what we need, namely reconciliation between local social cohesion and global economic organisation. The actions and strategies of local lead firms can only be a part of the story. Indeed, Zeitlin, a much-cited author in the "local lead firms" approach, did describe the emergence of large lead firms in the district as just one of the *possible outcomes* in the context of increased global competition. According to Zeitlin, an equally important outcome was "more continuous and more formalized collaboration among economic actors."[62] In other words, paying attention to lead firms is important, but I should also factor local collaboration and collective action into the external relations of the district. However, now we are back to square one. How does local collective action fit into the commodity chain?

The Commodity Chain as a Conceptual Tool

Even though we should be aware that commodity chain theory and industrial district theory have differences that are difficult to reconcile, such a combination is not impossible. A possible reconciliation lies in the flexible usage of commodity chains as a conceptual tool. Steven Topik has made the case that "historians can use it [commodity chains] as a conceptual tool for understanding the complicated business of global trade rather than as a normative theory capable of generating refutable hypotheses."[63] Topik underscored the importance of approaching commodity chains as concrete social relations between historical actors.[64] The flexibility usage of the commodity chain resolves a number of problems mentioned above. Most importantly, agency is restored since looking at the impact of local transformations upon the organisation of international trade are central to his analysis: "Topik shows how changing patterns of popular consumption in foreign markets, as well as particular characteristics of the locations in which production takes place shape the geography of international production and trade networks."[65] Importantly, commodity chains as a perspective or a tool "are attentive to the influences of the global on the local and vice versa."[66] Indeed, many historians seeking to map the interaction between the local and the global, or in crafting a global history of a single commodity, like cotton or diamonds, have embraced the commodity chain as a conceptual device.[67] The commodity chain perspective and its interactive view on the local and the global allow us to examine the industrial district and the outside world.

The emphasis on the entanglement between the local and the global, which such perspectives have in common, resolves some of the theoretical issues raised above as well as practical ones. It follows from this perspective that every commodity chain is unique in the sense that it is rooted in varying social contexts. Therefore world markets or global commodity chains are social constructions too. According to Kenneth Pommeranz, "the market structures that are basic to our world were not natural or inevitable, always latent and waiting to be opened up, rather markets are, for better or worse, socially constructed and socially embedded."[68] Just like every individual industrial district has it owns particularities, every commodity chain develops its own logic.[69] This flexibility and variety bring us back to a central premise employed by both the chain and industrial district perspectives, namely that "economic activities are coordinated through non-market relationships."[70] In other words, just as the economic action in the district is socially situated, commodity chains contain the basic premise that "all economic action is socially embedded" as well.

Of course, a view that the economic system runs on "noneconomic" bases is far from new and can be traced back to as early as Polanyi, who noted that "man's economy as a rule is submerged in his social relations."[71] Both commodity chain analysis and industrial district theory are indebted to this view but they have situated the existence of social relations in different spheres, in global networks on the one hand and local networks on the other. However, the view that both local embeddedness and world markets are socially constructed offers the potential to research the interaction between those levels. This allows us to think about "world markets" as social constructions, forged by global and local actors. Following Dejung and Petterson, it is precisely the local and global interactions that define global markets, the rules of which are "constructed by public and private, local, national and global actors."[72] Accordingly, social action shapes markets and economic relations at different levels: local, national, and global. This view has two implications. Local collective action can have a bearing on the outside world, shaping the rules, norms, and practices of the world market. Equally, the structure of the world market can deeply affect local communities. In other words, processes of local embedded interaction were constitutive to the world market, and the industrial district was not invulnerable to exogenous developments. This social perspective on world markets best reflects a combination of micro- and macro-level analysis on the problem of economic organisation and scale. In constructing such a framework, this book is indebted to those "commodity-centred views" that have provoked a growing body of literature on the history of economic globalisation and capitalism.

The Leipzig Fur Capital as an Industrial District and the Problem of World Market Transformation

I have proposed the Leipzig fur industry as the subject of this research because it nicely represents the dualism between decentralised production and openness to the world market that was sketched out in the theoretical framework and was one of the central characteristics of Saxony's economy. The Leipzig industry was a typical Saxon business system. Specialisation among the many small and medium-sized firms of the fur industry, which numbered around 1,000 in 1925, was the norm. Steffen Held characterised the fur district as a symbiotic concentration of wholesale merchants, factories for dressing and dyeing skins, and fur tailors in small to medium-sized workshops.[73] The Leipzig fur industry took the form of an industrial district during the long nineteenth century and it was the most dynamic in the years leading to the First World War and in the 1920s. Its demise began after the economic and financial crisis of 1930–1931.

Importantly, the industrial district of the Leipzig fur industry emerged while being part of a highly globalised trade. The fur trade was responsible for the largest frontier expansion in world history since demand for furs pushed traders and explorers into the Siberian frontiers and the woodlands of North America.[74] By the end of the nineteenth century, the fur trade was still internationally oriented, involving peripheral subarctic regions, new areas of production in Central Asia and South America, and emerging marketplaces and manufacturing centres in North America, Great Britain, and continental Europe. Consumers of furs were to be found virtually everywhere on both sides of the Atlantic. Just when the fur industry emerged in Leipzig, the international fur trade was undergoing rapid transformation. Due to intensive hunting and growing demand, resources became scarcer, which pushed price levels upwards.[75] Furthermore, fur garments were no longer exclusively destined for the upper classes but came into the reach of an ever-increasing range of customers. Consequently, global competition over resources intensified. Fur companies entered frontier zones and new markets surfaced, especially in North America.[76] The transformation of the international trade in the nineteenth century, particularly the increase in consumption, undoubtedly offered opportunities, but heightened global competition was potentially threatening. Nevertheless, the fur industry in Leipzig somehow dealt with changing international patterns and managed to operate in a highly volatile world market.

It is in regards to the industrial district of the Leipzig fur industry between 1870 and 1939 that I pose my central research question: why did a business structure characterised by a plethora of small businesses become so successful while participating in a volatile world market? This main question has been split in two major subquestions that form the core of the book. Firstly, how do economic agents of the industrial district deal with exogenous challenges? Secondly, how do firms of the district participate in processes of internationalisation? In following a commodity perspective on the industrial district, I will employ an actor-oriented approach to processes of collective action, the behaviour of individual firms in the district, and how such patterns interacted with the structure of the world market. Local developments will still form the main thread of the narrative but will be connected to broader macroeconomic developments produced by international linkages of the commodity chain. Employing a commodity perspective means examining the world that is brought together by the commodity of furs, the main actors that held it together (lead firms, governments, economic institutions, and market conventions), and how these institutions interacted with the local business system.

It is my central hypothesis that responses to external challenges, most particularly collective action and interfirm collaboration, were inherent characteristics of the industrial district. Collective action and interfirm collaboration will thus be central to the analysis. As Carnevali argued, collective action formed a "strategic choice" and was not simply a natural by-product of firm interconnectivity in the industrial district.[77] Mechanisms and forms of cooperation were actively and intentionally constructed and remodeled. It thereby follows that collective and creative action was also potentially developed towards exogenous challenges. Such an intentional view on collective action is stressed in economic sociology. Herrigel noted that "joint creative action" of economic actors takes place in various social contexts "confronted with global pressures" in order to modify inherited organisational forms and governance mechanisms.[78] Joint creative action against global pressures arises because actors collectively define, understand, and resolve challenges in a common environment.[79]

In order to reconstruct reactions against world market transformation, the book will employ a broad sweep on collective action in the industrial district. Besides focusing on interfirm networks in the fur industry, it will integrate networks with other local stakeholders from related industries or services that were arguably embedded in the local structure or somehow connected to the fur cluster. As such, collective action encompasses many actors gathered around the local fur industry, like financial institutions, university scientists, political stakeholders, and related industries. Indeed, local banking is often identified as an important agent of local business systems.[80]

The connection of district firms to such stakeholders and associated economic agents was also connected to the growing complexity of global markets, which increasingly depended upon knowledge, scientific development, the availability of financial resources, and the standardisation of payment traffic. As such, I hope to encompass the full complexity of local dynamics and interactions with global developments. The forms of collaboration will be exhibited via typical interfirm cooperation, whether formal or informal. In addition, collective action also entails the creation of new economic institutions, the conversion of old institutions, and interpersonal networks.

Nevertheless, while stressing the importance of collective action, the book continues to pay attention to the behaviour of individual firms and the heuristic potential of the so-called lead firm as a pioneer of new projects and global relations. Lead firms are autonomous on the world market and capable of developing strategic decisions with a strong impact locally.[81] As it was impossible to gather comparable information on each business, the concept of the lead firm was a useful guideline in representing material on individual firms. Five of these firms were selected for this research, namely Biedermann, Eitingon, Ariowitsch, Friedrich Erler and Theodor Thorer. They were chosen primarily on the basis of their international autonomy but are not exhaustive given the source material available. However, they reflect different business traditions (industrial, Jewish, gentile, etc.) of which the business district was composed. Most of them also had a strong local affiliation, but it will be questioned in the book how their international role dovetailed with local embeddedness. Through the lens of lead firms, I hope to gain a deeper insight into processes of collaboration and collective action and also international developments. The lead firms selected for this research, and the business origins they reflect, are discussed more in depth in the next chapter.

Ambitions and Pitfalls

On a final note, I should address a number of potential pitfalls that one can come across while examining the relationship of the district and the outside world. Firstly, it would be risky to present industrial districts as entities that automatically exhibit a high degree of social homogeneity and harmony.[82] To avoid uncritically painting a picture wherein actors cooperated willingly in order to overcome internal and exogenous challenges, a critical stance vis-à-vis the nature of collaborative networks and attention to potential conflicts is required. Somewhat related to this is the problem of performance and collective action. Business history is generally more interested in success than failure.[83] As such, research into industrial districts runs the danger of overstating the dynamism and flexibility of the district. However, success is not the ultimate yardstick by which dynamism in the industrial district can be measured. In fact, declining districts and regions can develop the same mechanisms for sharing and collaboration as successful ones.[84]

The analysis will be aware of the failure and ineffectiveness of joint efforts in order to enhance our understanding of the interaction between the local and the global.

Jewish entrepreneurship, secondly, is another aspect of this research, especially in relation to the cluster as a social structure, that needs specific attention. A large percentage of the Leipzig fur cluster existed of Jewish entrepreneurs originating from different waves of immigration to Saxony. They were mostly active in the commercial segment of the Leipzig fur industry, representing 50% thereof.[85] Nevertheless, Jews in the Leipzig fur industry were one of the few sectors in Germany in which their concentration was strongly pronounced. Their occupation in the international fur commerce made them not different from German-Jewish entrepreneurship more generally, which excelled in making transnational links and integrating (German) industries and trade abroad. Being internationally oriented, Jewish entrepreneurship often evokes the stereotypical image of 'rootless capitalism,' and therefore seems at odds with firm embeddedness. Many have already argued against this rather one-sided stereotypical image. Mosse stated that Jewish entrepreneurs generally combined international orientation with national and local sympathies. He argued that Jewish entrepreneurs more often worked as integrative forces, integrating local industries with new national and international import, export and capital markets.[86] In addition, Jewish entrepreneurs also played a role in 'horizontal' integration, being very active in business and trade associations. What is more, from an international point of view, Jewish entrepreneurs were often to be found back in cluster-like and place-bound activities, like diamond cutting and garment production. This is perhaps less so in Germany, but here also Jewish entrepreneurs played constitutive roles in several historical (and internationally oriented) German business clusters, albeit to lesser extents than in the Leipzig fur industry, like the Solingen steel industry, the textile industry in Baden-Württemberg and closer, the book-printing industry in Leipzig.[87] So a combination of 'internationally oriented' Jewish entrepreneurship and local embeddedness is not mutually exclusive.

Admittedly, the omnipresence of Jewish entrepreneurs undoubtedly gave the fur cluster, in comparison to other business clusters, an advantage in constructing links to the world market. Yet, this book will seek to clarify the relationship between their international, cosmopolitan even, orientation and the embeddedness of the fur cluster. The book will therefore additionally analyse the role of Jewish entrepreneurship in the fur cluster as a social structure, as an integrative force both locally and internationally of the fur cluster. The book will adhere to the view that Jewish entrepreneurs were not exponents of rootless capitalism, but an essential part of the fur district engaging in its many forms of collective action, and actively engaging in relations with gentile as well Jewish firms. In other words, many of these firms exhibited lead firm behaviour but were active participants in local collective action. At first glance, there is good reason to propose this subhypothesis.

Their presence followed the life cycle of the district as an essential part of the cluster when tides were shifting in the 1920s; only with the deliberate obstruction and later annihilation of Jews in Germany, the Jewish character of the Leipzig fur cluster tragically disappeared.

The third obvious pitfall is that every collective action initiative in the district is read in the light of exogenous change. Certainly, it is not my aim to explain all collective action and local modifications from the point of view of external developments. In fact, industrial district processes are conditioned by multi-layered developments and always need to be situated in local, national, and global contexts. The fact of the matter is that the last category has been hitherto omitted. The intent of this work is precisely aimed to highlight the interaction of local business systems with the outside world. Nevertheless, I do not downplay the important and often unique character of local developments. Rather, the book hopes to contribute to the literature by pointing to the transregional and even global dimensions of local action, the international impact of small business, and exogenous factors that play a much larger role in the emergence and dynamism of industrial districts and regional business systems than has been previously assumed.

It is exactly this regional dimension of processes of world market integration that needs further elaboration. The fact that Saxony was at the forefront of processes of globalisation adds an important dimension to historical globalisation debates, which are largely biased towards examining the national context in interaction with the global. Sebastian Conrad argued that globalisation profoundly restructured national politics and societal processes in Wilhelminian Germany.[88] The same goes for businesses and economic actors. Cornelius Torp described how "the challenges of globalisation" caused major cleavages in Germany's economic policy, thereby exacerbating internal struggles.[89] The fact that regions like Saxony were at the forefront of processes of globalisation seems to be the missing link in this new research. However, proponents of the globalisation perspective are not unaware of this. Conrad, for one, added that it would be useful to add localities and regions to the "nation and globalisation" debate by examining "how globalisation not only caused the restructuring of the nation, but also left its traces at the level of the local, and indeed was simultaneously shaped by local developments. . . ."[90] The book hopes to increase our understanding of regional insertion into processes of globalisation.

Structure of the Book

Rather than following a chronological 'rise and fall' narrative that follows the Leipzig fur industry from its rapid emergence in the second half of the nineteenth century to its demise after World War II, the chapters of the book are divided into three large parts that centre on several patterns of collaboration that surfaced because of exogenous pressures. Such a structure also ekes out some of the foreign operations of the firms of the industrial district. In this Part I, "Local Business Systems and Global Trade (1850–1914)," the introduction presented here is followed by two main chapters in which a transnational perspective is employed to look at the emergence of the Leipzig fur industry as an industrial district in the period from 1850 until World War I. Central to the analysis is the question of why the district emerged whilst being part of a changing world market in furs and how regional openness shaped the emergence of the fur industry. Chapter 2 focuses largely on endogenous factors that determined the emergence of the Leipzig fur industry but also looks at how local processes of interfirm cooperation were constitutive in participating in global commerce. Chapter 3, then, more closely analyses the internationalisation strategies pursued by fur firms in the district, which allowed the integration of the capital in the rapidly changing world market of furs.

The three chapters of Part II, "Finding World Market Alternatives 1903–1939," are devoted to district dynamics of a completely different nature. These chapters examine how Leipzig firms reacted to structural resource shortages and world market disruptions. It deals with the sourcing of new resources required because of exogenous pressures on the supply of raw materials to the district. These are presented as alternatives to the world market. They have one major theme in common: all these chapters highlight the importance of collective action on the one hand and links between the fur district and scientific research on the other hand. The association between the fur industry and scientific research allowed for one of the most profound innovations in the modern fur industry, that of fur farming. The experimental niche of fur farming offered a series of tremendous opportunities to the local business system in overcoming problems connected to international resource markets. Chapter 4 highlights a peculiar case of fur farming in the German empire, that of sheep farming in the German colony of South West Africa and the role of the Leipzig fur industry in this colonial project. Chapter 5 discusses the impact of World War I upon the industrial district. The chapter focuses on processes of resource substitution as well as problems of business organisation in times of war in order to acquire a better understanding of the district in the period between the wars. Chapter 6, the last chapter of this part, investigates the impact of the debut of modern fur farming inside Germany in the 1920s. The links between farming and the agricultural sciences with the industrial district are also considered.

Part III, "World Market Restructuring and the Fur Capital," examines the industrial district in a time when the global trade in furs had undergone some major modifications. The three chapters highlight several aspects of the way in which the fur industry in Leipzig managed these exogenous challenges. Chapter 7 examines the impact of world market restructuring in the early 1920s upon individual businesses in the district. It delves into the problem of local lead firms, investigating whether several emerging lead firms disturbed firm balance in the business community and to what extent they contributed to the restoration of international links. Chapters 8 and

9 then look at how patterns of collective action allowed for the renewal of links between the Leipzig business community and the outside world. Chapter 8 discusses interfirm cooperation in the creation of new market institutions that re-established the position of Leipzig as an international centre of the fur industry. Chapter 9 discusses the dynamism of interfirm cooperation in the construction of an international trade exhibition, the IPA in 1930, which was designed as an international promotion campaign for the Leipzig fur industry. The book ends with an analytical conclusion, preceded by an epilogue that discusses the decline of the industrial district in the 1930s and places emphasis on continuing, if eroding, patterns of collaboration in the Leipzig fur industry in times of economic turmoil and political upheaval.

Notes

1 Zeitlin, "Industrial Districts and Regional Clusters," 234.
2 Applegate, "A Europe of Regions: Reflections on the Historiography of Sub-National Places in Modern Times."
3 Becattini, "Italian Industrial Districts: Problems and Perspectives," 84.
4 Becattini, Bellandi, and De Propris, "Critical Nodes and Contemporary Reflections on Industrial Districts: An Introduction," xvi.
5 Asheim, "Industrial Districts: The Contributions of Marshall and Beyond," 419.
6 Becattini, "Italian Industrial Districts," 83.
7 Daumas, "Dans la 'boîte noire' des districts industriels," 15.
8 Daumas, "Territoire et Dynamique Industrielle: Des Configurations Historiquement Différenciées (France, XIXe–XXe Siècles)," 76.
9 Zeitlin, "Industrial Districts and Regional Clusters," 222.
10 Porter, "Locations, Clusters, and Company Strategy," 254.
11 Zeitlin, "Industrial Districts and Regional Clusters," 226. However, the authors stress that cooperation is not a 'natural feature' of the ID and that mechanisms to resolve conflicts and institutions to foster cooperation are consciously created.
12 Zeitlin, "Industrial Districts and Regional Clusters," 225.
13 Todaro and Smith, *Economic Development*, 321.
14 Porter and Ketels, "Clusters and Industrial Districts: Common Roots, Different Perspectives," 181. "Clusters are a much broader concept, encompassing many possible configuration of companies and institutions. Clusters encompass the configuration found in IDs, so that IDs are one type of a cluster."
15 Swedberg, *Principles of Economic Sociology*, 65.
16 Carnevali, "Crooks, Thieves, and Receivers: Transaction Costs in Nineteenth Century Industrial Birmingham," 534.
17 Judet, "La genèse du district industriel de la vallée de l'Arve: la construction sociale d'un territoire sur la longue durée (fin XVIIIème–début XXème siècles)."
18 Popp and Wilson, "Districts, Networks and Clusters in England: An Introduction," 15.
19 Sabel and Zeitlin, "Historical Alternatives to Mass Production," 143–4.
20 Zeitlin, "The Historical Alternatives Approach," 121.
21 Sabel and Zeitlin, *World of Possibilities*, 31.
22 Scranton, *Endless Novelty*, 18–19.
23 Zeitlin, "Industrial Districts and Regional Clusters," 234.
24 Daumas, "Districts industriels," 142.
25 Ibid., 152.
26 Fridenson, "Conclusion," 428–9.

27 Becattini, Bellandi, and De Propris, "Critical Nodes and Contemporary Reflections on Industrial Districts," xxi.
28 Scott and Storper, "Regions, Globalization, Development," 193.
29 Bathelt, "Cluster Relations in the Media Industry," 110.
30 Amdam and Bjarnar, "Globalization and the Development of Industrial Clusters." In their article, the authors chiefly considered the interaction between clusters and globalisation since the 1960s.
31 Jones, "Globalization," 153.
32 Petersson, "Das Kaiserreich in Prozessen Ökonomischer Globalisierung," 59.
33 Retallack, "Society and Politics in Saxony in the Nineteenth and Twentieth Centuries," 396.
34 Hahn, *Die industrielle Revolution in Deutschland*, 29.
35 Kiesewetter, "Bevölkerung, Erwerbstätige und Landwirtschaft im Königreich Sachsen 1815–1871," 103.
36 Blaschke, "Grundzüge sächsischer Geschichte zwischen der Reichsgründung und dem Ersten Weltkrieg," 22.
37 Herrigel, *Industrial Constructions*, 1.
38 Ibid., 20. Along with other regions like Württemberg, Baden, the Bergland, the Siegerland, and the left bank of the Rhine.
39 Ibid., 45.
40 Warren, *The Red Kingdom of Saxony; Lobbying Grounds for Gustav Stresemann, 1901–1909*, 2.
41 Schramm, *Konsum und regionale Identität in Sachsen 1880–2000*, 35.
42 Karlsch and Schäfer, *Wirtschaftsgeschichte Sachsens im Industriezeitalter*, 113–17; Keiderling, *Aufstieg und Niedergang der Buchstadt Leipzig*.
43 Szejnmann, *Nazism in Central Germany*, 6.
44 Bramke, "Einleitung," 19.
45 Müller, *Der Kaffeesatz im Löschpapier*.
46 Schäfer, *Familienunternehmen und Unternehmerfamilien*, 11.
47 Bramke, "Einleitung," 19.
48 Szejnmann, *Nazism in Central Germany*, 6.
49 Schäfer, *Familienunternehmen und Unternehmerfamilien*, 32.
50 McKay, *Pioneers for Profit*, 50.
51 Schäfer, *Familienunternehmen und Unternehmerfamilien*, 204.
52 Gross, "Selling Germany in South-Eastern Europe," 29.
53 Tavoletti and te Velde, "Cutting Porter's Last Diamond," 308.
54 Hopkins and Wallerstein, "Commodity Chains in the World-Economy Prior to 1800," 159.
55 Gereffi, Korzeniewicz, and Korzeniewicz, "Introduction: Global Commodity Chains," 2.
56 Reinert et al., *The Princeton Encyclopedia of the World Economy*, 180.
57 Gereffi, Humphrey, and Sturgeon, "The Governance of Global Value Chains," 84.
58 Hunter, "Commodity Chains and Networks in Emerging Markets," 278.
59 Bair, "Analysing Global Economic Organization," 340.
60 Humphrey and Schmitz, "How Does Insertion in Global Value Chains Affect Upgrading in Industrial Clusters?" 1019.
61 Chiarvesio, Di Maria, and Micelli, "Global Value Chains and Open Networks: The Case of Italian Industrial Districts," 334.
62 Zeitlin, "Industrial Districts and Regional Clusters," 231.
63 Bair, "Global Commodity Chains: Genealogy and Review," 17.
64 Topik, Marichal, and Frank, "Commodity Chains in Theory and in Latin American History," 14.
65 Bair, "Global Commodity Chains," 17.
66 Bentley, "Regional Histories, Global Processes, Cross-Cultural Interactions," 7.

67 Beckert, *The Empire of Cotton*; De Vries, *Diamonds and War*.
68 Pomeranz and Topik, *The World That Trade Created*, x.
69 Topik and Wells, "Warenketten in einer globalen Wirtschaft," 684.
70 Humphrey and Schmitz, "How Does Insertion," 1019.
71 Polanyi, *The Great Transformation*, 48.
72 Dejung and Petersson, "Introduction: Power, Institutions, and Global Markets," 7.
73 Held, "Juden in der Leipziger Rauchwarenwirtschaft," 269.
74 Brook, *Vermeer's Hat*, 44.
75 Richards, *The Unending Frontier an Environmental History of the Early Modern World*.
76 Osterhammel, *Die Verwandlung der Welt*, 555.
77 Carnevali, "Crooks, Thieves, and Receivers'," 535.
78 Herrigel, *Manufacturing Possibilities*, 2.
79 Ibid., 7.
80 Bonin and Eck, "La Problématique de L'adaptabilité Du Banquier," 15. The criterion is whether such actors collectively defined challenges from abroad and derived a sense of belonging to the industrial district.
81 Chiarvesio, Di Maria, and Micelli, "Global Value Chains and Open Networks, 335.
82 Zeitlin, "Productive Alternatives: Flexibility, Governance, and Strategic Choice in Industrial History," 75.
83 Rossfeld and Köhler, "Bausteine des Misserfolgs: Zur Strukturierung eines Forschungsfeldes," 10.
84 Zeitlin, "Industrial Districts and Regional Clusters," 222.
85 Kowalzik, *Jüdisches Erwerbsleben in der inneren Nordvorstadt Leipzigs 1900–1933*, 66.
86 Mosse, "Jewish Entrepreneurship in Germany," 63.
87 Rosenthal, "Jews in the Solingen Steel Industry Records of a Rhineland City"; Keiderling, *Aufstieg und Niedergang der Buchstadt Leipzig*.
88 Conrad, *Globalisation and the Nation in Imperial Germany*, 2–3.
89 Torp, *Die Herausforderung der Globalisierung*, 21.
89 Conrad, *Globalisation*, 397.
90 Ibid.

References

Amdam, Rolv Petter, and Ove Bjarnar. "Globalization and the Development of Industrial Clusters: Comparing Two Norwegian Clusters, 1900–2010." *Business History Review* 89, no. 4 (January 2015): 693–716.

Asheim, Bjorn T. "Industrial Districts: The Contributions of Marshall and Beyond." In *The Oxford Handbook of Economic Geography*, edited by Gordon L. Clark, Maryann P. Feldman, and Meric S. Gertler, 413–31. Oxford, England; New York: Oxford University Press, 2000.

Bair, Jennifer. "Analysing Global Economic Organization: Embedded Networks and Global Chains Compared." *Economy and Society* 37, no. 3 (2008): 339–64.

———. "Global Commodity Chains: Genealogy and Review." In *Frontiers of Commodity Chain Research*, edited by Jennifer Bair, 1–35. Stanford, CA: Stanford University Press, 2009.

Bathelt, Harald. "Cluster Relations in the Media Industry: Exploring the 'Distanced Neighbour' Paradox in Leipzig." *Regional Studies* 39, no. 1 (2005): 105–27.

Becattini, Giacomo. "Italian Industrial Districts: Problems and Perspectives." *International Studies of Management & Organization* 21, no. 1 (April 1, 1991): 83–90.

Becattini, Giacomo, Marco Bellandi, and Lisa De Propris. "Critical Nodes and Contemporary Reflections on Industrial Districts: An Introduction." In *A Handbook of Industrial Districts*, edited by Giacomo Becattini, Marco Bellandi, and Lisa De Propris, xv–xxv. Cheltenham, UK: Edward Elgar, 2009.

Beckert, Sven. *The Empire of Cotton*. London: Macmillan, 2004.

Bentley, Jerry H. "Regional Histories, Global Processes, Cross-Cultural Interactions." In *Interactions: Transregional Perspectives on World History*, edited by Jerry H. Bentley, Renate Bridenthal, and Anand A. Yang, 1–14. Honolulu: University of Hawaii Press, 2005.

Blaschke, Karlheinz. "Grundzüge sächsischer Geschichte zwischen der Reichsgründung und dem Ersten Weltkrieg." In *Sachsen im Kaiserreich: Politik, Wirtschaft und Gesellschaft im Umbruch*, edited by Simone Lässig and Karl Heinrich Pohl, 11–29. Weimar: Böhlau, 1997.

Bonin, Hubert, and Jean-François Eck. "La Problématique de L'adaptabilité Du Banquier." In *Les Banques et Les Mutations Des Enterprises: Le Cas de Lille-Roubaix-Tourcoing Aux XIXe et XXe Siècles*, edited by Hubert Bonin and Jean-François Eck, 13–25. Villeneuve d'Ascq: septentrion, 2012.

Bramke, Werner. "Einleitung." In *Wirtschaft und Gesellschaft in Sachsen im 20: Jahrhundert*, edited by Werner Bramke, 9–27. Leipzig: Leipziger Universitätsverlag, 1998.

Brook, Timothy. *Vermeer's Hat: The Seventeenth Century and the Dawn of the Global World*. New York: Bloomsbury Press. Distributed to the trade by Macmillan, 2008.

Carnevali, Francesca. " 'Crooks, Thieves, and Receivers': Transaction Costs in Nineteenth Century Industrial Birmingham." *Economic History Review* 57, no. 3 (2004): 533–50.

Chiarvesio, Maria, Eleonora Di Maria, and Stefano Micelli. "Global Value Chains and Open Networks: The Case of Italian Industrial Districts." *European Planning Studies* 18, no. 3 (2010): 333–50.

Conrad, Sebastian. *Globalisation and the Nation in Imperial Germany*. Cambridge; New York: Cambridge University Press, 2010.

Daumas, Jean-Claude. "Dans la 'boîte noire' des districts industriels." In *Les territoires de l'industrie en Europe,1750–2000: entreprises, régulations et trajectoires: actes du colloque international de Besançon, 27, 28 et 29 octobre 2004*, edited by Jean-Claude Daumas, Pierre Lamard, and Laurent Tissot, 9–36. Besançon: Presses universitaires de Franche-Comté, 2007.

———. "Districts industriels: du concept a` l'histoire: Les termes du débat." *Revue économique* 58, no. 1 (2007): 131–52.

———. "Territoire et Dynamique Industrielle: Des Configurations Historiquement Différenciées (France, XIXe–XXe Siècles)." In *Les Banques et Les Mutations Des Enterprises: Le Cas de Lille-Roubaix-Tourcoing Aux XIXe et XXe Siècles*, edited by Hubert Bonin and Jean-François Eck, 75–97. Villeneuve d'Ascq: septentrion, 2012.

Dejung, Christof, and Niels P. Petersson. "Introduction: Power, Institutions, and Global Markets-Actors, Mechanisms and Foundations of Worldwide Economic Integration, 1850–1930." In *The Foundations of Worldwide Economic Integration: Power, Institutions, and Global Markets, 1850–1930*, edited by Christof Dejung and Niels P. Petersson, 1–21. Cambridge: Cambridge University Press, 2013.

De Vries, David. *Diamonds and War: State, Capital, and Labor in British-Ruled Palestine.* New York: Berghahn Books, 2010.

Fridenson, Patrick. "Conclusion." In *Les territoires de l'industrie en Europe, 1750–2000: entreprises, régulations et trajectoires: actes du colloque international de Besançon, 27, 28 et 29 octobre 2004 [Conseil régional de Franche-Comté]*, edited by Jean-Claude Daumas, Pierre Lamard, and Laurent Tissot, 401–23. [Besançon]: Presses universitaires de Franche-Comté, 2007.

Gereffi, Gary, John Humphrey, and Timothy Sturgeon. "The Governance of Global Value Chains." *Review of International Political Economy* 12, no. 1 (2005): 78–104.

Gereffi, Gary, Miguel Korzeniewicz, and Roberto Korzeniewicz. "Introduction: Global Commodity Chains." In *Commodity Chains and Global Capitalism*, edited by Gary Gereffi and Miguel Korzeniewicz, 1–14. Westport: Greenwood, 1994.

Gross, Stephen. "Selling Germany in South-Eastern Europe: Economic Uncertainty, Commercial Information and the Leipzig Trade Fair 1920–40." *Contemporary European History* 21, no. 1 (2012): 19–39.

Hahn, Hans-Werner. *Die industrielle Revolution in Deutschland.* München: R. Oldenbourg, 1998.

Held, Steffen. "Juden in Der Leipziger Rauchwarenwirtschaft." In *Leipzigs Wirtschaft in Vergangenheit Und Gegenwart: Akteure, Handlungsspielräume, Wirkungen (1400–2011)*, edited by Susanne Scholz, 269–85. Leipzig: Leipziger Universitätsverlag, 2012.

Herrigel, Gary. *Industrial Constructions: The Sources of German Industrial Power.* Structural Analysis in the Social Sciences 9. Cambridge, UK: Cambridge University Press, 1996.

———. *Manufacturing Possibilities: Creative Action and Industrial Recomposition in the United States, Germany, and Japan.* Oxford: Oxford University Press, 2010.

Hopkins, Terence K., and Immanuel Wallerstein. "Commodity Chains in the World-Economy Prior to 1800." *Review (Fernand Braudel Center)* 10, no. 1 (July 1, 1986): 157–70.

Humphrey, John, and Hubert Schmitz. "How Does Insertion in Global Value Chains Affect Upgrading in Industrial Clusters?" *Regional Studies* 36, no. 9 (2002): 1017–27.

Hunter, Ian. "Commodity Chains and Networks in Emerging Markets: New Zealand, 1880–1910." *Business History Review* 79, no. 2 (2005): 275.

Jones, Geoffrey. "Globalization." In *The Oxford Handbook of Business History*, edited by Geoffrey Jones and Jonathan Zeitlin, 141–71. Oxford: Oxford Handbooks Online, 2008.

Judet, Pierre. "La genèse du district industriel de la vallée de l'Arve: la construction sociale d'un territoire sur la longue durée (fin XVIIIème–début XXème siècles)." In *Les territoires de l'industrie en Europe, 1750–2000: entreprises, régulations et trajectoires: actes du colloque international de Besançon, 27, 28 et 29 Octobre 2004*, edited by Jean-Claude Daumas, Pierre Lamard, and Laurent Tissot, 323–41. Besançon: Presses universitaires de Franche-Comté, 2007.

Karlsch, Rainer, and Michael Schäfer. *Wirtschaftsgeschichte Sachsens im Industriezeitalter.* Leipzig: Edition Leipzig, 2006.

Keiderling, Thomas. *Aufstieg und Niedergang der Buchstadt Leipzig*. Beucha: Sax-Verlag, 2012.

Kiesewetter, Hubert. "Bevölkerung, Erwerbstätige Und Landwirtschaft Im Königreich Sachsen 1815–1871." In *Region Und Industrialisierung*, edited by Sidney Pollard, 89–104. Göttingen: Vandenhoeck & Ruprecht, 1980.

Kowalzik, Barbara. *Jüdisches Erwerbsleben in der inneren Nordvorstadt Leipzigs 1900–1933*. Leipzig: Leipziger Universitätsverlag, 1999.

McKay, John P. *Pioneers for Profit: Foreign Entrepreneurship and Russian Industrialization, 1885–1913*. Chicago: University of Chicago Press, 2011.

Mosse, Werner. "Jewish Entrepreneurship in Germany." In *Jüdische Unternehmer in Deutschland Im 19. Und 20. Jahrhundert*, edited by Werner Mosse and Hans Pohl, 54–67. Stuttgart: Franz Steiner Verlag, 1992.

Müller, Rita. *Der Kaffeesatz im Löschpapier: sächsische Industrie-Geschichten*. Chemnitz: Chemnitzer Verl., 2006.

Osterhammel, Jürgen. *Die Verwandlung der Welt: eine Geschichte des 19. Jahrhunderts*. München: C. H. Beck, 2009.

Petersson, Niels. "Das Kaiserreich in Prozessen Ökonomischer Globalisierung." In *Das Kaiserreich Transnational: Deutschland in Der Welt 1871–1914*, edited by Sebastian Conrad et al., 49–68. Göttingen: Vandenhoeck & Ruprecht, 2004.

Polanyi, Karl. *The Great Transformation: The Political and Economic Origins of Our Time*. Boston, MA: Beacon Press, 2008.

Pomeranz, Kenneth, and Steven Topik. *The World That Trade Created: Society, Culture, and the World Economy, 1400 to the Present*. Amonk, NY: M. E. Sharpe, 2006.

Popp, Andrew, and John Wilson. "Districts, Networks and Clusters in England: An Introduction." In *Industrial Clusters and Regional Business Networks in England, 1750–1970*, edited by John Wilson and Andrew Popp, 1–19. Burlington, VT: Ashgate, 2003.

Porter, Michael E. "Locations, Clusters, and Company Strategy." In *The Oxford Handbook of Economic Geography*, edited by Gordon L. Clark, Maryann P. Feldman, and Meric S. Gertler, 253–75. Oxford: Oxford University Press, 2000.

Porter, Michael E., and Christian Ketels. "Clusters and Industrial Districts: Common Roots, Different Perspectives." In *A Handbook of Industrial Districts*, edited by Giacomo Becattini, Marco Bellandi, and Lisa De Propris, 172–87. Cheltenham, UK: Edward Elgar, 2009.

Reinert, Kenneth A., Ramkishen S. Rajan, Amy Joycelyn Glass, and Lewis S. Davis. *The Princeton Encyclopedia of the World Economy*. Princeton, NJ: Princeton University Press, 2010.

Retallack, James. "Society and Politics in Saxony in the Nineteenth and Twentieth Centuries." *Archiv Für Sozialgeschichte* 38 (1998): 396–547.

Richards, John F. *The Unending Frontier an Environmental History of the Early Modern World*. Berkeley: University of California Press, 2003.

Rosenthal, Heinz. "Jews in the Solingen Steel Industry Records of a Rhineland City." *The Leo Baeck Institute Yearbook* 17, no. 1 (January 1, 1972): 205–23.

Rossfeld, Roman, and Ingo Köhler. "Bausteine Des Misserfolgs: Zur Strukturierung Eines Forschungsfeldes." In *Pleitiers Und Bankrotteure: Geschichte Des Ökonomischen Scheiterns Vom 18. Bis 20. Jahrhundert*, edited by Ingo Köhler, 9–37. Frankfurt: Campus Verlag, 2012.

Sabel, Charles F., and Jonathan Zeitlin. "Historical Alternatives to Mass Production: Politics, Markets and Technology in Nineteenth-Century Industrialization." *Past & Present* 108, no. 1 (August 1, 1985): 133–76.

———, eds. *World of Possibilities: Flexibility and Mass Production in Western Industrialization.* Cambridge, UK: Cambridge University Press, 1997.

Schäfer, Michael. *Familienunternehmen und Unternehmerfamilien: zur Sozial- und Wirtschaftsgeschichte der sächsischen Unternehmer, 1850–1940.* München: C. H. Beck, 2007.

Schramm, Manuel. *Konsum und regionale Identität in Sachsen 1880–2000: die Regionalisierung von Konsumgütern im Spannungsfeld von Nationalisierung und Globalisierung.* Stuttgart: Steiner, 2003.

Scott, Allen J., and Michael Storper. "Regions, Globalization, Development." *Regional Studies* 41, no. sup1 (2007): S191–205.

Scranton, Philip. *Endless Novelty: Specialty Production and American Industrialization, 1865–1925.* Princeton, NJ: Princeton University Press, 1997.

Swedberg, Richard. *Principles of Economic Sociology.* Princeton, NJ: Princeton University Press, 2003.

Szejnmann, Claus-Christian W. *Nazism in Central Germany: The Brownshirts in 'Red' Saxony.* New York: Berghahn Books, 1999.

Tavoletti, Ernesto, and Robbin te Velde. "Cutting Porter's Last Diamond: Competitive and Comparative (Dis)advantages in the Dutch Flower Cluster." *Transition Studies Review* 15, no. 2 (2008): 303–19.

Todaro, Michael P., and Stephen C. Smith. *Economic Development.* Boston, MA: Addison-Wesley, 2012.

Topik, Steven C., Carlos Marichal, and Zephyr Frank. "Commodity Chains in Theory and in Latin American History." In *From Silver to Cocaine: Latin American Commodity Chains and the Building of the World Economy, 1500–2000*, edited by Steven Topik, Carlos Marichal, and Frank Zephyr, 1–25. Durham, NC: Duke University Press, 2006.

Topik, Steven C., and Allen Wells. "Warenketten in einer globalen Wirtschaft." In *1870–1945: Weltmärkte und Weltkriege*, edited by Emily S. Rosenberg, 589–815. München: C. H. Beck, 2012.

Torp, Cornelius. *Die Herausforderung der Globalisierung: Wirtschaft und Politik in Deutschland 1860–1914.* Göttingen: Vandenhoeck & Ruprecht, 2005.

Warren, Donald. *The Red Kingdom of Saxony: Lobbying Grounds for Gustav Stresemann, 1901–1909.* The Hague: M. Nijhoff, 1964.

Zeitlin, Jonathan. "The Historical Alternatives Approach." In *The Oxford Handbook of Business History*, 120–40. London: Oxford University Press, 2007.

———. "Industrial Districts and Regional Clusters." In *The Oxford Handbook of Business History*, edited by Geoffrey Jones and Jonathan Zeitlin, 219–44. Oxford: Oxford University Press, 2008.

———. "Productive Alternatives: Flexibility, Governance, and Strategic Choice in Industrial History." In *Business History Around the World*, 62–80. Cambridge, UK: Cambridge University Press, 2003.

2 The Making of the Fur Capital Leipzig (1850–1914)

Introduction

In the introduction, I located a tension in the economic structure of Saxony in the perplexing combination of business embeddedness and its orientation towards foreign markets. This 'missing link' in the history of the region as well as in industrial district theory is analysed here in one of its most active and successful industrial districts. As mentioned before, the Leipzig industrial district emerged while being dependent upon one of the most historical world markets. In the mid-1920s, Leipzig city official Walter Leiske (who would later be the postwar mayor of Frankfurt am Main) called it one of the most valuable industries of the city. At this point, the luxury fur industry employed 3.2% of the Leipzig workforce and one out of four garment businesses in the city was occupied with fur manufacture.[1] Along with London and New York, Leipzig had developed into one of the largest markets in the world trade of furs. The fur district had thus emerged as one of the main sectors in the urban economy during the long nineteenth century. How and why could such a structure emerge in this strongly globalised industry?

Before turning to the global position of the Leipzig fur capital, a number of endogenous factors will be explored in this chapter, such as the presence of human capital, the process of industrialisation, and the importance of pre-existing economic institutions. All of these facilitated the growth of Leipzig fur industry. To begin with, the role of the strong guilds in Saxony, which persisted well after the introduction of freedom of commerce in 1861, will be examined.[2] How did the craft tradition influence the process of industrialisation in the Leipzig fur industry? This and other factors, like mobility and the cross-fertilisation between the fur industry and local finance, will be starting point in describing how a cluster of fur businesses emerged in and around the city of Leipzig. Given the openness of the district, however, it is impossible to maintain a purely endogenous view. Firstly, a number of features, like industrialisation and local networks between economic actors, will be studied by looking at their interplay with exogenous developments, such as economic globalisation, mobility, and the expansion of the international fur trade. In particular, the symbiosis between local finance in Leipzig and the fur industry will be shown to have been instrumental to processes of internationalisation. Secondly, the chapter also explores the importance of inward mobility in terms of replenishing entrepreneurship in the expansive district.

The Local Tenets of the Leipzig Fur Capital

From Artisans to Industrialists

Fur manufacturing already constituted an essential part of the crafts industry in Leipzig in the Middle Ages. However, fur crafting in Leipzig was not unusually large in comparison with other German cities. In 1555, Leipzig had 45 master furriers. However, Breslau (107 masters in 1536) and Augsburg (92 masters in 1499) had a much larger fur sector. Breslau was an important marketplace for trade with the East whereas Leipzig belonged to the smaller cities (only 1,745 inhabitants in 1529) of the Holy Roman Empire. In subsequent centuries, little changed in terms of either the size or the distribution of the fur craft in Leipzig. In 1800, the number of masters had barely increased to 64 furriers; however, this was still 20 more than 250 years previous.[3]

Between 1849 and 1861, just before the introduction of the freedom of commerce, the number of masters increased only slightly but there was a significant rise in the number of journeymen and apprentices working in the Saxon fur industry.[4] In 1849, the fur industry in Leipzig numbered around 97 fur workshops, employing about 197 workers. In 1850, a strike in the British fur industry served as an important impetus to the development of the fur dyeing and dressing industries as more skins from the London market arrived in Leipzig and its environs. Nevertheless, growth in the fur industry was gradual. By 1861, the number of fur workshops reached 100 in Leipzig and its immediate surroundings while the number of journeymen and apprentices reached roughly 329. These figures indicate that the growth of fur manufacturing in Leipzig was at first situated in the growth of traditional furrier workshops.

Industrialisation and Growth

While the expansion of local fur manufacturing remained connected to the realm of artisanship, industrialisation drastically changed the production process and introduced wage labour on a large scale into the fur industry. In contrast to early industry in other Saxon sectors, the industrialisation of the fur industry occurred relatively late, in the 1870s and 1880s, because it was strongly linked to shifts in production connected to the second industrial revolution, such as synthetic dyeing.

In order to fully understand its impact, let us explore the ramifications of industrialisation on the production process. The fur production process consisted of two successive procedures, known technically as dressing and dyeing. Both dressing and dyeing can include a variety of practices but generally boil down to the following. Fur dressing, the first stage, involves the careful cleaning of fat and any remaining flesh from the skin and, crucially, treating the skins with a series of chemicals that softens and preserves them. Basic preservatives were most often applied to raw furs before their introduction into the fur market, although this was usually insufficient or unsystematic. Further preservation was thus required. A large variety of preservation methods existed. They differed in the composition of the preservative (the ratio between salt and chemicals), which depended on the procedures developed in the dressing plants. Preservation was accomplished by turning the skins in tubs containing the substance for a couple of hours. Treatment with chemical substances was introduced much later. A preindustrial method of preserving the skins with perspired salt was generally known as the "Leipzig dressing method."[5] From the beginning of the nineteenth century, this part of the process was industrialised: the manually performed turning was replaced by tons driven by steam engines.[6] Later, preservatives and treatment solutions were also systematically improved by utilising advances in applied chemistry.

Fur dyeing, the next stage of production, involves the application of colorants. The application of dyes can differ significantly depending on the quality of the material. When the quality of the natural fur is excellent, only minor adjustments like blending and "reinforcing" are required. For furs of substandard quality, the process can also entail complete over-dyeing. In other words, dyeing could be used to evenly spread the fur's natural colour but often it entailed the imitation of colourations. Fur dyes are usually applied in a dye bath. Fur dyers finalise the production process by giving the dyed skins a sawdust treatment in order to eliminate unwanted residue. The development of synthetic dyeing rendered the time-consuming process of applying natural dyes obsolete and constituted a watershed in the history of fur dyeing. It also enhanced the potential for imitating prime fur colorations. A German chemist named Hugo Erdmann received one of the first patents for the process of hair and feather dyeing in 1888.[7] Like in dressing, the composure and ratios of the chemical substance and the duration of oxidisation were often kept secret.

The first 'factories' in Leipzig to industrialise the production process of furs were established from the 1870s onwards. By 1875, Leipzig had 10 fur factories that employed 259 employees. The first fully independent dyeing factories, four in total, were also in place by this time. At first, these enterprises employed no more than 40 persons. Industrialisation therefore continued to co-exist with manufacturing workshops. Indeed, after freedom of commerce was enacted, the number of workshops exploded, swelling to 125 enterprises employing over 553 workers.[8] In sum, when industrialisation kicked in, manufacturing in fur workshops still represented a much larger proportion of the industrial district than the new factories.

Photograph 2.1 A Fur Dressing Workshop in Leipzig (1920–1940). Reproduced with permission of the Stadtarchiv Leipzig (BA 1977, nr. 3272).

This slow transition from traditional to modern manufacturing was not unusual in Saxony. Before 1848, the proportion of artisans in Saxony was much higher than the rest of Germany even though traditional manufacturing went in irreversible decline after 1865.[9] In the transition phase of fur manufacturing, the furrier remained an important part in the formation of the industrial district. Artisans continued to lead small workshops whilst others maintained themselves as tailors. The latter turned factory dressed and dyed furs into custom garments. Such finishing activities thus also had a prominent position within the district. The artisans and furrier workshops continued to occupy an important position in Leipzig, adding to the specialisation and division of labour typical of an industrial district.

Even though transformation went slowly, the introduction of the freedom of enterprise and the final abolition of guild privileges in 1861 gave an important impetus to the formation of new factories. Many of them were established by 'outsiders.' This was the case for two future lead firms. The firm Theodor Thorer was established by a furrier from Görlitz who came immediately after the introduction of free enterprise. Thorer constructed a factory in the early 1880s in Lindenau, on the outskirts of Leipzig. It immediately turned into one of the most successful factories: in 1883, the Thorer factory was a source of employment for more than 100 workers.[10] In 1847, Friedrich Erler, an apprentice from Frankfurt am Main, established a workshop in Leipzig. Later, he experimented with modern dyeing techniques in collaboration with the chemist Adolf Stieglitz. Together they founded the dyeing company Adolf Stieglitz & Co in Plagwitz in 1876 and it was placed under the supervision of the chemist.[11] The Stieglitz firm moved to Leipzig-Lindenau a few years later and remained closely connected to Erler well into the 1930s.[12]

After 1880, industrial fur production grew even more spectacularly. The industrial census of 1882 confirms the existence of 788 fur factories in Saxony employing 2,150 workers. The fur factories in Saxony were clearly concentrated in Leipzig and its environs, an area that contained precisely 212 firms and 1,381 workers.[13] Furthermore, many fur factories were domiciled in towns that bordered Leipzig, like Schkeuditz, Ötzschz, Markleeberg, Markranstädt, and Plagwitz. The Leipzig fur industry was arguably a Saxon phenomenon: it emerged within the region of Saxony, with Leipzig functioning as the undisputed epicentre. In turn, Saxony formed the core of the German fur industry. Indeed, about 16.1% of German fur workers in 1882 were employed in Saxony and the number of factories represented 11.1% of the Reich's total. In turn, the labour force in the Leipzig fur industry represented 64% of Saxony's fur industry and roughly 10% of the German fur industry in its totality.[14] The Saxon fur industry grew at a more rapid pace than the Reich's average, a fact that contributed to the regional concentration of the German fur industry. In 1907, despite a decrease in factories to 742, the fur industry in Saxony now represented 15.7% of the Reich's total (5,070 companies). Furthermore, 4,643 labourers worked in Saxony's fur industry, which was about 25.5% of the Reich's 18,232 labourers.[15] In the census year 1907, 36% or 272 of Saxon fur factories were domiciled in Leipzig and 40% of the Saxon labourers in the fur industry were Leipzig fur workers (against 64% in 1882). Still, one out of 10 German fur workers worked in Leipzig. Leipzig had expanded its status as both the Saxon and national fur capital, although manufacturing was now more pronouncedly a Saxon phenomenon.

The First World War was but a small interlude in the growth of the industrial district. In fact, by the mid-1920s, the fur industry in Saxony reached its zenith. In 1925, 1,091 fur factories employed over 11,170 workers, including 5,520 female workers. This figure could even expand to 18,397 workers (8,160 male, 10,237 female) during the peak of the fur season,

Table 2.1 Fur Workers in Germany (1882–1925)

	LEIPZIG	*SAXONY*	*REICH*
1882	1,381	2,150	13,345
1907	1,857	4,643	18,232
1925	5,881	11,170	30,002

Table 2.2 Number of Fur Firms in Germany (1882–1925)

	LEIPZIG	SAXONY	REICH
1882	212	788	4,907
1907	272	742	5,070
1925	519	1,091	5,166

since approximately a pool of 7,000 workers belonged to a seasonal labour force.[16] According to the 1925 census, the German fur industry was as large as 5,166 firms, employing 30,002 non-seasonal fur workers in total.[17] Some 37% of all German fur workers were concentrated in Saxony (against 25.5% in 1907). Leipzig was still the epicentre of the Saxon fur industry with 519 fur companies employing 5,881 labourers (2,865 male and 3,016 female workers). The Leipzig labour pool thus represented roughly 20% of Germany's fur workers and 52% of Saxony's. The fur industry in Saxony and Leipzig would never be larger than during the mid-1920s.

The Commercial Segment of the Cluster

It is impossible to examine the emergence of the industrial district without looking at another important field of business specialisation, fur trading. Simultaneous with the development of the industry, the commercial segment of the district emerged in Leipzig. At the beginning of the nineteenth century, Leipzig housed only 30 wholesale fur traders in total. By 1907, Saxony had about 350 fur trading firms employing 1,243 persons. Saxony's fur trading firms thereby represented 35% of the Reich's total and the number of employees represented 42% of all workers active in the Reich's fur trading activities. The spectrum of entrepreneurs here ranged from small traders to commissioners and brokers who worked on behalf of foreign trading companies. According to the contemporary trader Wilhelm Harmelin, a minority of these firms (roughly 30 to 50) were classified as leading fur trade companies. It is clear that Leipzig was the undisputable heart of the Saxon fur trade, housing about 794 fur traders in the city by 1930.[18]

Unlike the processing industry, the commercial segment of the fur district was not widely dispersed in and around Leipzig, but centralised on the street called "Brühl" and in the adjacent Nikolaistrasse in downtown Leipzig. The Brühl was therefore the billboard for the German fur industry, much like the Sentier was for the Parisian fashion industry. The fur trading houses, most of which were constructed between 1860 and 1914, even evinced a distinct architectural style. The so-called *"Pelzkontorhaus"* typified the Brühl and the Nikolaistrasse in Leipzig, of which only a few have survived the tides of history into the present day.[19] Typical fur merchant houses could be recognised by their rich decoration and their large exhibition spaces and were connected to a common inner courtyard where deliveries were accepted.

As said, fur commerce in Leipzig was strongly associated with Jewish entrepreneurship. Of the 794 fur traders active in downtown Leipzig in 1930, it was estimated that at least 460 of them were of Jewish origin. The presence of Jewish entrepreneurs was in the first place strongly linked to trade historical fairs in Leipzig. Indeed, Jewish middlemen historically played a leading role in connecting the fur trade in Russian fairs to those in Leipzig.[20] In particular, the Jews of Brody, part of the Austrian empire after the division of Poland in 1772, were important as fur importers to Leipzig.[21] They bought furs in Russia and Poland and transported them via Brody to the fairs in Leipzig. Authorities in Leipzig realised the importance of Jewish middlemen, especially in regards to the fur trade, and therefore relaxed the rather strict regulations that governed the movement of Jews in Saxony, although only moderately. In 1747, for instance, the city council allowed for the settlement of Polish and Russian Jews without paying taxes "in recognition of their contribution toward the import of raw materials for the hide and fur industries."[22] The city council also granted Jews the status of "fair brokers," an official permit that legalised their stay in Leipzig during the fairs.[23] Until around 1830, however, Saxon laws largely curtailed Jewish business and property rights. Leipzig therefore only had 22 Jewish inhabitants in 1785, but that number had grown to 76 in 1834.

When the fairs became gradually less important for commerce in furs—modernised transportation allowed for permanent mercantile activities—several Jewish entrepreneurs decided to settle permanently in the city of Leipzig.[24] A change in Saxon laws in the mid-1830s further facilitated the settlement of this first generation of Jewish business. Marcus Harmelin, a supplier from Brody, established one of the first prominent Jewish companies in Leipzig in 1830, followed by the Felsenstein brothers. The arrival of Harmelin and the Felsensteins in the Brühl preceded many more traders. Many traders originated from Brody, the Galician city that served as East-West trade junction. Fein Nachmann (1842) and Saul Finkelstein (1857) ranked amongst the most prominent Jewish traders from Brody.[25]

The full emancipation of Jews, which came in the wake of Saxony's integration into the North German confederation, triggered the arrival of a new cohort of Jewish entrepreneurs who mostly originated outside the tradition of the fairs. The Jewish community grew from 713 members in 1858 to 6,171 in 1900. A third wave of Jewish immigrants after World War I gave the Leipzig Jewish community its strongest-ever presence. In 1925, 12,594 persons belonged to the Jewish community in Leipzig (or 1.8% of the urban population).[26] Many of the second wave Jewish migrants were already businessmen who had established firms abroad or elsewhere in Germany before opening branches on the Brühl. Most noteworthy was the successful Moscow-based business of Chaim Eitingon (1857–1932), who was one of the lead firms of the district. Having analysed the waves of Jewish immigration, the importance of outsiders and migrants in the creation of the industrial district has to be emphasised, both in trade as well as manufacturing.

Finally, I should note the occupational structure of the Jewish population in Leipzig. Jewish migrants in Leipzig mainly contributed to the fur industry as traders and entrepreneurs whereas comparatively few of the Jewish migrants were employed as fur workers. This is a significant difference from Jewish occupational patterns in the fur industry elsewhere. In both European and American fur centres, Jewish immigrants tended to be more active in sweatshops and in the manual labour workforce than in Germany. For

Photograph 2.2 The Brühl in Leipzig (taken between 1920 and 1940). Reproduced with permission of the Stadtarchiv Leipzig. (Stadtarchiv Leipzig, BA 1977 761. s.d.)

instance, in 1912, 7,000 of the 10,000 fur workers in the US (predominantly in New York) were of Jewish descent.[27] In Germany, Jewish settlers were mostly self-employed since German administrative policy clearly favoured the settlement of more well-to-do migrants. According to Nancy Green, German migration authorities employed a more 'utilitarian' policy that focused on the economic surplus the Jewish migrant could produce.[28] Merchants therefore represented the majority of Jewish settlers in Saxony.[29] The policy determined the supply of entrepreneurs to the Leipzig fur business. In 1925, of the 4,693 Jews in Leipzig with a gainful occupation, 805 worked on the Brühl. Thus, almost one out of four Jews worked in the Leipzig fur business. Of the 805 Jews associated with the Brühl, 396 were independent merchants and 268 worked as white-collar workers in one of the many trading houses. Conversely, only 79 Jews worked as furriers and even fewer, 62, as labourers in the fur industry.[30] The absence of Jewish fur workers in the Leipzig fur industry marked a major difference between Leipzig and other international fur centres: these tended to be more strongly characterised by an 'all-around presence' of sweatshop workers and a Jewish proletariat next to successful entrepreneurs.

Patterns of Local Cooperation: Interfirm Networks, Trade Associations, and Bank Firm Relationships

The Symbiosis Between Manufacturing and International Trade

A body of merchants settled permanently in the city and organised the supply of furs at roughly the same time as industrialisation triggered the formation of highly specialised production units in Leipzig. What were the links between these subsectors and between individual firms representing them? There are strong indications that fur trading and fur manufacturing reinforced each other as the central components of the fur district. Steffen Held characterised the Leipzig fur industry as "a symbiosis between wholesale trading, the dressing and dyeing of skins in factories, and also small furrier businesses, primarily involved with fur tailoring."[31] Two elements of the symbiosis should be emphasised. Firstly, fur trading, and the international links forged by Jewish entrepreneurs, arguably influenced the emergence of the fur cluster since it provided the raw material to be processed in these production units. In fact, trading necessarily involved links to the wider world. Fur traders forged connections with resource producing areas and discovered foreign sales markets. The following numbers reveal the foreign dimension of the Leipzig fur trade. The joint trade volume of the Leipzig fur industry amounted to 100 million marks in 1908: according to Benndorf, around 75–80% of that figure was earned from the turnover of foreign commerce.[32]

Secondly, the fur trade was not only beneficial because of the connections it constructed to the outside world. There existed many connections between industry and commerce, on the level of the firm. Many fur trade companies built partnerships with existing fur factories or established manufacturing units by themselves in order to expand the profits made by fur trading. As a result, few fur factories in Leipzig operated independently from commerce. They accepted work on behalf of other companies or depended upon the import of raw furs from larger enterprises specialised in commerce. For instance, in 1883, the trade firm Theodor Thorer opened a dyeing factory (Thorer & Co) in Leipzig-Lindenau, specialised in the industrial dyeing of karakul and Astrakhan sheepskins. Despite this vertical integration, the Thorer family chiefly focused on the trading affairs of their business in North America, Central Asia, and Russia. The Thorer family therefore granted the factory a significant degree of autonomy. After 1925, a kinsman from the renowned Leipzig machine construction company Rudolf H Sack KG was appointed as the manager of the fur dyeing Thorer & Co factory.[33] The factory ranked as one of the largest in Leipzig since it employed 500–600 workers (the number of labourers could fluctuate depending on seasonal activities). The trade firm itself, strongly in the hands of the Thorer family, employed 80 labourers and white-collar workers.[34]

A similar division of labour applied to Friedrich Erler & Co. As mentioned above, the partnership with the chemist Adolf Stieglitz in the 1870s led to the construction of a fur dyeing factory. Stieglitz developed not only synthetic dyeing procedures but was also appointed manager of Erler's factory, first in Plagwitz and later in Leipzig-Lindenau.[35] Although the Stieglitz firm retained its connection to the Erler firm well into the 1930s, it was not exclusively a part of it. Indeed, the Erler firm had transformed from a fur workshop into a wholesale trading business. Similar collaborative structures between trading and manufacturing emerged between the trading firm Friedrich Maerz in the Brühl and the dyeing factory of Adolf Arnold AG. Links were created the other way around as well. Walter AG in Markranstädt, one of the largest fur dyeing factories and the only German fur company that was listed on the stock exchange, had a semi-independent trading division in the city centre of Leipzig.[36] Links between Jewish entrepreneurs and production emerged as well. Ferdinand Salm, a medium-sized Jewish trading firm, owned a factory of about 100–110 workers in Wahren, which, like Walter AG in Markrandstädt, illustrates the connection of international trading with Leipzig's industrial hinterland and the wider Saxon region.[37] The Eitingon family invested in production facilities after World War I. In sum, the fur industry was compartmentalised along the lines of vertical specialised activities and they were not integrated in one overarching business but operated semi-independently from one another, based on ownership and cooperative links.

Having established that there remained a high level of business specialisation, if with strong ties between the firms typical for an industrial district, it is now time to take a look at the size distribution of the firms. At first glance, the figures tend to reveal an increase in scale. Between 1882 and

1907, the number of workers increased more rapidly than the number of manufacturing plants. Still, the number of production units that employed more than 50 labourers only represented 2.5% of the total number of firms in 1907. However, the number of labourers working in firms with more than 50 labourers had climbed to 42.9%, indicating the scale increase in Saxony. Moreover, this percentage is far above the Reich's average: only 15% of the workers were employed in factories with over 50 labourers whereas 52.8% of the fur workers worked in small workshops. This contrasts significantly with a figure of 17.7% in Saxony. A fur factory in Saxony tended to be larger on average (105 workers) than one outside Saxony (101 workers).[38]

At first sight, these figures run contrary to the image of Saxony as a region characterised by a decentralised mode of production where firms were on average much smaller than in the Reich.[39] However, the reason for this difference has to be sought within the national structure of the fur industry itself. Most importantly, Saxony was the industrial powerhouse of the German fur industry. Leipzig developed as the centre for fur production whereas business activity across the Reich tended to focus on specialised functions like tailoring or retailing manufactured furs from Leipzig. Every city in the Reich had at least a few fur shops, small workshops, or retailers. Industrial concentration, on the other hand, only took place in Saxony, and to a lesser extent perhaps in Berlin. This is a plausible explanation for the difference in size distribution of the firms.

Even though firms were larger than the Reich's average, moreover, the fur industry in and around Leipzig still corresponds to the features of an industrial district in terms of decentralisation. Firstly, firms were highly specialised, and as mentioned above often linked to one another, which led to high degrees of specialisation. Businesses were active in industrial production, as well as other businesses involved in related activities like fur tailoring, brokerage, and trading. Secondly, the discrepancy in national figures does not mean that big business was the norm in the Saxon fur industry. In the mid-1920s, at the apex of the Saxon fur industry, the overwhelming majority of firms were extremely small. To begin with, 309 firms (28%) employed no workers other than the owner of the workshop. In addition, about 313 firms (29%) employed one to three labourers. In all likelihood, these units represented the segment of artisanal production at the very end of the production chain, which had been transformed into an integral part of the industrial district. Moreover a large part of the labour force worked in small to medium-sized enterprises. The largest group, consisting of 3,479 workers (31%), were employed in middle-sized firms that had between 11 and 50 employees.[40] Some 26% of the labourers worked for companies that employed between 51 and 200 workers. There was little big business. Only six fur firms employed more than 200 workers, but these firms provided work for 20% of the workforce (see Figure 2.1).

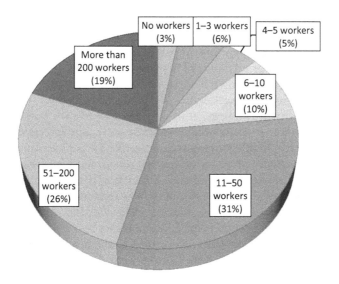

Figure 2.1 Average Number of Employees in Saxon Fur Companies in 1925

Leipzig as a Capital for the Organised Fur Business

Leipzig was not only the commercial and industrial epicentre of the German fur business but also gradually emerged as the 'capital' of the German fur industry from an organisational perspective. All of the major national business associations of the fur industry established headquarters in Saxony's commercial centre, even if they were not strongly associated with the region. The Leipzig Fur Guild (*Kürschnerinnung zu Leipzig*) ranked as one of the oldest because it represented the old guild established in 1425. Around 1900, it represented the interests of about 40 independent artisans, who employed 75 journeymen and 60 apprentices.[41] Like most heirs to the old guild organisations after freedom of enterprise, the furrier guild was predominantly involved in a rearguard fight against the dismantlement of corporatism in Germany and the preservation of the venerable handwork tradition.[42] The relative decline of the guilds and the industrialisation of the fur industry fostered the development of new organisations. The Association of German Fur Dressers and Dyers (*Verband Deutscher Rauchwaren Zurichtereien und Färbereien*) was established in 1899. This organisation remained rather small. In 1925, 27 industrialists had joined the Association of Fur Dressers and Dyers, 20 of whom were domiciled in Leipzig.[43]

The most important association in Leipzig, the Leipzig Fur Merchant Association (*Verband Leipziger Rauchwarenfirmen*) was established in 1908 and 42 firms immediately joined the trade association. A diverse number of items characterised the agenda of the association, ranging from the standardisation of trade practices to the protection of the international position of Leipzig's fur companies.[44] This business association most clearly incorporated Jewish and non-Jewish entrepreneurs. Some of the founding members were Jewish enterprises, whereas important Jewish entrepreneurs of lead firms, like Max Ariowitsch, served as members of the board.[45] As such, Jewish entrepreneurs were a driving force behind the horizontal integration of the fur cluster, which was not exceptional, as mentioned before, to the behaviour of Jewish entrepreneurs in Germany more generally. It suggests a role for Jews in the district beyond than that of cosmopolitan entrepreneurs only interested in international commerce. In other German clusters, like the Solingen cutlery industry, Jewish entrepreneurs played a prominent role in local business associations as well.[46] The Leipzig Fur Merchants Association witnessed its largest expansion after World War I. The Association was renamed the German Fur Merchants Association (*Reichsverbandes der Deutschen Rauchwaren-firmen*) and included firms from outside Leipzig. Membership rose from 148 firm-owners in 1919 to about 688 in 1925. Nevertheless, the headquarters remained in Leipzig. Since 480 members were Leipzig firms, the Leipzig division arguably formed the nucleus of the German Fur Trade Association.[47]

Remarkably, none of these organisations succeeded in representing firms across specialised activities, despite the fact that partnerships between firms often cut across such specialisations. Instead, trade associations followed the vertical division of labour that characterised the fur district. Every segment of the industry was represented by a separate trade association: furriers, retailers, the trading houses, and finally the dressing and dyeing companies. Since traders had the largest interest in foreign trade, this association also collectively addressed problems connected to transborder activities of the Leipzig district, admittedly somewhat timidly before World War I but more firmly thereafter.

The Local Bank and Fur Industry Nexus in Leipzig (1900–1914)

Another key element of the fur business cluster in Leipzig was the easy and advantageous access to financial resources. Although cross-fertilisation between the financial system and concentrated industrial development on the local level is often implicitly assumed, knowledge about the interaction between finance and industry in Saxony remains tentative at best. Frank Zschaler has shown that private banking in Saxony persisted for a relatively long time in comparison to other industrialising regions. The persistence of private banking is said to have influenced the formation of the smaller businesses that pervaded in the region.[48] The argument is based on the assumption that private banking was prone to invest in the smaller and specialised firms in the local areas whereas joint-stock banking investments flowed into the larger businesses.

It is however unlikely that private banking was responsible for the pronounced business specialisation in the fur district. After all, Leipzig formed the exception to the rule in Saxony as a centre of banking. The commercial magnitude of the city attracted the presence of both private banks and the larger joint-stock banks. One of the first German joint-stock banks, the Leipziger Bank, was established there as early as 1839. By the beginning of the twentieth century, Leipzig had developed as the financial centre of Saxony and was second only to the financial capital of the Reich, Berlin. In 1911, besides a *Reichsbankhauptstelle*, 31 private banks and bank branches were to be found in Leipzig. All major German joint-stock banks opened branches in the city: the Allgemeine Deutsche Creditbank (ADCA, present from 1856), Mitteldeutsche Regionalbank, the Hamburger Commerz und Discontobank (from 1911), the Deutsche Bank, and the 'Bank für Handel und Industrie' (Darmstädter Bank).

The presence of large joint-stock banks in Leipzig was however not inimical to the clustering of small-scaled and specialised fur firms. Joint-stock banks did not leave investment in the fur industry to private banks: rather, private and joint-stock banks divided the credit market. All the joint-stock banks took an interest in the rapidly growing fur district, particularly the ADCA, the Dresdner Bank, the Deutsche Bank and, to a lesser extent, the Commerzbank. The fur industry was also closely linked to private banks, most importantly the Bankhaus Meyer & Co. Firms could rely on several bank connections and profited from bank offers that aimed to extract the fur firms from rival banks. Bank competition, rather than the *nature* of the banks, seemed to have been influential in regards to business organisation.

Competition between joint-stock banks over the fur industry was particularly strong in the case of the branches of the Dresdner and the Deutsche Banks in Leipzig. Their rivalry was also the best documented. Both banks entered the financial market of Leipzig relatively late. Whereas the Dresdner Bank had its roots in Saxony, the Leipzig branch was established only in 1909, significantly later than the establishment of branches abroad (London, 1895) or commercial centres in Germany of comparable magnitude like Hamburg (1892).[49] The opening of a branch in Leipzig was thus part of an expansive policy of transforming itself into a universal bank with the aim of creating a dense network of branches in the Reich and abroad. Importantly, the new branch first opened in the epicentre of the fur trade, at the Brühl 37/39.[50]

The Dresdner Bank was still interested in investing in its home region, despite the fact that it had gradually evolved into a nationwide bank at the turn of the century. In 1913, von Klemperer, the director of the Dresdner Bank in Leipzig, wrote, "Despite its role as a large and international bank, the Dresdner Bank is still a Saxon institute and one of its first goals is the support of Saxon trade and industry."[51] Given this self-declared commitment to Saxony, the lack of customers in Leipzig was a painful lacuna in the banking affairs of the Dresdner Bank. As the bank had to start from scratch in Leipzig, the fur industry featured prominently in the 'conquest' of the local lending market. This can be seen in the somewhat self-laudatory memoirs of von Klemperer: "I began with the fur sector and found success because of our international contacts and our willingness to provide credit and accept 'special desires.' I succeeded in bringing in first class firms as customers and thereby I had overcome!"[52] The first customers were Chaim Eitingon, König-swerther, and Ullmann: after only a few months, most of the fur firms had become customers of the Dresdner Bank.[53] Locally clustered activities were of great interest to the Dresdner Bank. After the fur industry, von Klemperer won many new accounts in the book-printing industry, the other main business cluster in the Leipzig region. The result was that the Dresdner Bank in Leipzig assigned a staggering 70% of its credit activities between 1924 and 1929 to the local fur industry and the book-printing sector.

The Deutsche Bank entered the Leipzig market much earlier (1901), where it occupied the vacuum left by the bankruptcy of the first joint-stock bank in Leipzig, the Leipziger Bank.[54] Competition between banks in Leipzig sharpened after the opening of the Deutsche Bank's division. The Leipzig division of the Deutsche Bank followed a similar strategy to the Dresdner Bank in order to gain a foothold in the trade fair city. On the business credits market, the Deutsche Bank focused on luring customers from the Allgemeine Deutsche Credit-Anstalt (ADCA). In 1901, it gained Ariowitsch as a customer. Soon, the Brühl came to represent the largest circle of customers of the Deutsche Bank in Leipzig.[55] Continuity of leadership preserved the entanglement between banks and the fur industry. Von Klemperer led the Leipzig division of the Dresdner Bank from its opening in 1909 until 1934. Eugen Naumann headed the Deutsche Bank in Leipzig between 1909 until 1930. Before the directorship, he had been vice-director of the Leipzig branch between 1901 and 1909: earlier, he had learnt banking in the London and Hamburg branches. Both directors were advocates of investment in the local fur industry. They remained in the highest positions of local finance for almost 30 years.

Little is known about the relationship between the banks and the fur industry before World War I, yet several factors indicate that banks tailored their financial products to the (international) requirements of the fur industry. In 1906, for instance, the Deutsche Bank granted the Theodor Thorer firm 300,000 marks of unsecured credit, which was extended with short-term loans to the sum of "200,000 marks during the large fairs and auctions in the world."[56] Thorer did not solely depend on the credit of the Deutsche Bank. Indeed, the opposite was true. By October 1913, the credit provided to Thorer by the Leipzig banks (which he spent in London and Nizhnii Novgorod) amounted to 2,310,000 marks; 500,000 marks had been provided by the Deutsche Bank.[57] The fur industry was able to profit from the competition between the banks. Firms could accrue credit from multiple sources because of the laws of supply and demand on the bank market. Let us not forget that this system carried advantages for banks too. Joint credit offers spread over a number of fur firms diminished the financial risk of the banks.

The element of competition can be found in other cases as well. In particular, two other examples will be given in connection to the Deutsche Bank. Before Thorer, the Ariowitsch account was the most important to the Deutsche Bank and its commitment toward this Jewish trade firm consisted of around 600,000 marks in unsecured credit that the firm could freely use for purchasing. With the banking affairs of the firm amounting to 3,000,000 marks, it represented the flagship account of the new branch. It was noted that "we are the only bank connection and much of the profitable foreign commerce goes through our hands."[58] Ariowitsch entertained connections to one bank only and the Deutsche Bank in Leipzig tried to keep it that way. The effects of competition worked here as well nonetheless. In 1913, the Ariowitsch family could easily exert pressure on the Deutsche Bank when they needed additional unsecured credit: "Two other banks have offered these gentlemen unsecured credit but they want to stay with us, and will refrain from opening a second credit line."[59] However, this was on the condition that the Deutsche Bank extended the unsecured credit by an additional 150,000 marks.

As part of its expansion policy, the Deutsche Bank connected to the Biedermann firm, one of the pioneering companies in the fur trade in Russia's Far East, as early as 1908.[60] The trade volume of the Biedermann firm was worth 2,600,000 marks and therefore it was one of the largest fur firms on the Brühl. Although the Biedermann firm had considerable financial resources, steadily increasing prices forced Biedermann to support his commercial activities in Russia on bank credits. Biedermann divided his banking affairs between the Deutsche Bank and, to a lesser extent, the Bank für Handel und Industrie and the Bankhaus Meyer & Co, a private Saxon bank. In 1910, the Deutsche Bank, like the Bankhaus Meyer, approved commercial credit of 100,000 marks, which Biedermann could spend at the Nizhnii fairs. Later, in 1913, Biedermann demanded that his credit be increased in order to keep up with the rise in prices. The head office in Berlin regarded Biedermann's credit request as 'inconvenient' (*unbequem*) since the international fur industry was undergoing problems in 1913. Upon the advice of Berlin, the Deutsche Bank in Leipzig therefore declined his request in order "curb his entrepreneurial spirit." However, Biedermann, whose trade volume had increased to 11,000,000 marks, then opened negotiations with the Dresdner Bank, the main competitor of the Deutsche Bank, for some short-term loans.[61] Biedermann held that bank credit for buying in Russia was paramount for the survival of his firm. With the threat of the Dresdner Bank lurking, the Deutsche Bank gave in. Naumann increased Biederman's unsecured credit from 100,000 to 300,000 marks. Bank competition offered considerable opportunities to the fur firms in Leipzig and made it difficult for banks to curb 'risky' business expansion.

The heavy competition on the local lending market is further illustrated in the communication of the Deutsche Bank between the branch in Leipzig and the head office in Berlin. Criticism towards the policy of the Leipzig office had long been looming but finally erupted in 1913. In that year, the trade cycle in furs was rather slack and Berlin panicked about the position of its Leipzig office in the local economy. It posed restrictions on the Leipzig office, which had been overly transfixed on the success of several fur firms. Nonetheless, the head office understood the pressure that Naumann had experienced when breaking into the local lending market: "We understand that under the circumstances it is not easy to pose limits on your customers in the fur industry, which are courted heavily by your competitors and whose commercial success tempts you to further expand your business activities."[62] In the years before the war, the head office aimed to reverse the policy of the Leipzig office. Berlin instructed that the Leipzig branch should "limit its credit to the local industry and decline new requests for credit, particularly from the fur industry."[63]

The nervousness during the 1913 slump reveals the lopsided balance between the fur industry and the banking system. The Gotha Privatbank, for instance, had almost blindly granted 300,000 marks of credit to Theodor Thorer from 1906 on the advice of the Deutsche Bank. In the troubled year of 1913, the private bank suddenly worried about the risks it had undertaken: "The connection is now somewhat uncomfortable since we are not able to learn more about this firm and we cannot supervise it. Moreover, they have multiple connections to banks besides us. . . ."[64] Regarding the panic that had engulfed the banking system in 1913, the director of the Deutsche Bank in Leipzig noted that "several of the banks . . . especially the Bank für Handel and Industrie, Mitteldeutsche Privatbank, Bankhaus Meyer & Co . . . have gratuitously and even light-headedly granted credit to a number of companies in the district that do not even deserve to exist and will scatter once trade imposes restrictions."[65] The Deutsche Bank believed in a purifying effect of credit restrictions: "The new conditions have the effect that many traders will be unable to purchase at the fairs: all the strong firms will survive and the weaker ones will go down. It is a traditional phenomenon at the Brühl that a 'purification' of the market occurs without having negative effects upon the stronger elements."[66] However, such a policy remained dead letter and banks continued a policy of extensive credit, allowing the businesses of the fur capital to grow and participate on the international market.

Conclusion

As can be seen in the above discussion, the competition between Leipzig banks positively influenced the development of firms in the district since banking competition had a downward effect on lending conditions. However, the entanglement of the banking system and the fur industry cannot be seen as a purely endogenous factor, since the clustering of business and finance can also be read as a reaction towards macroeconomic developments. Banks followed the requirements of firms that were imposed on the latter by foreign commerce, like short-term credit for annual fairs. In addition, by the end of the nineteenth century, a decreasing supply of prime furs caused a steady rise of wholesale prices.[67] The local banking system not only supported the growth of the fur industry: the availability of credit was of seminal importance for the fur industry since such allowed them to participate in the international fur boom of the early twentieth century. It is hereby illustrated again that the formation and endurance of the industrial district and interfirm networks cannot be solely explained by endogenous factors. Like most Saxon industries, the Leipzig fur industry was strongly oriented towards the world market. In other words, to understand the formation of the fur district, we are obliged to further examine the structure of the world market that the local economy was embedded in.

Notes

1 Rückert, *Leipziger Wirtschaft in Zahlen*, 806.
2 Green, *Fatherlands*, 31.
3 Fellmann, *Der Leipziger Brühl*, 43.
4 Kiesewetter, *Industrialisierung und Landwirtschaft*, 377.
5 Hunger, *Industrial Dyes*, 446.
6 Mechthild, "Lexikon des alten Handwerks," 137.
7 Austin, *Principles and Practice of Fur Dressing and Fur Dyeing*, 156; Lockemann, "Erdmann Hugo."
8 König, "Das Zurichten Und Färben Der Pelze," 5.
9 Green, *Fatherlands*, 31.
10 Fellmann, "Schlaufüchse und Blaufüchse vom Brühl," 444.
11 Der Rauchwarenveredler, Beiblatt zum Rauchwarenmarkt, 3. Jg. 23., 6.05.1933, p. 1. Adolf Stieglitz.
12 StA-L, Dresdner Bank in Leipzig 21018, nr. 296, Kreditakten (Otto Erler), Entwurf. Leipzig 1935.
13 Only seven years earlier, the number of fur workers in Leipzig had not reached 1,000.
14 König, "Das Zurichten und Färben der Pelze," 2.
15 Benndorf, *Weltwirtschaftliche beziehungen der sächsischen industrie*, 293. See Tabelle 147.
16 Statistisches Jahrbuch für den Freistaat Sachsen, Jg 1924/1926., p. 98.
17 Statistisches Jahrbuch für das Deutsche Reich 1928, p. 107. Die Gewerblichen Betriebe (örtliche Betriebseinheiten) im Deutschen Reich nach Gewerbegruppen.
18 Harmelin, "Juden in Der Leipziger Rauchwarenwirtschaft," 267.
19 Schubert, "Die Pelzgewerbehäuser in Der Leipziger Innenstadt," 61.
20 Falke, Dieter et al. *Deutsche und Russen im Gouvernement Nishnij Nowgorod: Geschichte und Gegenwart*, 64.
21 Kuzmany, "La Ville de Brody Au Cours Du Long XIXe Siècle: L'histoire D'une Contre-Performance?"
22 Berenbaum and Skolnik, "Fur Trade and Industry," 313.
23 Reinhold, "Vom Messmakler zum etablierten Kaufmann," 431.
24 Kahan, *Russian Economic History*, 36.
25 Harmelin, "Die Juden in Der Leipziger Rauchwarenwirtschaft," 273–82.
26 Plowinski, "Die jüdische Gemeinde Leipzigs auf dem Höhepunkt ihrer Existenz: Zur Berufs und Sozialstruktur um das Jahr 1925," 79.
27 Berenbaum and Skolnik, "Fur Trade and Industry," 314.

28 Green and Altman, "Introduction," 10–11. Green estimates the number of working-class Jews in imperial Germany to be around 20,000 to 30,000, which was fairly small in comparison with Great Britain and France.

29 Höppner, "Ostjude ist jeder, der nach mir kommt . . . " 347.

30 Plowinski, "Die jüdische Gemeinde Leipzigs auf dem Höhepunkt ihrer Existenz: Zur Berufs und Sozialstruktur um das Jahr 1925," 81.

31 Held, "Juden in Der Leipziger Rauchwarenwirtschaft," 269.

32 Benndorf, *Weltwirtschaftliche beziehungen der sächsischen industrie*, 288.

33 Schäfer, *Familienunternehmen und Unternehmerfamilien*, 96.

34 *Theodor Thorer, Thorer & Co., Leipzig*, 2.

35 Der Rauchwarenveredler, Beiblatt zum Rauchwarenmarkt, 3. Jg. 23, 6.05.1933, p. 1, Adolf Stieglitz.

36 Schubert, "Die Pelzgewerbehäuser in Der Leipziger Innenstadt," 13.

37 StA-L, Deutsche Bank, Filiale Leipzig 21017, nr. 496, f. 15, Leipzig, den 20.05.1924.

38 Benndorf, *Weltwirtschaftliche beziehungen der sächsischen industrie*, 292.

39 Herrigel, *Industrial Constructions*, 45.

40 Statistisches Jahrbuch fûr den Freistaat Sachsen, 47. Ausgabe. 1927/1928. pp. 148–9.

41 Rückert, *Leipziger Wirtschaft in Zahlen*, 866.

42 Stadt-Al, Kürschnerinnung D 19, 22.10.1906.

43 Rückert, *Leipziger Wirtschaft in Zahlen*, 888.

44 Malbin, *Der internationale rauchwarenhandel vor und nach dem Weltkriege unter besonderer berücksichtigung Leipzigs*, 37.

45 Kowalzik, *Jüdisches Erwerbsleben in der inneren Nordvorstadt Leipzigs 1900–1933*, 120.

46 Rosenthal, "Jews in the Solingen Steel Industry Records of a Rhineland City," 214.

47 Rückert, *Leipziger Wirtschaft in Zahlen*, 888.

48 Frank Zschaler, "Das Bankhaus Meyer & Co in Leipzig," 235.

49 Meyen, *120 Jahre Dresdner Bank*, 57.

50 Andreas Graul, *Gustav und Victor von Klemperer*, 95.

51 StA-L, Dresdner Bank in Leipzig 21018, Nr. 1. Leipziger Zeitung v. 29.01.1913.

52 Meyen, *120 Jahre Dresdner Bank*, 58.

53 Graul, *Gustav und Victor von Klemperer*, 95.

54 Tilly, "Die Deutsche Wirtschaftskrise von 1900/01 Und Der Fall Der Leipziger Bank."

55 *Die Deutsche Bank in Leipzig*, 60.

56 StA-L, Deutsche Bank in Leipzig, 21017, Filialbüro Berlin an die Direktion der Leipziger Filiale der Deutschen Bank, Leipzig, 16.07.1906.

57 StA-L, Deutsche Bank, Filiale Leipzig 21017, nr. 544, Filiale Leipzig an die Deutsche Bank Filialbureau, Berlin. 4.09.1913. These credits were divided among Deutsche Bank (500,000), ADCA (500,000), Darmstädter (500,000) and some smaller banks: Gotha Bank (300,000), Meyr & Cie (450,000), Frühling & Goschen (25,000), Rüffers (15,000), and finally Kleinworte (20,000).

58 StA-L, Deutsche Bank in Leipzig 21017, nr. 208, f. 13.

59 Ibid.

60 StA-L, Deutsche Bank in Leipzig, 21017, nr. 258, f. 2.

61 Ibid., f. 10.

62 StA-L, Deutsche Bank Filiale Leipzig, nr. 208. Deutsche Bank Filialbureau an die Direktion der Deutschen Bank Filiale Leipzig, 2.12.1913.

63 StA-L, Deutsche Bank 21017, Filiale Leipzig, nr. 208, ff. 12–15.

64 StA-L, Deutsche Bank in Leipzig, 21017, Abschrift, Gotha, den 01.09.1913. An Deutsche Bank Filial-Bureau Leipzig.

65 StA-L, Deutsche Bank in Leipzig 21017, nr. 544, Filiale Leipzig an die Deutsche Bank, Filial Bureau Berlin. 04.09.1913.
66 StA-L, Deutsche Bank in Leipzig 21017, nr. 544, Filiale Leipzig an die Deutsche Bank Filial-Bureau Berlin. 04.09.1913.
67 Ray, *The Canadian Fur Trade in the Industrial Age*, 61.

References

Austin, William E. *Principles and Practice of Fur Dressing and Fur Dyeing.* New York: Van Nostrand, 1922.

Benndorf, Erich. *Weltwirtschaftliche beziehungen der sächsischen industrie.* Jena: G. Fischer, 1917.

Berenbaum, Michael, and Fred Skolnik, eds. "Fur Trade and Industry." *Encyclopedia Judaica.* Detroit: Macmillan Reference USA, 2007.

Cassis, Youssef. "Private Banks and the Onset of the Corporate Economy." In *The World of Private Banking*, edited by Philip Cottrell and Youssef Cassis, 43–61. Farnham, UK: Ashgate, 2009.

Falke, Dieter et al. *Deutsche und Russen im Gouvernement Nishnij Nowgorod: Geschichte und Gegenwart.* Höppner, Solvejg. "Ostjude ist jeder, der nach mir kommt . . . " In *Wirtschaft und Gesellschaft in Sachsen im 20: Jahrhundert*, 343–70. Leipzig: Leipziger Universitätsverlag, 1998.

Fellmann, Walter. *Der Leipziger Brühl: Geschichte und Geschichten des Rauchwarenhandels.* Leipzig: VEB Fachbuchverl, 1989.

———. "Schlaufüchse und Blaufüchse vom Brühl." In *Leipzigs Messen: 1497–1997: Gestaltwandel-Umbrüche-Neubeginn*, edited by Berit Bass, Annett Hietzke, and Hartmut Zwahr, 439–51. Köln: Böhlau Verlag, 1999.

Graul, Andreas. *Gustav Und Victor von Klemperer: Eine Biographische Skizze; Mit Bildern Und Dokumenten Aus Dem Besitz Der Familie von Klemperer.* Dresden: Eugen-Gutmann-Ges., 2005.

Green, Abigail. *Fatherlands: State-Building and Nationhood in Nineteenth-Century Germany.* Cambridge, UK: Cambridge University Press, 2001.

Green, Nancy L., and Patrick Altman. "Introduction." In *Jewish Workers in the Modern Diaspora*, edited by Nancy L. Green and Patrick Altman, 1–11. Berkeley: University of California Press, 1998.

Harmelin, Wilhelm. "Die Juden in Der Leipziger Rauchwarenwirtschaft." *Juden in Sachsen* 2, no. February (2009): 6–40.

———. "Juden in Der Leipziger Rauchwarenwirtschaft." *Tradition* 11 (1966): 249–82.

Held, Steffen. "Juden in Der Leipziger Rauchwarenwirtschaft." In *Leipzigs Wirtschaft in Vergangenheit Und Gegenwart: Akteure, Handlungsspielräume, Wirkungen (1400–2011)*, edited by Susanne Scholz, 269–85. Leipzig: Leipziger Universitätsverlag, 2012.

Herrigel, Gary. *Industrial Constructions: The Sources of German Industrial Power.* Structural Analysis in the Social Sciences 9. Cambridge, UK: Cambridge University Press, 1996.

Hunger, Klaus. *Industrial Dyes: Chemistry, Properties, Applications.* Weinheim: Wiley-VCH, 2003.

Kahan, Arcadius. *Russian Economic History: The Nineteenth Century.* Chicago: University of Chicago Press, 1989.

Kiesewetter, Hubert. *Industrialisierung und Landwirtschaft: Sachsens Stellung im regionalen Industrialisierungsprozess Deutschlands im 19. Jahrhundert.* Köln: Böhlau, 1988.

König, Friedrich. "Das Zurichten Und Färben Der Pelze." *Angewandte Chemie* 27, no. 72–75 (September 18, 1914): 529–32.

Kowalzik, Barbara. *Jüdisches Erwerbsleben in der inneren Nordvorstadt Leipzigs 1900–1933.* Leipzig: Leipziger Universitätsverlag, 1999.

Kuzmany, Börries. "La Ville de Brody Au Cours Du Long XIXe Siècle: L'histoire D'une Contre-Performance?" *Discussions* 5 (2010): 1–28.

Lockemann, Georg. "Erdmann Hugo." In *Neue Deutsche Biographie*, edited by Historische Kommission bei der Bayerische Akademie, 572. Berlin: Dittel-Falck, 1959.

Malbin, Max. *Der internationale rauchwarenhandel vor und nach dem Weltkriege unter besonderer berücksichtigung Leipzigs.* Oschatz: F. Oldecops erben (C. Morgner), 1927.

Mechthild, Wiswe. "Kürschner." In *Lexikon des alten Handwerks: vom Spätmittelalter bis ins 20. Jahrhundert*, edited by Reinhold Reith, 134–139. München: C. H. Beck, 1990.

Meyen, Hans G. *120 Jahre Dresdner Bank: Unternehmens-Chronik 1872 bis 1992.* Frankfurt am Main: Dresdner Bank, 1992.

Plowinski, Kerstin. "Die jüdische Gemeinde Leipzigs auf dem Höhepunkt ihrer Existenz: Zur Berufs und Sozialstruktur um das Jahr 1925." In *Judaica Lipsiensia: zur Geschichte der Juden in Leipzig*, edited by Manfred Unger, 79–91. Leipzig: Edition Leipzig, 1994.

Pohl, Manfred, and Angelika Raab-Rebentisch. *Die Deutsche Bank in Leipzig: 1901–2001.* München: Piper, 2001.

Ray, Arthur J. *The Canadian Fur Trade in the Industrial Age.* Toronto: University of Toronto Press, 1990.

Reinhold, Josef. "Vom Messmakler zum etablierten Kaufmann." In *Leipzigs Messen 1497–1997: Gestaltwandel, Umbrüche, Neubeginn*, edited by Hartmut Zwahr, Thomas Topfstedt, and Günter Bentele, 431–9. Köln: Böhlau, 1999.

Rosenthal, Heinz. "Jews in the Solingen Steel Industry Records of a Rhineland City." *The Leo Baeck Institute Yearbook* 17, no. 1 (January 1, 1972): 205–23.

Rückert, Hans. *Leipziger Wirtschaft in Zahlen: Sammlung der Statistik aus dem Leipziger Wirtschafts-Handbuch.* Leipzig: Industrie- und Handelskammer Leipzig, 1930.

Schäfer, Michael. *Familienunternehmen und Unternehmerfamilien: zur Sozial- und Wirtschaftsgeschichte der sächsischen Unternehmer, 1850–1940.* München: C. H. Beck, 2007.

Schubert, Jens. "Die Pelzgewerbehäuser in Der Leipziger Innenstadt." Magisterarbeit: Leipziger Universität, 2003.

Theodor Thorer, Thorer & Co., Leipzig. Berlin [SW 68, Alexandrinenstr. 134]: Adolf Ecksteins Verl., 1929.

Tilly, Richard. "Die Deutsche Wirtschaftskrise von 1900/01 Und Der Fall Der Leipziger Bank." In *Bankenkrisen in Mitteleuropa Im 19: Und 20. Jahrhundert*, edited by Richard Tilly, 69–100. Stuttgart: Steiner, 2000.

Zschaler, Frank. "Das Bankhaus Meyer & Co in Leipzig. Eine Sächsische Bankiersfamilie Zwischen 1814 Und 1972." In *Unternehmer in Sachsen: Aufstieg-Krise-Untergang-Neubeginn*, edited by Ulrich Hess and Michael Schäfer, 253–69. Leipziger Studien Zur Erforschung von Regionenbezogenen Identifikationsprozessen 4. Leipziger: Leipziger Universitätsverlag, 1998.

3 Linking the Capital to the Outside World

The purpose of this chapter is to analyse the global trade relations in which the business of the Leipzig fur capital was engaged and how these relations constructed links to the outside world. The chapter will investigate the changing structure of the world market in furs during the long nineteenth century, defining and retracing its main movements and developments. As many business sectors and commodity chains in the long nineteenth century, the main movements that defined the world market in furs were globalisation and commodity market integration. However, every commodity chain has its peculiarities and specificities. What made the fur trade in particular an interesting case, in terms of globalisation, is that the commodity had been a driving force in global expansion and trade networks for centuries. It is therefore necessary to employ a long-term perspective on the history of the fur trade, in order to understand how the early modern trade in furs entered and transformed into the era of globalisation.[1]

Next to sketching the world market in furs, importantly, the chapter will make links with how these developments intersected with the history of the fur capital and its emergence. Firstly, the chapter endeavours to retrace the position of Leipzig on the world market. Secondly, a specific focus will be put upon how firms created links with the outside world. As sketched in the introduction, the claim of this chapter is that most of the firms of the capital engaged in global networks and showed the creativity and resourcefulness to participate in the world trade of furs. Next to traditional methods of firm branching, the importance of mobility will be stressed again. In particular the phenomenon of transnational entrepreneurship will be given attention as an alternative method of internationalisation. Transnational entrepreneurs are entrepreneurs that maintain business links within multiple communities across state borders: "Transnational entrepreneurs by travelling both physically and virtually, simultaneously engage in two or more socially embedded environments."[2] Indeed, the district was not only a net recipient of inward mobility of primarily entrepreneurs, but also to a lesser extent labourers. It was also a sending context. How did migration and mobility construct links and in what ways was it different from firm branching?

The Changing Structures of the World Fur Trade (1800–1914)

In order to study the position of the district in relation to the outside world, it is obviously necessary to place Leipzig within the context of global trade—in other words, within the commodity chain of furs in which it was embedded. However, a difficulty immediately arises when talking about a single commodity chain in furs. It makes more sense to subdivide the commodity chain into two larger subchains. The first chain originated from the heartlands of Siberia and went across the Urals to fur markets in western Russia, where the furs ended up in the hands of foreign buyers. The second one started in the woodlands of North America with London as its central hub in terms of both trade and manufacture. Both had a number of striking historical similarities and both changed significantly during the long nineteenth century.

The global commodity chains of furs on both continents were created relatively early in terms of world economic history and featured prominently in processes of frontier expansion. Since the late Middle Ages, traders from the state of Muscovy systematically integrated the vast Siberian woodlands into what would become the largest continental empire in world history. Russian traders set out en masse to explore the Siberian woodlands and installed an imperial exploitation system that was subsequently monopolised by the state.[3] Similarly, European demand for furs was largely responsible for attracting hunters and explorers to North America beginning from the sixteenth century and frontier expansion continued well into the late 1900s. An important difference between the Siberian and North American trades was the way in which sales were organised. The Siberian fur trade was organised into a system of trading at fairs. Foreign and local merchants specialised in furs connected the Leipzig trade fair to the system of fur procurement in Russia. From these Siberian outposts, barrels and packages of fur travelled to busier markets, like Irkutsk, Irbit, and Nizhnii Novgorod.[4] From the beginning of the eighteenth century, the Nizhnii fairs became an indispensable commercial event in Russia, with sales worth around 150–200 million rubles on average. The Nizhnii fairs attracted averagely 1.5 million visitors during the summer.[5] European traders, notably Germans, were welcome guests there every summer. The Irbit fairs, east of the Urals, were smaller, making around 25–40 million rubles in sales: they were strongly focused on select commodities like tea and furs.[6]

In contrast, the sale of North American furs was organised at auctions. In auctions, the seller 'puts the pricing in the hands of the buyers,' hoping that competition will set an acceptable price. Therefore, it is a useful system if there are a large number of potential buyers.[7] Auctions were tailored to the quasi-monopolistic Hudson's Bay Company (HBC), the chartered company that had the Canadian fur trade in its hands for centuries, and its top-down trade structure. On the other hand, fairs enabled multiple buyer-seller transactions and the presence of many smaller firms, as was the case in the Russian fur trade. Auctions were a typically British phenomenon too. Auction houses like Sotheby's emerged in eighteenth-century England and governed the transaction of other imperial commodities, like the tea offered by the British East India Company.[8]

A major trend that affected both commodity chains was that the world market prices of furs went uncontrollably upwards, especially after the turn of the century. According to Arthur Ray, fur prices in Canada remained relatively stable between 1870 and 1900. However, in 1905 prices reached 130% of the 1870 level and in 1910 prices ascended even further to 180%. Prices of raw furs reached record heights in 1913 at 230% of the 1870 price level.[9] The trend in Russian furs is remarkably similar. Russian trade figures reveal that earnings made from exports went up while procurement stagnated and quantities remained thus largely the same. At the turn of the century, fur exports were worth 3.3 million roubles on average: between 1900 and 1906, this figure reached 9.5 million and then 15.6 million between 1907 and 1913.[10] Scarcity and growing consumption in particular were driving world market prices to new heights.

Consequently, rising commodity prices and growing consumption increased global competition over furs. Both in North America and in Siberia, more capitalistic businesses came to divide control the fur trade. In Canada, the Hudson's Bay Company had to tolerate the intrusion of foreign competitors that made use of the transcontinental railway and steamboat shipping. Most leading American, British, and German merchant houses had sent agents or installed branches in Canada's boreal zones, particularly so in the second half of the nineteenth century.[11] The French Revillon Frères company in particular became one the most dynamic competitors of the HBC in North America. The intrusion of numerous firms in Canada meant heavy competition for the London auctions. At the turn of the century, roughly 50% of Canadian furs were exported to the US and the other half to Great Britain. Prior to 1900, almost 80% flowed to the fur auctions in London.[12] In Siberia, a similar pattern of competition emerged on the frontier. Business interests intruded Siberia and its markets like Irbit because of the construction of parts of the Trans-Siberian railway. The Revillon Frères company opened departments in the Siberian heartlands and in Central Asia in 1908.[13] Siberia became more 'open' too.

By the turn of the century, global competition in manufacturing surfaced more strongly as well. Aside from Leipzig, fur manufacturing emerged prominently in Great Britain and North America. However, the British fur dressing and dyeing industry, concentrated chiefly in London's East End, remained significantly smaller than its German counterpart. In 1907, Britain's fur industry employed 2,386 male and 2,305 female workers, a figure that is almost identical to the number of labourers in Saxony (4,643) in the same year and significantly smaller than the 18,232 German fur workers in total.[14] A key shift was the increase in fur consumption in the US and the associated emergence of fur manufacturing in American cities like Chicago and New York at the turn of the century. By 1912, the American fur industry employed around 10,000 labourers, amongst which were 7,000 of Jewish origin.[15] Fur manufacturing in Toronto and Montreal was said to be of a lesser magnitude.

The emergence of Leipzig as an industrial district has to be placed within a context of increased global fur manufacturing and trading. It emerged in a world market that was in full expansion. Both chains had changed considerably during the nineteenth century in the sense that they became more globalised. The international fur trade that had been characterised by early modern trade patterns, based on the fairs and dominated by quasi-monopolistic actors like the HBC, was in full transition. Capitalist business increasingly defined the organisation of trade in both chains. I have already mentioned that historically the fur trade in Leipzig was strongly oriented towards Russian business. Nonetheless, economic institutions like the fairs were under pressure. How was the Leipzig industrial district embedded within this changing structure of global trade and in the dual commodity chains? Did firms simply focus upon the Russian market or were they interested in other markets as well? How did long-term development and chain institutions govern the conditions under which the Leipzig firms operated?

Leipzig on the World Market

Where can we position the business cluster Leipzig in this expanding world market of furs reigned by fierce competition? It is difficult to procure trade figures from the city of Leipzig itself, so we have to start from some overarching figures. An important observation is that the German fur industry imported furs from multiple sources. A major shift was the falling imports from Great Britain, and the sharp increase in commerce with America. The constant trend in the figure is however is the strong trade relations with Russia, showing a contraction in the years leading to World War I, which was largely caused by overexploitation. Illuminating is the drop in the number of caught sables (100,000 to 35,000) and martens (80,000 to 30,000) between 1896 and 1913.[16] Furs were central to bilateral German-Russian trade relations. In 1913, 64.3% of Russia's total fur exports (which accounted for roughly half of world production) arrived in Germany.[17]

Moreover, the German fur industry also controlled Russia's internal fur market by re-exporting manufactured furs, since synthetic dyeing was largely underdeveloped in Russia. Michael Dohan noted that 84% of all Russia's processed leather and fur imports came from Germany. This led to the situation where German garments, made from Siberian furs, were sold in St. Petersburg and Moscow. Despite being one of the largest fur producers in the world, Russia was essentially transformed into a net importer of furs at the beginning of the twentieth century. According to the tsarist customs houses, the value of these processed furs was roughly 2.8 times higher than raw furs.[18] Furs joined the commodity list of Russian products, like flax and platinum, which the Germans could use to dominate internal markets in Russia through re-export with added value.[19]

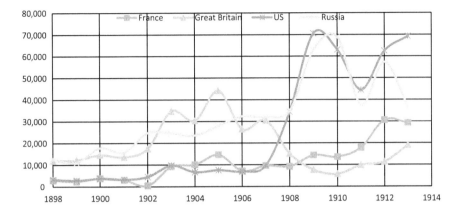

Figure 3.1 Import of Raw Furs to Germany (1898–1913) in thousand marks[20]

Most of the firms and merchant banks that dominated the Russian trade in the nineteenth century were of German origin. In fact, German merchants and merchant houses had replaced the British as the main trading partner of Russia, especially after the Crimean War.[21] Between 1899 and 1910, around 45% of Russia's exports on average were destined for Germany whereas 45% of Russian imports originated from the Reich. In contrast, Britain ran a small deficit with tsarist Russia: it imported 18% of Russian goods but only sold 13%.[22] A considerable number of key Russian export commodities were in the hands of German traders, like barley (61.5%), grain (31%), and oil (40%), and also furs (64%). Conversely, between 1907 and 1910, 45% of all goods that Russia imported came from Germany, foremost machinery and dyes.

Eastern Promises: Transnational Entrepreneurship and Mobility

What explains the success of German merchants and firms in doing business with Russia before World War I? Apart from the impact of international events like the Crimean War on rival British businesses, Margaret Miller noted that this "peaceful penetration" was based on a German willingness to adapt to local customs: "German merchants studied the language, customs, desires, and needs of their customers to a much greater extent than did their English colleagues."[23] The same tendency to meet Russian desires extended to the level of trading practices. For instance, German traders complied with the Russian penchant for selling on credit, which British merchants strongly disliked.[24] In contrast to the complacent representatives of British firms, the Germans were quicker to appear in cities and areas that required trading services, to adapt to local customs, and to make themselves proficient in the Russian language.

The Leipzig fur businesses operated in Russia according to the same lines. First, the entanglement between banking and the fur trade allowed fur traders to comply with the Russian preference for payment in advance. Banks in Leipzig gave considerable credit to purchase furs at the fairs in Nizhnii, thus covering the time between buying in Russia and selling in Leipzig. In addition, the gradually increasing prices did not affect the firms' abilities to operate on the Russian markets since competition between banks in Leipzig pushed credit to the same heights. Secondly, firm owners in the fur business showed at least a similar devotion to adapt to Russian trade customs as their colleagues in other trades. All the major Leipzig firms possessed branches in Russia or had brokers working for them. However, the specialisation in the Russian business also made way for a different mode of entrepreneurship, one that was closely linked to a transnational lifestyle.

The devotion to operate on the Russian market can be illustrated by analysing the foreign activities of several Leipzig entrepreneurs. Fur merchant houses in Leipzig traditionally sent family and employees on long journeys through Russia. Joseph Garfunkel, employed by the Marcus Harmelin firm and also a member of the Harmelin family through marriage, mentioned a journey as a young adolescent to Nizhnii Novgorod in 1889 with his father. Later, Joachim Harmelin, one of the youngest descendants of Marcus Harmelin, joined Garfunkel on a trip to Nizhnii. In 1892, Garfunkel undertook travel to the February fairs in Irbit, which was still uncharted territory for many foreign merchants. This was an advantageous strategy because it meant that the firm could circumvent the intermediary trade that took the furs from Irbit to Nizhnii Novgorod.[25] At the turn of the century, the Harmelin firm possessed an agency even deeper in Siberia, close to the source of raw furs.[26]

The Jewish Fränkel family also organised business according to the large sales events in the Russian fur trade, thereby demonstrating the features of transnational entrepreneurship. The Fränkel family were Jews who had moved in the 1850s to Leipzig from Brody and established the Julius N. Fränkel company. Hugo Fränkel, who was born in Leipzig, inherited the business much later. Whilst maintaining the branch in Leipzig, he moved back to Moscow and spent most of his time in Russia. However, Fränkel conducted most of his business outside of Moscow. His 14-year-old son Jury mentioned in his memoirs that his father took him to the fairs in Irbit in the winter of 1913–1914, the beginning of a long sequence of tiresome trips.[27] In Irbit, Fränkel and his son encountered many members of the Brühl, one of whom was David Biedermann. After Irbit, Fränkel sent his furs back to Moscow. With the furs shipped from Moscow to Germany, he and his son travelled in the spring to Leipzig, where they stayed with their family still residing close to the Brühl. In the summer, however, the Fränkels went back to Moscow and travelled forth to Nizhnii in order to attend the fairs. The analysis of the business activities of this family firm reveals that the phenomenon of transnational entrepreneurship was seminal in the commercial links between the East and Leipzig. Such merchant families were certainly rooted in more than one social context and they maintained global trade relations of the Leipzig fur trade.

As can be seen from the example of the Fränkel family, the Moscow-Leipzig axis turned into an operating base for fur trading in Russia. Moscow was a growing hub for foreign business: a large German community was domiciled in Moscow and Nizhnii Novgorod could easily be reached from there.[28] The Chaim Eitingon AG in Leipzig, which was established by the Eitingon family in 1893, retained an important division in Moscow, which after 1910 was called the Moskauer AG für Rauchwarenhandel and was headed by a nephew of Chaim Eitingon.[29] Chaim, similar to the Fränkel family, was a transnational entrepreneur in the sense that he lived in both cities: only just before World War I he decided to reside permanently in Leipzig. Middle-sized firms also had branches in Moscow, like Koenigswerther (1910–1914) and Munisch Rapaport, a fur trader who had agents in Moscow and Nizhnii Novgorod.[30] Other Leipzig firms penetrated deeper into the Siberian heartlands in order to increase the efficiency of trade. In addition to the Moscow branch, Ariowitsch established a branch in Slobodskoi after 1904.[31] But also transnational entrepreneurship and international family networks were important for the Ariowitsch firm too, established in Leipzig in 1871. Julius Ariowitsch's father Mordechai preferred to stay in Russia: he died while visiting the Nizhnii Novgorod fair of 1878.[32]

With regard to the organisation of Russian exports, Leipzig thus profited from the presence of merchants of Jewish origins, some of whom not only held contacts in Russia but were also Russians themselves. Aside from branching, links between Russian and Leipzig were maintained through mobility. Many of the Jewish entrepreneurs clearly led transnational lives, with Leipzig being one of their social contexts. However, gentile firm owners who specialised in the trade with the East demonstrated similar behaviour. Theodor Thorer, the founder of the Theodor Thorer firm, took his son and successor Paul Thorer, aged 17, to the Russian fur centres Moscow and Nizhnii Novgorod. In order to avoid middlemen, Paul Thorer took the business further into Asia. He sent agents to Bukhara in order to buy Astrakhan and karakul sheep skins on the local market, thus circumventing the Russian trade. In 1902, Paul Thorer himself undertook a journey to Bukhara in order to expand his trade infrastructure. During his journey, he met the emir of Bukhara personally.[33] Personal contacts and travelling were of the highest importance in securing profitable supplies of furs. The structure of the Russian fur trade required personal efforts and a transnational lifestyle.

Some of the Leipzig firms were truly global firms based on this organisational pattern. An intriguing example in terms of organising Russia's foreign trade was the firm of David Biedermann (1869–1930), a Russian Jew who lived in Leipzig, which supported an impressive trade infrastructure on the Far Eastern frontier. Although he never travelled there in person, Biedermann's firm was a pioneer in organising exports from the Russian Far East, usually through the Chinese border. Biedersmann's Far East headquarters was situated in Urga (Ulan Bator), a major trade centre in Central Asia where the fur trade played an essential part. From Urga, Biedermann's Russian representatives bartered with hunters and sent caravans stuffed with supplies, tea, sugar, leather, and silver to native tribes and hunter communities in Central Asia. It was therefore one of the few Leipzig firms directly involved in cross-cultural trade. The provisions were traded for furs, wool, and animal hair.[34] While Urga was the centre of the firm's fur and wool trade, Biedermann possessed branches in Manchuria, Harbin, Chialar, and Uljajutas in Mongolia. Indeed, cities like Harbin and Tainjin had flourishing Jewish communities that traded in furs, amongst other things.[35] Biedermann integrated Leipzig into the Jewish-Chinese fur trading business. As well as having a lucrative trade passage to China, the Biedermann firm also operated through the traditional channels, participating in the fairs of Nizhnii Novgorod and Irbit. David Biedermann left the dealings of the firm at these important fur fairs to his brother in Moscow.

In terms of the Russian business, it has been established that a small business community in Leipzig constructed many ties with the East and Central Asia. Evidence regarding the activities of Leipzig merchants in Russia is patchy and certainly not exhaustive but nonetheless confirms a larger picture of dynamic German merchants in Russia prior to World War I. Leipzig merchants were successful in the Russian fur trade because of their great knowledge of local markets, customs, and networks. In addition, it has been illustrated that trade customs, like the credit system, were appropriated by local dynamics. Bank competition was beneficial to the international operations of Leipzig firms in the sense that it led to larger amounts of credit. Classic instruments like branching and agents were supplemented by transnational entrepreneurship. Many of the entrepreneurs who linked the industrial district were in fact members of more social contexts than just the Leipzig district, leading lives that took them abroad for a considerable period of time. Such a strategy was effective, although time-consuming.

Interest in the US Market

While the export of Siberian furs was dependent upon foreign business and particularly German merchants, the German fur trade was not dependent on the exports of furs from Russia. Leipzig firms increasingly turned to the US for fur importing, leaving aside London. The reason was that American firms and centres increasingly dealt in Canadian furs, eroding the HBC monopoly.[36] In this context, a few Leipzig fur firms opened branches across the Atlantic simultaneously with the shifting trade flows in Canadian furs from Great Britain to the US. Ariowitsch established a New York division that opened in 1910 and was renamed as the J. Ariowitsch Corporation in 1914. However, it was liquidated immediately after World War I. The new office in New York complemented activities on other markets, especially in

Paris (Société d'Importation de Pelleteries, Paris), London (London: Ariowitsch & Jacop Fur Co Ltd), and to a lesser extent in Stockholm (Svenska-Norska Pälsvaru-Actiebolaget).[37] The Eitingon business, originally centred around the Leipzig-Moscow connection, also opened a branch in New York in 1912; the Russian nationality of the Eitingon family saved it from liquidation during World War I.[38]

Theodor Thorer was one of the pioneers of the New York market. Alexander Thorer (the fourth son of Theodor) established the New York business in 1884; it was known as Thorer Hollender Inc. after the First World War. The New York house completed Thorer's business empire. Before 1914, he had representatives in all the major fur markets: New York, London (Raw Furs Ltd), and Paris. This was all governed from Leipzig. Maintaining a multinational business across the Atlantic was not without its problems. Alexander Thorer lacked the business acumen of his father and left America again for Germany in 1896. Between 1896 and 1904, Carl Praetorius, a local German entrepreneur, was given leadership over the New York division. In 1904, the company appointed Edward M. Speer as a manager.[39] However, relations between the head office in Leipzig and the management in New York remained dysfunctional. In 1913, the company was faced with what Thorer called himself the "worst year in company history." It made a substantial loss of around 414,000 marks, a part of which was ascribed to buy out the last shares of Praetorius in the New York branch. In February 1914, Paul Thorer and Paul Hollender reorganised the multinational structure by giving more autonomy to the New York branch, thus transforming it into a freestanding subsidiary with a capital base of $200,000. Thorer had his qualms about the activities in the US: "In recent years, it has been proven that Leipzig management over the New York division cannot be achieved in a satisfactory way. From the greater autonomy of the branch, I expect a return of the profitability of Thorer in New York."[40] Even though the management of transatlantic business was not straightforward, a few major Leipzig houses had representation in New York before World War I.

Global Competition and Collective Action

The orientation to the American market was not only caused by the fact that Canadian furs were traded by American fur companies or the increasing transatlantic business connections, but also because of the growing competition between Leipzig and London. The scant source material on the German fur industry in the years leading to World War I points to an atmosphere of conflict between the Leipzig business community and London. Above all, participation in the British auction system was a source of major discontent. Auction fees could amount to 10% of the total price of the goods.[41] However, while the auction fees were certainly galling, the main problem was that the crowded auction calendar increasingly interfered with the Leipzig fairs. The London raw fur market was saturated in the years leading to

World War I. Firms that hitherto played a secondary role in the London fur market organised important auctions as well. Next to the HBC and the Lampson & Co auctions, the A & W Nesbitt firm took a larger interest in the fur trade and the merchant banker Frederick Huth & Co organised auctions in London from 1912, which likewise dealt in North American furs.[42] The boom in London fur auctions caused concern among Leipzig trade firms, who feared for the marginalisation of their international market institutions, especially the Leipzig trade fairs. In order to counter the London auctions, fur businesses in Leipzig endeavoured to create new market institutions. Such attempts were made early on. In the 1870s, the Leipzig merchant Heinrich Lomer tried to organise auctions in order to create a Leipzig market for the distribution of North American furs, thereby undermining the leading position of London.[43] However, the attempt failed.

Interestingly, protecting the Leipzig fur trade against the British auctions was identified by individual firms as a common goal. Here, the importance of local associations came into play. In 1913, the Leipzig Fur Merchants Association opened negotiations with Lampson, one of the new players in London, in order reshape the agenda of the fur season. This led to the first meeting of international fur trade representatives in London at the Cannon Street Hotel. The Leipzig Fur Merchant Association demanded a merger between the Lampson & Co fur auctions and those of the Hudson's Bay Company in March. This would allow the Leipzigers to preserve the importance of the Easter fairs, which were at that point "enclosed" between those large auctions, the HBC March auctions, and the Lampson June auctions. However, the meeting failed to produce a satisfactory result for the Leipzig trade. The British offered minor adjustments that only eased competition between the London firms but failed to do so on an international level.[44] In 1914, the Leipzig Fur Merchant Association called for a boycott of Lampson's June auctions.[45] In Leipzig, 137 firms abided by this boycott, and 32 companies also joined them, not all of them of German origin. Incited by a sphere of war tension, rivalry on the level of international business formed the basis for cooperation between firms in the fur district. Collective action was undertaken to preserve the importance of the local economic institution that defined the position of the locality in the system of international trade.

Branching and Transnational Entrepreneurship: Leipzig and the Export Business

A final point we need to address is the position of Leipzig in terms of export markets. Figure 3.2 presents the export structure of the German fur industry at the beginning of the twentieth century, representing the same duration of the import structure. The statistics here also confirm the trend of intensified trading with the US. Exports to resource providers are particularly noteworthy. Great Britain, the US, and Russia were not only the major providers of raw furs but also important consumers of German-made furs. Nevertheless, it is clear that France was the most important customer of the German fur industry. Especially after 1904, France became the largest consumer of furs dyed in Germany by far. How was it that France was the principal customer for German furs? The answer is difficult to ascertain. Proximity was undoubtedly important since neighbouring countries, such as Belgium and Austria-Hungary, formed important markets too. The lack of fur manufacturing and an absence of a fur market in France might have played a role as well. In all likelihood, the strong presence of Leipzig-affiliated firms helped conquer the Paris sales market. It could also be argued that immigrant or transnational entrepreneurship played an important role in proximate sales markets like Paris. Before the Franco-Prussian War, a large community of German furriers was already present in the city.[46] German immigration to Paris was temporarily declined immediately after that war but ultimately returned to older levels. Around the turn of the century, several firms opened branches again: a factory from Berlin, Wolff, Wilhelm Reinecke, Herpich Söhne, and Gebr. Breslauer, a Breslau firm, are cited as new German fur firms operating on the Parisian market.[47] Leipzig firms like Konigswerther, Haendler Nathan, Ariowitsch, and Thorer followed suit.

A clearer example in which transnational entrepreneurship played an important role in conquering a foreign sales market was that of Belgium. A significant number emigrants from Saxony, mostly labourers or high-ranked employees from a Leipzig fur business, established themselves in Brussels as entrepreneurs. In Brussels, they profited from the rising consumption of manufactured furs by the expanding urban elite. Around 60 of the 136

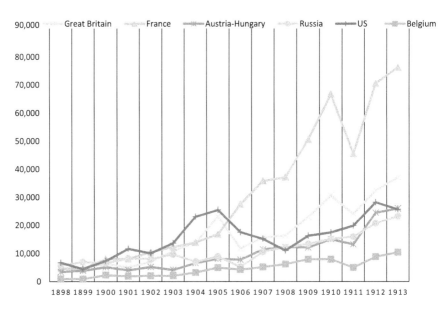

Figure 3.2 Export of German Furs (1898–1913) in thousand marks[48]

fur companies in Brussels in 1910 were in German hands.[49] Most German immigrants operated as brokers in Brussels for larger Leipzig firms, but also the larger businesses had contacts with the fur capital. Under the impulse of these entrepreneurs, German exports rose from 2.3 million marks in 1900 to 10.3 million marks in 1913.[50] This ultimately made Belgium the sixth-largest customer of German fur products (Figure 3.2). The link with the fur capital gave the entrepreneurs a competitive edge over their Belgian competitors. Similarly, the Leipzig firms derived advantages from working with local immigrant entrepreneurs. The newly settled entrepreneurs were an interesting alternative to foreign direct investment or firm branches. The migrants took the risks but were also the better judge of the local markets given their experience. Consequently, by World War I a strong transnational border-crossing network emerged between firms in Leipzig and Brussels. In addition, mobility was not only a method for procuring furs on the Russian market, but also for setting up export and sales networks abroad.

It is difficult to find a satisfactory answer regarding the role of the Saxon fur industry in the total export figure. Rough estimates have placed the proportion of the Leipzig manufactured furs at about 45% of total German exports in the years leading to World War I.[51] However, figures on Leipzig exports to the US are available and indicate the magnitude of fur manufacturing in Leipzig (see Table 3.1). The reports of the American consulate in Leipzig recognised that the largest share of imported processed furs originated from Leipzig after 1904. In fact, firms in Leipzig almost exclusively served the American import market for manufactured furs in the years immediately preceding World War I. The share of processed furs from the Leipzig fur industry in American imports was much larger than the dressing industry in Great Britain. In 1912, $7,280,000, or 40% of the

Table 3.1 American Fur Imports (1901–1912) in millions of dollars

	TOTAL FUR IMPORTS	FROM GERMANY	FROM LEIPZIG	FROM GREAT BRITAIN
1901	11.01	3.28	2.76	3.46
1902	15.62	5.32	4.23	4.61
1903	15.3	4.86	3.86	4.26
1904	14.76	5.15	4.76	3.67
1905	18.3	7.44	5.92	4.03
1906	21.85	7.65	5.65	5.04
1907	21.88	8.03	5.46	5.03
1908	15.91	5.51	4.68	3.37
1909	21.08	8.19	6.97	4.14
1910	26.59	9.31	6.92	4.72
1911	23.61	8.01	7.65	4.42
1912	24.98	9.43	7.28	4.35

total American fur imports, had been processed in the Leipzig fur cluster.[52] The value of the Leipzig exports to America equalled 29,120,000 marks and represented a 14% share of the total German fur exports. Thus, in several markets like the American one, the Leipzig industry was disproportionately large. It can be assumed that the Leipzig fur industry possessed a similar magnitude in exports to other countries as well.

Concluding Remarks

The previous Chapters 2 and 3 have discussed the formation of the industrial district in Leipzig that took place during the long nineteenth century. The fur industry was a typical Saxon industry, a consumer goods industry mainly composed of small to medium-sized businesses that was also open, pronouncedly transnational, and dependent on the world market. The argument developed in the chapter supports the observation that the formation of the industrial district cannot be separated from the external macroeconomic changes that governed the international fur industry. In fact, the chapter has demonstrated that the fur district grew when the world around the commodity was undergoing significant changes. At the same time, the chapter has engaged with the difficult task of understanding how processes of globalisation defined and determined the actions of district firms.

A number of important international trends have been identified. Firstly, the international fur trade experienced a bonanza throughout the nineteenth century. Fur consumption was clearly on the rise while at the same time the process of expansion into the fur frontiers came to its ultimate conclusion. In addition, new markets across the Atlantic Ocean were established. The result of the former was a spectacular increase in wholesale prices, whereas the latter unleashed fierce international competition. This global context of commercial expansion and competition reinforced the formation of an industrial district, activating local factors already present. These were the Leipzig trade fairs, which had aggregated local expertise in fur trading and crafting. The furrier workshops were the places where expansion in manufacturing started in the early nineteenth century. Small factories emerged out of workshops or furriers abandoned the workshop altogether but stayed in city as tailors. The surge of new businesses in Leipzig by the end of the nineteenth century was as powerful as the rising value of the international fur commerce.

However, the fur industry in Leipzig also constructed this worldwide transformation as much as it was essentially a result of it. For instance, the interplay of local economic actors not only had a positive effect on the internal dynamics of the fur district but also was often tailor-made to meet the conditions of distant commerce and transborder business activity. This was arguably the case with the role of the local banks in financing the local fur industry. Whilst firms profited from financial services to establish themselves on the local markets, tough competition forced banks to serve the 'special needs' of fur firms, allowing them to adapt to international trade parameters. The availability of credit allowed the firms to pursue an expansionist policy towards trade in Russia, where trading on credit was preferred by local traders. In other words, the large local credit market not only facilitated the opening of new business in the district, it also enabled fur entrepreneurs to pursue profits in the uncharted territory of the Siberian heartlands and the Far East frontier. What appears to be a symbiosis between two local economic actors in fact harboured a significant international dimension. It allowed the firms to construct a world market.

The dialectic between local and international dynamics in the formation of the industrial district is also evinced by entrepreneurship, particularly by transnational entrepreneurship. Foreign entrepreneurs, especially former fair visitors, were not merely attracted by the local expansion of the fur trade and industry; rather, their arrival further played a decisive role in connecting Leipzig to the outside world. Foreign entrepreneurs continued to lead transnational lives and were thereby constitutive of processes of globalisation from below.[53] Once settled in Leipzig, many foreign entrepreneurs behaved like transnational entrepreneurs, travelling or dividing their time between several offices. In the summer, a lengthy visit to the Nizhnii fairs was deemed essential for business. The same applied for the many auctions in London. Entrepreneurs and their family members further integrated Leipzig into an economic space that was a part of land-based trade network reaching deep into Siberia and Central Asia. In terms of export, transnational entrepreneurship was seminal in constructing firm links with proximate markets, like Brussels.

Even though transnational orientations marked Jewish entrepreneurs in particular, it has also been noted that they were also an integrative force on the local level. Jewish entrepreneurs participated actively in local business associations to deal with local matters and actively engaged in interfirm relations with both Jewish and gentile firms. It was thus not inimical to embeddedness. In addition, transnational entrepreneurship marked the businesses of gentile firm-owners as well. German entrepreneurs participated in the Russian trade but also migrated to proximate markets like Paris and Brussels. As such, mobility thus defined the capital in its entirety, for both gentile and Jewish entrepreneurs.

Notes

1 Osterhammel, *Die Verwandlung der Welt*, 555.
2 Drori, Honig, and Wright, "Transnational Entrepreneurship," 1001.
3 Martin, *Treasure of the Land of Darkness*, 166.
4 Kerblay, "Chasseurs et marchands de fourrures en Russie au début du XXe siècle," 356.
5 Evtuhov, "Nizhnii Novgorod in the Nineteenth Century: Portrait of a City," 268–9.
6 Kahan, *Russian Economic History*, 36.

7 McMillan, *Reinventing the Bazaar*, 76.
8 Chaudhuri, *The Trading World of Asia and the English East India Company*, 396.
9 Ray, *The Canadian Fur Trade in the Industrial Age*, 14.
10 Dohan, 104–5.
11 Ray, *The Canadian Fur Trade in the Industrial Age*, 67.
12 Ibid., 65.
13 Mallet, *Kakoot*, 7.
14 The Fur World, 1913. January. No. II. Vol. 3. Seasonality of the fur trade.
15 Berenbaum and Skolnik, "Fur Trade and Industry," 313.
16 Weiner, *Models of Nature*, 10.
17 Dohan, "Soviet Foreign Trade in the NEP Economy and Soviet Industrialization Strategy," 153.
18 Kerblay, "Chasseurs et marchands de fourrures en Russie au début du XXe siècle," 363. One ton of raw furs averagely carried the value of 2,390 roubles, whereas the processed furs of the same quantity when they entered Russia again valued 6,770 roubles.
19 Dohan, "Soviet Foreign Trade in the NEP Economy and Soviet Industrialization Strategy," 151–2. See FN. 96.
20 Statistischen Jahrbuch für das Deutsche Reich. 1914, p. 196. "Spezialhandel der wichtigeren Waren". In 1906, only between December and March.
21 Jones, *Merchants to Multinationals*, 24.
22 Lewis, "Foreign Economic Relations," 199.
23 Miller, *The Economic Development of Russia, 1905–1914*, 63.
24 Davenport-Hines and Jones, *British Business in Asia Since 1860*, 79.
25 Kahan, *Russian Economic History*, 36.
26 Harmelin, *Marcus Harmelin, Rauchwaren und Borstenkommission Leipzig*, 31.
27 Fränkel, *"Einbahnstraße" Bericht eines Lebens*, 32–3.
28 Dahlmann, "Before the Great War: German Entrepreneurs in Russia—Russian Scholars in Germany: Two Types of Russian-German Relations in the Decades before the First World War," 13. In 1897, the German community in Moscow had 17,538 members or 1.7% of the city's total population. Rougly 2,000 of them were economically self-sufficient.
29 StA-L, Dresdner Bank in Leipzig 21018, nr. 267. Leipzig, den 22.11.1912.
30 Harmelin, "Juden in Der Leipziger Rauchwarenwirtschaft," 277.
31 StA-L, Dresdner Bank in Leipzig, nr. 220. J. Ariowitsch Rauchwaren. Kreditakte. 23.08.1930.
32 Unger, *Judaica Lipsiensia*, 269.
33 *Theodor Thorer, Thorer & Co., Leipzig*, 2.
34 StA-L, Dresdner Bank in Leipzig 21018, nr. 258, f. 22. Leipzig an Deutsche Bank Berlin. Leipzig, den 4.02.1914.
35 Messmer, *China*, 124.
36 Ray, *The Canadian Fur Trade in the Industrial Age*, 64.
37 StA-L, Deutsche Bank, Filale Leipzig 21017, nr. 207. Bericht über. J. Ariowitsch, Rauchwaren, Leipzig, C1, Brühl 71, Leipzig, 04.09.1929.
38 Harmelin, "Juden in Der Leipziger Rauchwarenwirtschaft," 275.
39 Nauen, *350 Jahre Thorer*, 40.
40 StA-L, Deutsche Bank Filiale Leipzig 21017, Nr. 550. Theodor Thorer an die Deutsche Bank Filiale Leipzig, 06.03.1914.
41 Feistle, *Rauchwarenmarkt und rauchwarenhandel*, 48.
42 TNA, Hudson Bay Company Archives (Microfilm Copy). Public Record Office, (BH 3454), A 93.37. London correspondence: confidential. Lectures on the Fur Trade. Delivered at the City of London college by J.D. Forbes, October/December 1929. p. 23.

43 Gottlieb, *Der Pelzmarkt Leipzig*, 4.
44 TNA, Hudson Bay Company Archives (Microfilm Copy). Public Record Office, (BH 3454), A 93.37. London correspondence: confidential. Lectures on the Fur Trade. Delivered at the City of London college by J.D. Forbes, October/December 1929. p. 23.
45 Die Kürschnerzeitung. Nr. 12, 07.06.1914. "Zum Nichtbesuch der Londoner Juni-Auktionen." The exact reason behind the boycott is not straightforward to establish. Sentiments about the 'London monopolists' oscillated between technical matters, like practical aspects of the organisation of Lampson's auctions, and the subjective feeling that the Leipzig firms were disadvantaged in London. The technical aspects concerned the following: Lampson & Co was gradually downsizing the lots of furs to be sold, which, in turn, increased the competition between dealers as the smaller size of the lots opened possibilities for smaller firms—firms with a smaller capital basis than the traditional visitors.
46 König, "Brüche als gestaltendes Element: Die Deutschen in Paris im 19. Jahrhundert," 22.
47 Brass, *Aus dem Reiche der Pelze*, 276.
48 Data retrieved from: Statistisches Jahrbuch für das Deutsches Reich (years 1898–1913).
49 Declercq, "Transnational Entrepreneurs? German Entrepreneurs in the Belgian Fur Industry (1880–1913)," 57.
50 Statistisches Jahrbuch für das Deutsches Reich, 1901–1914.
51 Kowalzik, *Jüdisches Erwerbsleben in der inneren Nordvorstadt Leipzigs 1900–1933*, 66; Held, "Juden in Der Leipziger Rauchwarenwirtschaft," 274.
52 Benndorf, *Weltwirtschaftliche beziehungen der sächsischen industrie*, 291.
53 Ebner, "Transnationales Unternehmertum," 156.

References

Benndorf, Erich. *Weltwirtschaftliche beziehungen der sächsischen industrie*. Jena: G. Fischer, 1917.
Berenbaum, Michael, and Fred Skolnik. "Fur Trade and Industry." In *Encyclopaedia Judaica*, edited by Berenbaum Michael and Fred Skolnik, 313. Detroit: Macmillan Reference USA, 2007.
Brass, Emil. *Aus dem Reiche der Pelze*. Berlin: Im Verlage der "Neuen Pelzwaren-Zeitung und Kürschner-Zeitung," 1925.
Chaudhuri, Kirti N. *The Trading World of Asia and the English East India Company: 1660–1760*. Cambridge, UK: Cambridge University Press, 1978.
Dahlmann, Dittmar. "Before the Great War: German Entrepreneurs in Russia–Russian Scholars in Germany. Two Types of Russian-German Relations in the Decades before the First World War." In *Russian-German Special Relations in the Twentieth Century: A Closed Chapter*, edited by Karl Schlogel, 11–31. Oxford: Berg, 2006.
Davenport-Hines, R.P.T., and Geoffrey Jones. *British Business in Asia Since 1860*. Cambridge, UK: Cambridge University Press, 2003.
Declercq, Robrecht. "Transnational Entrepreneurs? German Entrepreneurs in the Belgian Fur Industry (1880–1913)." *Zeitschrift Für Unternehmensgeschichte* 1, no. 60 (2015): 52–75.
Dohan, Michael Repplier. "Soviet Foreign Trade in the NEP Economy and Soviet Industrialization Strategy." 1969.

Drori, Israel, Benson Honig, and Mike Wright. "Transnational Entrepreneurship: An Emergent Field of Study." *Entrepreneurship Theory and Practice* 33, no. 5 (September 1, 2009): 1001–22.

Ebner, Alexander. "Transnationales Unternehmertum: Wirtschaftssoziologische und institutionenökonomische Perspektiven." *Zeitschrift für Unternehmensgeschichte / Journal of Business History* 58, no. 2 (2013): 149–62.

Evtuhov, Catherine. "Nizhnii Novgorod in the Nineteenth Century: Portrait of a City." In *The Cambridge History of Russia 1689–1917*, edited by Dominic Lieven, II, 264–83. Cambridge, UK: Cambridge University Press, n.d.

Feistle, Otto. *Rauchwarenmarkt und rauchwarenhandel.* Stuttgart: W. Kohlhammer, 1931.

Fränkel, Jury. *"Einbahnstraße" Bericht eines Lebens.* Murrhardt: Rifra-Verl., 1973.

Gottlieb, Albrecht. *Der Pelzmarkt Leipzig.* Bottrop: Inaugural Dissertation Wirtschaftlichen Staatswissenschaften, 1931.

Harmelin, Wilhelm. "Juden in Der Leipziger Rauchwarenwirtschaft." *Tradition* 11 (1966): 249–82.

———. *Marcus Harmelin, Rauchwaren und Borstenkommission Leipzig: 1830–1930; zum hundertjährigen Bestehen.* Leipzig: Leipziger Universitätsverlag, 1930.

Held, Steffen. "Juden in Der Leipziger Rauchwarenwirtschaft." In *Leipzigs Wirtschaft in Vergangenheit Und Gegenwart: Akteure, Handlungsspielräume, Wirkungen (1400–2011)*, edited by Susanne Scholz, 269–85. Leipzig: Leipziger Universitätsverlag, 2012.

Jones, Geoffrey. *Merchants to Multinationals: British Trading Companies in the Nineteenth and Twentieth Centuries.* Oxford: Oxford University Press, 2000.

Kahan, Arcadius. *Russian Economic History: The Nineteenth Century.* Chicago: University of Chicago Press, 1989.

Kerblay, Basile. "Chasseurs et marchands de fourrures en Russie au début du XXe siècle." *Cahiers du Monde Russe* 19 (1978): 339–70.

König, Mareike, ed. "Brüche als gestaltendes Element: Die Deutschen in Paris im 19. Jahrhundert." In *Deutsche Handwerker, Arbeiter und Dienstmädchen in Paris: eine vergessene Migration im 19. Jahrhundert*, edited by Mareike König, 9–27. München: Oldenbourg, 2003.

Kowalzik, Barbara. *Jüdisches Erwerbsleben in der inneren Nordvorstadt Leipzigs 1900–1933.* Leipzig: Leipziger Universitätsverlag, 1999.

Lewis, Robert. "Foreign Economic Relations." In *The Economic Transformation of the Soviet Union, 1913–1945*, edited by R. W. Davies, Mark Harrison, and S. G. Wheatcroft, 198–216. Cambridge, UK: Cambridge University Press, 1994.

Mallet, Thierry. *Kakoot: récits du pays des caribous.* Sillery: Les éditions du Septentrion, 2000.

Martin, Janet. *Treasure of the Land of Darkness.* Cambridge, UK: Cambridge University Press, 1986. http://dx.doi.org/10.1017/CBO9780511523199.

McMillan, John. *Reinventing the Bazaar: A Natural History of Markets.* London: W. W. Norton & Company, 2003.

Messmer, Matthias. *China: Schauplätze west-östlicher Begegnungen.* Vienna: Böhlau Verlag Wien, 2007.

Miller, Margaret Stevenson. *The Economic Development of Russia, 1905–1914: With Special Reference to Trade, Industry, and Finance.* London: Psychology Press, 1967.

Nauen, Otto. *350 Jahre Thorer.* Frankfurt am Main: Thorer & Hollender, 1962.

Osterhammel, Jürgen. *Die Verwandlung der Welt: eine Geschichte des 19. Jahrhunderts*. München: C. H. Beck, 2009.

Ray, Arthur J. *The Canadian Fur Trade in the Industrial Age*. Toronto: University of Toronto Press, 1990.

Theodor Thorer, Thorer & Co., Leipzig. Berlin [SW 68, Alexandrinenstr. 134]: Adolf Ecksteins Verl., 1929.

Unger, Manfred. *Judaica Lipsiensia: zur Geschichte der Juden in Leipzig*. Leipzig: Edition Leipzig, 1994.

Weiner, Douglas R. *Models of Nature*. Pittsburgh, PA: University of Pittsburgh Press, 2000.

Part II

Finding World Market Alternatives (1903–1939)

4 The Karakul Farming Experiment in South West Africa (1903–1933)

Introduction

The chapter opens the section on how businesses of the Leipzig fur industry created and found alternatives to the world market. The creation of alternatives by the Leipzig fur industry are presented here as the result of various exogenous developments that took place between 1900 and 1930. As described above, resource scarcity and the fierce competition over resources characterised the modern fur industry at the turn of the century. The first example of the sourcing of an alternative supply chain, namely karakul farming in the German colonies, will be presented as a reaction against global competition. The mass production of rabbit skins as a process of resource substitution during World War I is presented in Chapter 5 and fox breeding in Weimar Germany as an autarkic response to resource scarcity in Chapter 6. The section on sourcing new resources will shed light on local processes of collaboration and the actions of individual district firms in dealing with external developments.

This chapter deals with the transplantation of karakul sheep to South West Africa and how the Leipzig industry was involved in this activity. Karakuls were a popular type of fur for the fur industry by the end of the nineteenth century; they were however difficult to procure, obtainable only from a few number of distant markets (emirate of Buchara, Afghanistan). It is in this context that karakul farming as a colonial project surfaces. With this chapter, the history of the Leipzig fur capital interacts with Germany's colonial history. In terms of scholarly research, there is not much to build on. Most studies of German colonial business have stressed the economic irrelevance and unprofitability of the empire, thereby explaining the lukewarm interest of German business in the exploitation of their territories.[1] Small and large businesses alike were apparently absent from processes of imperial exploitation. However, a growing body of literature reveals that such interests did exist. Rather than registering business activities in the broad sweep of colonial trade statistics, such treatments offer a qualitative reading of colonial exploitation by seeing business interests in relation to scientific imperialism and the colonial state. Especially revealing in terms of business history is the attention that has been paid to business involvement in the creation of imperial infrastructures and "new production paradigms."[2] The work of Zimmerman and Beckert is worth mentioning in this regard: they have described the endeavours of the German colonial administration and industrial representatives in the Colonial Economic Committee to create a cotton plantation industry for German Africa.[3] Such projects of colonial improvement and development, although often unexecuted, were strongly connected to networks of science as well. The karakul industry created by the fur industry, if largely unknown in historiography, was one of the most successful in the context of the German empire.

The chapter will investigate how district firms pursued such imperial ambitions. Who were the main actors in the industrial district? Was it the result of individual firms or local collective action? Given their specialised nature, how did firms organise the creation of a new production paradigm in the colonies? Even the largest firms in the district arguably lacked the funds to attract agricultural experts or provide for the costly transport and the acquisition of farmland. It is assumed here that the fur business was involved in ways that were not significantly different from those of other business enterprises with an interest in the German empire. Businesses worked in close collaboration with the colonial state and with experts and scientists, who carefully examined the possible economic future of newly acquired colonies. The link with expert knowledge will especially be emphasised. As Joseph Morgan Hodge has noted, imperialists turned to scientific expertise in order to deal with the problems of production and resource management both at home and abroad.[4] This was certainly the case for South West Africa, one of the most desolate German colonies but also the centrepiece of settler colonialism.[5]

To a greater or lesser extent, this chapter is a chronological account of the creation of the karakul farming business in South West Africa. The key thread is the role of the industrial district in the sourcing of fur resources in the colony. I begin by portraying the global karakul trade at the end of the nineteenth century. Then I will devote attention to the link between the Leipzig fur business and agricultural science at the beginning of the twentieth century and how this alliance set in motion controlled karakul farming by 1914. It will be demonstrated that the history of karakul farming in relation to the Leipzig fur industry did not end with World War I. The settlers and karakul farmers in South West Africa were one of the few links that remained between Germany and its former empire.[6] However, the loss of empire necessitated a different approach towards fur farming in the interwar period.[7] Lacking the tools of empire, the fur industry both profited and was troubled by the expansion of karakul farming in South West Africa.

The Making of the German Karakul Industry (1903–1914)

The Limits of Global Trade and the Prospects of Agricultural Science

Native to the steppes of Central Asia, karakul and astrakhan sheep formed a niche in the international fur industry. Like the rest of the fur industry, it was a niche that was growing rapidly by the end of the nineteenth century. Karakul fur owed its attractiveness to the black curly locks of the lamb. Because these thick lamb curls rapidly changed into less valuable sheep wool, karakul lambs were usually slaughtered for their skins when 3 to 10 days old. Even more precious was the pelt of the stillborn foetal karakul lamb because of its so-called "moire pattern."[8] By far the most lucrative, the skins of the stillborn lambs were labelled and sold on the international fur market as "broadtails."

The karakul pelt became popular in Germany and Europe at the end of the nineteenth century. However, only a few firms in Leipzig were specialised in the manufacture of the karakul skin. A. Herzog established the first dyeing firm in Leipzig specialised in the processing of karakul and astrakhan lambskins.[9] The most important firm was undoubtedly that of Theodor Thorer. In 1882, Thorer developed a secret industrial dye to apply to this type of skin. Consequently, Thorer specialised in both the trading and processing of this commodity and led the Leipzig market in the black fur sector.[10] By the late 1880s, Thorer was one of the leading firms in the international manufacture of lambskins well into the 1930s. At a later stage, the Leipzig auction company RAVAG also played a role in the karakul trade. Thus, the karakul trade was limited to only a few firms of the Leipzig fur cluster.

The Thorer firm was also the most active in the international karakul trade. In 1905, Thorer imported 385,000 of these skins worth about 6,000,000 marks from Bukhara, the main procurement area in the world trade.[11] Commercial networks with the emirate of Bukhara were paramount in securing supplies. Paul Thorer, the oldest son of Theodor and owner of the firm between 1892 and 1920, personally undertook lengthy journeys to Bukhara to obtain karakul skins. Karakul and Astrakhan skins were also put on sale as well in the fairs of Nishnni Novgorod at the so-called "Wostostschnii bazaar." The sales were conducted by a trustee of the emir of Bukhara.[12] Nevertheless, the Thorer firm endeavoured to buy the skins directly at their source. In 1909, the director of the Deutsche Bank in Leipzig characterised Paul Thorer as "the authority in the world trade in Persian skins [karakuls]" and noted the exhausting travelling that came along with such eminence: "For many years, Paul Thorer has gone regularly to Bukhara, the country where Persian skins are produced, to acquire information on the situation and prospects of the karakul market."[13] In Bukhara, Paul Thorer was immersed in forging trade networks with local representatives who bought the skins from local dealers in the steppes and brought them to the Bukhara market. In addition, he set up a commercial network around Astrakhan furs in Tashkent. His closest business partner there was the German firm Wilhelm Durrschmidt.[14]

Although it seems that Thorer was quite successful in securing supply routes in Russia and Central Asia, the dependency on the stretched trade trajectories, the time-consuming travelling, and contact with the go-between traders in Bukhara produced irritation in the company's management. Particularly unpalatable to Thorer was the lack of dexterity among traders in the Emirate of Bukhara in preparing the skins for the export. He noted in 1913 that "this method [of preparing] is well known to me, but it is cumbersome, time consuming, not at all used properly and . . . dangerous to the value of the goods."[15] Reports on trading in Bukhara that circulated in Leipzig (the international success of the Thorer in the karakul market attracted a great deal of interest) complained about the unreliability of Bukharian traders and the difficult circumstances under which German traders operated in the Emirate.

As early as 1903, consequently, Thorer first suggested bringing karakul farming to Germany or its colonies during a speech about his travelling experiences to Bukhara. With demand for karakul garments steadily rising, Thorer was confronted by the prospects of stagnating supply and increased competition. In 1910, he wrote to Bernhard Dernburg, state secretary of the *Reichskolonialamt*, that "the increased consumption of fur garments in general makes it even more promising to enhance karakul production in the colonies . . . it appears that the Turkestan steppes will not be able to increase their stock for mass-production."[16] Therefore, the plans to install karakul farming in South West Africa cannot be understood without taking this global economic dimension into account. Rather than being dependent on unreliable trade partners, Thorer felt that control over the supply chain was of paramount importance for the development of his business. The idea to create a new source of resources was thus strongly linked to a single firm in the district. As such, Theodor Thorer acted as a lead firm in the global commerce of karakuls and played the most prominent role in advocating the creation of a new supply chain inside the German empire. However, the Thorer firm needed the help of other partners in executing the project.

The Value of Agricultural Expertise

While organising long-distance trade with the emirate caused Theodor Thoror problems, the transplantation of karakuls was certainly not a straightforward enterprise. It required cooperation beyond the fur business, with scientists and the colonial state. In the early stage of the project, networks with university science departments were the most important since karakul farming, and fur farming more generally, was a completely new industry. The firm chose to cooperate with a local partner, the agricultural institute in Halle (which was established in 1863 and was 35 kilometres from Leipzig). The director Julius Kühn was one of Thorer's personal acquaintances and an *éminence grise* in the German agricultural sciences.[17] For several decades, the Halle institute maintained its pivotal role in German karakul farming in South West Africa. It first tested karakul farming in Germany before introducing the black sheep in the colonies. In 1913, the German colonial administration finally appointed Halle as the official research institution for colonial karakul farming.[18]

The cooperative relationship between Halle and the fur industry was strongly linked to the emergence of genetics as the dominant paradigm in biology and life science at the beginning of the twentieth century.[19] Across Europe, studies on animal and plant genetics that strictly separated organism and inheritance were increasingly changing the field of biology and challenging earlier notions of biology, which saw the immediate surroundings as the determining factor of life forms. Animal genetics opened the door for improving and modifying life forms, but also the physical qualities of an animal. Genetics, and its main tool of artificial selection, was therefore indispensable in creating fur farming as a new source of resources.

Kühn, an advocate of Mendelian genetics, experimented on raising karakuls in Germany between 1903 and 1908.[20] Breeding an independent and standard karakul flock in Germany or its colonies required crossbreeding experiments with other types of sheep. The first experiments with karakuls were performed on four rams and 28 ewes; they were brought to Germany via Thorer's business contacts in Tashkent. The crossbreeding experiments took place on the Heidegut Timmerloh farm, located in the vicinity of Soltau.[21] Other agricultural scientists joined Kühn in his attempts to prove the feasibility of karakul farming. Leopold Adametz, a professor in the K.K. Hochschule für Bodenkultur in Vienna, had been studying the rearing and breeding of karakuls since the beginning of the twentieth century. Leopold Adametz, a professor in Vienna, argued for applied genetics as to propel successful Karakul farming: "A good breeder will be able to modify and enlarge the organism of the animals and to positively influence the characteristics of the karakul, especially the beautiful curls of the lamb, despite the absence of a dry domestic climate."[22] Scientists were also instrumental in making links to the world of agriculture. Kühn argued in 1906 for the promising future of karakuls in animal farming in the newspapers of the German Agricultural Society: "The nature of these pelts is so excellent that we can probably count on a continuous demand."[23]

The German interest in karakul breeding was not an isolated phenomenon. On the eve of World War I, agricultural experts across Europe had successfully introduced breeding stocks. The Russians in particular had successfully created and maintained flocks of half-breed karakul in particular areas. By 1912, large flocks of the Russian half-breeds grazed on the meadows of Bessarabia.[24] A few years later, Russian farmers kept karakuls in Iakovleva; with some 2,000 animals, they had at the largest karakul flock outside Bukhara.[25] In the US and in Great Britain, the results of crossbreeding experiments began to unveil the possibilities of karakul breeding in domestic agriculture. Thorer's business contacts mentioned the presence of American experts in Central Asia performing studies on the breeding of karakuls.[26] Confirmed exports of karakul sheep to the US took place in 1912.

Mendelian Genetics as the Handmaiden of the Fur Industry

The success of the Kühn experiments promoted by the Leipzig fur industry on karakul rearing in Germany quickly attracted the interest of the German colonial administration in Windhuk. Extensive karakul farming was 'naturally' suited to the arid lands of Namibia. In particular, the project evoked the interest of governor von Lindequist and he corresponded intensively with Paul Thorer from 1906. It did not take long for von Lindequist to order 120 ewes and 20 rams through Thorer's business channels in Tashkent.[27] The colonial administration's interest in fur farming took shape just when migration to the colony started to soar. Between 1907 and 1913, when the first karakuls arrived in South West Africa, the white population went from 7,110 to almost 13,000.[28] The first shipments of karakul sheep were sent to the German protectorate in Africa from 1908 to 1909. Small but numerous shipments formed the basis of the karakul herd in South West Africa. Another shipment was organised by the Thorer company in 1913. In addition, other firms also organised the import of karakul sheep to South West Africa; the famous animal trade firm Haegenbeck of Hamburg increased the size of the herd still further. At this stage, it is important to stress that the colonial project was no longer exclusive to the Thorer company: the Leipzig dyeing factory Herzog also entered the colonial project when it organised a small shipment of six additional rams to South West Africa.[29]

Transportation was a time-consuming process. Before karakuls were shipped from Bukhara across Russia, German agricultural experts carefully inspected the quality of the karakuls. These experts, most notably Simon von Nathusius (Jena University), were assisted by Theodor Thorer's business connections in Central Asia. Trains brought the karakul herds to Hamburg where they were put on steamers to the German protectorate. Once unloaded, the herd was brought to the Fürstenwalde state farm in the vicinity of Windhuk.[30] The karakuls remained under the control of agricultural experts working for the industry and the colonial state throughout the entire journey,

Tight expert supervision and the creation of the central agricultural station in Fürstenwalde were two of the demands of the fur industry and Paul Thorer in particular. Afraid that the project would drown in a quagmire of "amateurism," Thorer asked that the "*Stammherde*" be put under the supervision of "a strong and smart personality." Furthermore, Thorer stressed that those experts should make karakul rams available only to those farmers who were willing "to send goods of high quality to Germany."[31] As 'pure' karakuls were limited in the number, the success of karakul farming in South West Africa depended on the continuation of crossbreeding experiments. Under the leadership of its director Koeppel, the Fürstenwalde centre strictly monitored the sale of karakuls to German farmers. The strict control over karakuls was also necessary because of an insufficiency of 'breeding material.' Supply problems were the chief concern. As the trans-Caucasian passage was not suited for large animal shipments, cargo had to go by rail from Bukhara to Moscow.[32] Problems with the organisation of this long journey erupted when the Russians refused to cooperate in 1913.[33] According to the German colonial administration, the Russians wanted to protect their own karakul farming business. And secondly, the first karakul herds in South West Africa suffered from high mortality rates.

Due to these problems, it was finally decided to create a crossbreed based on the mixture between karakul and African sheep, like the Perser and Somali variants. Selective breeding according to Mendelian principles was the means to achieve this goal. The colonial state could control this operation via Fürstenwalde. It took measures to ensure that the karakul sheep sold to the colonists were used in accordance with these plans. Purchase contracts cited numerous stipulations with regard to the care and the mating of rams. Farmers signed a contract obliging them to use the rams only to "enhance" crossbreeding (*Aufkreuzung*) with domestic Perser and Somali "blood" (crossbreeding with other species of sheep was strictly forbidden).[34] Farmers had no choice other than to sign this contract as the karakul ram was a precious item: "Given the limited number of pure-blooded rams in the protectorate and the uncertainty of supply of the original animals, it is an essential task of the breeder to use the valuable ram from the state farm efficiently and keep it capable of reproducing as long as possible."[35] By 1913, German colonists owned about 335 pure karakul rams and 830 pure ewes.

Crossbreeding the karakul with African sheep made good progress in the years leading up to World War I. In 1913, Koeppel, the director of Fürstenwalde, personally inspected 15 farms in the east of South West Africa in order to assess the development of crossbreeding. The report made clear that German farmers had carefully followed the instructions by joining the karakul rams with the 'African' herds "until the last sheep is mixed with the karakul." Koeppel was optimistic about the results in the east of South West Africa: "In regards to the inheritance of colour and morphological characteristics, one can be really satisfied, since crossbreeding started here in January 1912 and it concerns first generation breeds."[36] Koeppel was strongly convinced that the "half-bloods" were adequately adapted to the arid environment of the south: "The crossbred sheep are more resistant, quieter in temperament, and more sociable."[37] By 1914, the distribution policy had created a herd of 21,000 mixed African karakul sheep, which would eventually form the core of the African fur supply for Leipzig.

The agricultural experts who collaborated with the fur trade in Leipzig made artificial selection the norm in the creation of the African karakul. Genetics and artificial selection therefore came to play a dominant role in the daily practice of colonial farming. In January 1913, Koeppel explained the importance of artificial selection in producing for the fur industry to the Agricultural Association in Windhuk. The main yardstick for the new species was fur: "The pattern of fur must be equally balanced, that is, the curls must extend evenly over the body and its extremities. Desired is the karakul curl that is both small and firm, with the tip turned inward."[38] The farmers received classification guidelines in order to enhance their breeding stock for karakul farming. According to these guidelines, farmers ought to achieve this goal by focusing on a number of physical characteristics, some of which were quite obvious (such as the pureness of the black colour, the so-called "*Far-benreinheit*") whilst others were of a more biometric nature (for instance, the shape of the nose). Colonial farmers were thereby given a very basic introduction to the tenets of applied Mendelian genetics. The classification system translated genetics into the observable qualities of living beings and served as a handbook for karakul farmers in South West Africa.

Experts sought to improve the classification system by attaching more precise biometric data to describe an ideal crossbreed karakul that would be suitable for further breeding. Von Nathusius, professor in agriculture at the Halle University, made the first attempt to deepen the rating system when he inspected karakuls awaiting dispatch in Hamburg. For von Nathusius, the smoothness of the skin was the indisputable yardstick for grading the karakuls, but he also realised that measurable data was required to judge characteristics. In order to create such biometric standards, the colonial administrators and scientists invited Herzog, an industrialist from the Leipzig fur industry. Under the influence of Herzog, it was decided that the classification system that formed the basis for artificial selection should focus on the "the character of the curly locks before the lamb reaches 12 days of age."[39] The biological result of crossbreeding was increasingly tailored according to the needs of the fur factory. As Herzog noted, "A solid fleece with less pronounced locks is preferred over a lose fleece with pronounced locks, since the former is better for dressing whereas the latter is lost during production process."[40] Mendelian genetics was an increasingly sophisticated instrument for the fur industry.

The additional discussions between experts and the fur industry led to the creation of a new uniform 'list' that gave scores to biometric data such as height, dimensions of the body parts, and shades of colour. At several junctions in the karakul's life span, the farmer ought to fill in this document by giving marks to various characteristics of the karakul. The ultimate aim was to create a biometric certificate system for the karakuls in South West Africa, with each karakul having its own biometric passport. The final step in the creation of the German-African karakul was separating 'inferior' crossbreeds from superior ones on the basis of fur quality.[41] The system of biometric karakul certificates was never put in place because of the outbreak of World War I. Nevertheless, it marked an advance for genetics as an applied science in agricultural business.

Furthermore, the selection systems and classification models mattered to colonial farmers from an economic point of view. Koeppel had already made clear to the Windhuk Agricultural Society that successfully practicing artificial selection was important for commercial success since the grading system of the fur industry was based on colour purity and the perfection of the curls. As an agricultural expert, Koeppel was in very close contact with the fur industry. When he gave his lecture to the German colonists, he had just returned from a work trip to Leipzig. At the demand of the colonial administration, Koeppel was instructed to spend his 1913 journey to Germany in Leipzig in order to gain insight into the Thorer factory and the "grading system for manufacturing the fur of the karakul."[42] Upon his return, he lectured to the farmers to the Windhuk Agricultural Society: "The production of a good, uniform, and even curl types of lambs . . . is the most important [thing]. A sufficient balance in terms of skin quality will lead to a rising and uniform wholesale price and, in other words, enhance the profitability of this branch of farming."[43]

Skin quality was the criterion in the development of a price-setting mechanism. The fur industry made five distinctions in quality: the first one, the stillborn pelt, was the highest type, and it exceeded the price of any other karakul pelt because of its perfect moiré pattern. The second category (I) met the production requirements for end products such as coats and other garments. Supplies graded as type II were destined for the trimming of fur jackets. Pelts graded lower than this were no longer highly valued and could only be used in low-value clothing products like hats (type III). Pelts that did not correspond to quality requirements were simply worthless (type IV). This classification system explicitly explained the low value of substandard types by reference to breeding and selection. Type III pelts were called 'inferior' whereas type IV skins were denounced as "unfit breeds."[44] The whole 'blueprint' for trade in African karakul skins was thus firmly undergirded by artificial selection. 'Good' breeders were to be rewarded and 'bad' breeders sanctioned. Successful reproduction of the black fur skin formed the basis of the price-setting mechanism adopted by the Leipzig houses like Theodor Thorer.

Other Influences from the Leipzig Industry

Stages of the new production process other than the breeding of animals were governed by similar patterns of cooperation between the colonial administration and the fur industry. Fur traders were regularly asked to deliver feedback on developments in the first wave of African karakul farming. The Leipzig fur industry, and the firms Theodor Thorer and Herzog in particular, issued a number of recommendations on the treatment and packaging of skins. The *Agricultural Review (Landwirtschaftliche Umschau)* in South West Africa published the recommendations of the fur industry concerning the drying, packing, and preventative treatment of the skins. On behalf of the A. Herzog dyeing factory, the *Umschau* also instructed that dried skins had to be treated with the environment-polluting naphthalene instead of a basic salt treatment.[45] Later, the fur industry modified its recommendations and suggested the use of trichlorbenzol instead of naphthalene.[46]

In 1914, the Theodor Thorer firm received a batch of 25 skins from Fürstenwalde. The feedback that the Thorer firm transmitted made it clear that the new supply chain was still suffering from deficiencies. According to Thorer, some of the procedures, packing for instance, were still poorly executed despite previous explanations: "In several cases, the leather of the skins has suffered from insufficient packing and the skins are therefore damaged in the dyeing process in our factory."[47] Thorer's recommendations show the German farmers' initial lack of dexterity in this new line of business. He gave clear instructions to the state farm concerning how the procured skins should be dried: "I have to advise, once again, that the skins have to dried, in stretched condition, protected from direct sunlight." The packing technique was also not satisfactory: "During shipping, skins have to be bound leather side on leather side and fur-side on fur-side in bunches of 10 or 20." According to Thorer, only one farmer so far had proven his dexterity in the treatment and packaging of the furs.[48]

The instructions of the fur industry and the interference of the colonial administration were paramount in the creation of the karakul farming business. For example, several farmers neglected the instructions and sought to produce crossbreeds largely for wool production, a fact that was most unpalatable for the fur traders. Mention was made of two farms in the east that kept karakuls for wool production. This illustrates that the creation of fur farming from scratch was not as straightforward as foreseen. Thorer testified later that: "distrust in farmer circles had to be overcome. The farmers felt comfortable with the production of meat and wool, to which the karakul was ill suited. Moreover, the introduction of karakul keeping was perceived by many German farmers as a great increase of work because of the slaughtering of the lambs and the refinement of skins. Overall, farmers lacked knowledge about this special breed. The karakul brought a change in their perception of extensive pasture, of which the conservative farmer was suspiciously reluctant."[49]

Nevertheless, the strategy of cooperation between the colonial state and a few fur firms was apparently successful. By 1913, about 1,155 pure breed and 21,000 crossbreed karakuls inhabited South West Africa. On the eve of World War I, the karakul skin trade was on the verge of becoming a major sector of intensive farming in South West Africa. During the war, the British acknowledged the positive results of the German endeavour to establish fur farms in Africa. The *Westminster Gazette* wrote in 1917 that "should German South-West Africa come under the British Flag, the caracul fur industry of that colony is likely to prove an asset of increasing value."[50] Furthermore, the promising results of karakul breeding led to heightened attention to the colonial opportunities that fur farming offered. In 1910, the Colonial Office's interest in creating new fur resources deepened when other eligible types of furbearing animals were discussed with representatives of the industry, zoologists, and agricultural experts.[51] The animal trading firm Hagenbeck and the fur trader Paul Thorer figured prominently as experts in this investigation. The colonial administration produced a lengthy report on "the possibility of elevating the production of fur and leather in Germany." Mention was made of the soaring prices in the international fur trade and it was held to be possible that "fur bearing animals could increase the value of some poor soils" both inside Germany and in its empire. However, the empire consisted mainly of tropical and arid areas,[52] which were not particularly well suited to keeping subarctic furbearing animals. The recommendations of the industry and university scientists were therefore limited to farming opossums and kangaroos. Nevertheless, it once again illustrates the link between the fur industry and imperialism in Germany.

Post-War Developments in the Karakul
Farming Industry (1914–1939)

The war had a disruptive impact on karakul farming in South West Africa. Farmers who joined the military neglected their herds and, more importantly, were cut off from the market in Leipzig and the support of the colonial administration. Allied forces fully conquered South West Africa in 1915 and transplanted the Fürstenwalde herd to Ojituesu, from whence many karakuls were sold to the South African agricultural school in Middelburg.[53] However, after the war, farmers in South West Africa took the initiative and tried to restore ties with Leipzig. A delegation of fur farmers visited Germany a few years after the war seeking to re-establish connections with the Leipzig industry. During the period 1920–1922, a few thousand pelts of South West African origin found their way to the Thorer factory.[54]

Despite the renewal of ties, it was difficult for the German fur industry and the colonial administration (Germany retained a colonial administration despite the loss of its empire) to support the karakul industry. German farmers were in dire need of new pure-breed rams in order to counter the "degeneration and inbreeding of the African stock."[55] However, new karakuls could only arrive in South West Africa in very small numbers. With Bukhara now an integral part of the USSR, the Soviets restricted the passage of karakuls in order to prevent the nurture of competing karakul flocks, just as tsarist administrators had done. Equally, the South African Union periodically blocked cattle imports from Germany, officially out of a veterinary concern for foot-and-mouth disease in continental Europe. The German Foreign Office sporadically managed to convince the Russians that imports were only destined for Germany and were desired only for research purposes in order to prevent the impression that the Soviets were supporting competitors in South West Africa.[56] Under this pretext, small numbers of karakuls managed to leave the Soviet Union for Germany and then ultimately went to South West Africa.

For the most part, the same actors were involved in supporting the karakul farmers in the former colony as before the war. Professor Frölich, who succeeded Julius Kuhn as the director of the Institute for Animal Breeding in Halle, Arndt Thorer (the son of Paul Thorer, who had died in 1920), and the Ministry of Foreign Affairs were actively involved in the transplantation of karakuls to the mandate. In 1927, they organised an expedition to Central Asia in order to choose a sample of karakul sheep. The *Reichszentrale für Pelztier und Rauchwarenforschung* (a research network sponsored by a number of firms in Leipzig), the Ministry of Foreign Affairs, and the Ministry of Education jointly financed the costs of the expedition.[57]

A further obstacle for the post-war karakul farming was the problematic situation of German colonists in South West Africa. In the early years of the mandate, the remaining colonists suffered from their incorporation into the Union of South Africa, as they had to abandon the German mark and accept the South African pound. In addition, Boers from South Africa crossed the border and took land from the troubled German colonists. Therefore, several herds owned by German farmers were in danger of falling into the hands of foreign buyers. To make matters worse, Namibia suffered from a severe drought in 1926.[58]

Unable to rely on the colonial administration, the problematic situation entailed more active involvement from the Leipzig fur industry in the former colony. From 1924 onwards, Thorer centralised his operations in South West Africa by establishing a subsidiary, the SWA-Karakul-Centrale (from 1928 called the SWA Karakul-Centrale Ltd). Besides the "Centrale," the Theodor Thorer firm purchased a large farm in the Rehoboth district of about 7,207 hectares. The Thorer branch thereby became an important link in the supply of karakul skins from South West Africa to Germany. In order to prevent the sale of land to non-German farmers, the Centrale purchased farms from colonists and ran them on the basis of shared ownership. These were the so-called "half-share flocks": the Thorer company became the co-owner of the flock while the farmer continued to manage it. Furthermore, the revenue was divided between the Centrale and the flock's manager. By 1931, the Karakul-Centrale owned six herds of this type, which were worth 76,228 RM in total.[59] The subsidiary acted also as a procurement centre for exports to the Leipzig fur industry.

The influence of the Karakul-Centrale in South West Africa was based on local cooperation with German farmers and with the local merchant bank Olthaver & List Trust Co, which was in charge of financial transactions and made monthly reports to the head office. Furthermore, the cooperation between Albert Voigt, a member of the board, and Otto Nauen, a manager of the Thorer company, was important. Voigt and his brother Gustav were pioneers in the breeding of karakuls and other non-domestic animals in South West Africa. The first karakuls were grazing on the Voigtland farm in 1908.[60] Furthermore, this farm was regarded as one of the best organised in South West Africa.[61] The Voigt brothers were not only experts in farming in Namibia, but also popular figures of German colonialism. As such, the connection with Voigt was useful for promoting the karakul industry inside Germany as well.[62] By cooperating with the Voigt brothers, the Thorer concern made an important alliance on the local level, buttressing their position in the South West African farm economy.

By buying land and procuring furs directly, the main goal of the Thorer intervention gradually shifted from reversing the demise of the karakul herds to stimulating supply to Leipzig. Paul Hollender, the manager of the Thorer business, wrote in 1932 that "the acquisition of land is not only done with the purpose of obtaining pastures for our karakul stock but also to influence the German breeders to send their skin produce to Leipzig."[63] The Thorer policy was also aimed at expanding the size of Karakul farming. The Centrale accomplished this long-term goal by extending credit to farmers, usually as advantages on future yields.[64] As such, the district firm Thorer actively intervened in Africa by setting up transcrossing trade flows. The Thorer firm was arguably more active in Africa after the loss of the empire.

The intervention of the Thorer business had a stimulating effect on karakul farming in South West Africa. Most importantly, credit advances remedied economic pressures on farmers who were killing the lambs for immediate profits. After 1924, several German farmers thereby managed to restore and even expand their flocks.[65] Farmers in South West Africa not only profited from the presence of Thorer; the South African government also heavily subsidised agriculture in its new territory. After the drought of 1926, for instance, the government allocated advance payments of up to £400 to replace losses.[66] In the long run, support from business as well as the state led to a more secure basis for breeding in South West Africa. By 1930, just before exports reached their crescendo, the former German colony was home to about 150,000 karakul sheep, spread among 1,200 farmers. To a certain extent, karakuls were relatively equally divided over these farms but some stood out with thousands of karakuls.[67] The breeding basis of karakuls grew exponentially thereafter: the stock of African karakuls numbered 369,359 in 1931, 514,629 in 1932, and 552,178 in 1933.

As the result of direct business and government intervention, karakul pelting finally turned into one of the most important export products of the South West African mandate. Exports of karakul skins for the world market increased from the early 1920s onwards but soared in the early 1930s. In the trade balance of mandate South West Africa, the karakul trade assumed a prominent position. In 1933, trade statistics estimated that about one-third of the mandate's total exports (£1,400,000) were generated by the karakul trade (£444,000).[68] The karakul industry continued to hold this position throughout the 1930s. Of a total export value of £3,689,800 in 1937, about £2,099,750 (57%) was ascribed to the agricultural sector. The karakul trade accounted for over half of all agricultural exports (58% or £1,222,629, a staggering 33% of total exports).[69] The trade reached its apex when it overtook diamonds in export value in 1938. It remained one of the largest export value creators of the Namibian economy in subsequent decades. The Thorer business profited from these exports, but also other businesses in Leipzig, foremost the RAVAG, a joint venture for importing and selling skins between a number of fur firms in Leipzig. On the long run however, the Leipzig businesses were unable to profit fully from the karakul boom in South West Africa, and market share was lost to the London fur trade. Currency restrictions and import quotas coincided with the sudden swell of African karakul business that took place in the early 1930s. In

1932, £100,000 of a total export value of £141,000 went to Leipzig while £40,000 went to London. A year later, the pendulum had swung in favour of London: £192,000 worth of karakul pelts were shipped to London. The total karakul export in that year was worth £433,000 but only £179,000 from this yield went directly to Leipzig.[70] By 1937, Leipzig only attracted 29% of the total karakul skins produced in South West Africa.

Conclusion

What does karakul farming reveal about the industrial district and its connections to the outside world? The empirical data in this chapter has established the importance of individual lead firms in the creation of karakul farming. The creation of karakul farming in the colonies was a reaction of a single firm towards global competition, not a collective one. Both the world trade and the organisation of karakul transplantation continued to lie in the hands of the Thorer firm. In the very first stage of experimental karakul farming, Thorer worked behind the scenes. Other firms, like the dyeing factory Herzog and the RAVAG, joined in at a much later stage. With the Fürstenwalde state farm in a pivotal role, business, science, and the state worked together in order to create the karakul industry in the South West African settler colony. As such, the organisation of karakul farming was not the result of the groups of firms or collaborative networks amongst firm owners that were so typical of the district. Rather, the role of independent lead dynamic firms in the construction of the new source of resources was fundamental.

The activities of lead firms did not necessarily disturb firm interdependency in the district, as this constituted a niche in the international fur business. As such, it allowed those firms specialised in the trade of lambskins to adjust their local specialisation to external changes in resource production. Importantly, from a more general perspective, the benefits of the karakul farming project were not restricted to the lead firms involved but fertilised the district economy in its entirety. In fact, the alliance of Mendelian genetics and agricultural science opened the pandora's box of exotic animal domestication. The domestication of such animals led to the creation of fur farming, which remains fundamental to the modern fur industry today. The ability to adapt life forms to the demands of luxury industries marked a new episode in the relationship between the (German) fur industry and nature. Indeed, although the creation of karakul farming was executed by a single lead firm, the spillover effects of creating new sources gave a tremendous advantage to the entire fur industry. The endeavour to create fur farming as a source of resources opened up the possibilities of creating world market alternatives and new geographies of production. The value thereof cannot be easily underestimated. The Thorer firm constructed a blueprint for future cooperation with science, connecting the problem of resource supply to the upcoming field of Mendelian genetics in German academia. Expert knowledge on

Mendelian breeding was an instrument to mould the colonial farmers in South West Africa into part of the supply chain of Leipzig's fur industry. The involvement in farming played a growing role in the future of the industrial district and provided fertile soil for interfirm cooperation, a theme that is further pursued in the next few chapters.

Notes

1 Louis, *Ends of British Imperialism*, 38.
2 Equally revealing are imperial business activities outside the empire: Barth, *Die deutsche Hochfinanz und die Imperialismen.*
3 Beckert, "Das Reich der Baumwolle: Eine globale Geschichte"; Zimmerman, *Alabama in Africa.*
4 Hodge, *Triumph of the Expert*, 42.
5 Bley, *Namibia under German Rule*, 107.
6 Graichen and Gründer, *Deutsche Kolonien*, 376.
7 Eckert, "Germany and Africa in the Late Nineteenth and Twentieth Centuries: An Entangled History?" 232.
8 Matter, Schöps, and Franke, *Breitschwanz-Karakul*, 15.
9 Arndt and Unger, *Leipzig in acht Jahrhunderten*, 100.
10 Der Rauchwarenmarkt, nr. 23, 5.06.1936, p. 3. Persianer.
11 BArch, Reichskolonialamt R 1001, nr. 85050. Der Sudwestbote: Sonntagsblatt, Windhoek 15.11.1911.
12 Fränkel, *"Einbahnstraße" Bericht eines Lebens*, 95.
13 StA-L, Deutsche Bank, Filiale Leipzig 21017, nr. 544. Deutsche Bank Filiale Leipzig, an das Filialbureau Leipzig, 29.07.1909.
14 Dürrschmidt owned a business network of about 20 companies divided between Chiwa, Tashkent, and Bukhara. Before the First World War, there were about 4,200 Germans living in Taschkent, 586 in Aschchabad, 96 in Merw, 378 in Samarkand and 24 in Kagan. Meissner, Neubauer, and Eisfeld, *Die Russlanddeutschen*, 107.
15 BArch, Reichskolonialamt R1001, nr. 8507. Thorer an der Staatssekretär des Reichs-kolonialamts, Tsingtau, den 11.03.1913.
16 BArch, Reichskolonialamt R 1001, nr. 8504, f. 205. Thorer an Excellenz dem Staatssekretär des Reichs-Kolonialamtes. Herrn Dernburg. Leipzig, den 29.01.1910.
17 "Landbauwissenschaften und landwirtschaftliches Hochschulwesen in Preussen vom Beginn des 19 Jahrhunderts bis in das 20 Jahrhundert," 24.
18 BArch, Kaiserliches Gouvernement in Deutsch SWA R 151 F, nr. N.V.a.1. Vertrag. Halle a;d.S. den 6. 12. 1913.
19 Nyhart, *Modern Nature*, 2.
20 BArch, Kaiserliches Gouvernement in Deutsch SWA R 151 F, nr. N.V.a.1, f. 12. Vortrag, 18.06.1906.
21 BArch, Reichskolonialamt R 1001, nr. 8503, f. 59.
22 BArch, Reichskolonialamt R 1001, nr. 8503, f. 30.
23 Ibid.
24 Bachrach, *A Practical Treatise*, 434.
25 BArch, Reichskolonialamt R 1001, nr. 8505, Kaiserliches Deutsche Generalkonsulat, Moskau an der Reichskanzler, den 8.10.1912.
26 BArch, Reichskolonialamt R 1001, nr. 8506, f. 119.
27 BArch, Kaiserliches Gouvernement in Deutsch SWA R 151 F, nr. N.VI.B.2. Der Staatssekretär des Reichskolonialamts an den Herrn Gouverneur Windhuk, Berlin, den 05.07.1908.

28 Schrank, "German South West Africa," 220.
29 BArch, Reichskolonialamt R 1001, nr. 8504, f. 59.
30 BArch, Kaiserliches Gouvernement in Deutsch SWA R 151 F, nr.N.VI.C.1, f. 49. Windhuk, 22.07.1912.
31 BArch, Kaiserliches Gouvernement in Deutsch SWA R 151 F, nr. N.VI.B.2. Band 1 Karakulschafzucht. 25.Abschrift. Leipzig, 2 Juni 1908.
32 BArch, Reichskolonialamt R1001, nr. 8503, f. 24. Abschrift.
33 BArch, Reichskolonialamt R 1001, nr. 8505, f. 119.
34 Barch, Kaiserliches Gouvernement in Deutsch SWA R 151 F, nr. N.VI.D.2, f. 37.
35 Ibid., f. 31; 37. Here: f. 37.
36 BArch, Kaiserliches Gouvernement in Deutsch SWA R 151 F. nr. VI.A.1, ff. 105–9. Here f. 108.
37 Ibid., f. 108.
38 BArch, Reichskolonialamt R 1001, nr. 8506, f. 175.
39 BArch, Kaiserliches Gouvernement in Deutsch SWA R 151 F, nr. N.V.a.1, f. 163.
40 Ibid.
41 BArch, Kaiserliches Gouvernement in Deutsch SWA R 151 F, nr. N.V. a.1, f. 174.
42 BArch, Kaiserliches Gouvernement in Deutsch SWA R 151 F, nr. N.VI.B.1, f. 14.
43 BArch, Reichskolonialamt R 1001, nr. 8506, f. 159.
44 Ibid., f. 175.
45 BArch, Kaiserliches Gouvernement in Deutsch SWA R 151 F. nr. N. XIII.f.1, f. 7.
46 BArch, Reichskolonialamt R 1001, nr. 8506, f. 163.
47 BArch, Reichskolonialamt R 1001, nr. 8508. Paul Thorer an das Reichskolonialamt 12.05.1914.
48 Ibid., Leipzig 12.05.1914.
49 Firma Thorer und Hollender, *350 Jahre Thorer*, 12.
50 BArch, Reichskolonialamt R 1001, nr. 8381. Abschrift. 06.04.1912.
51 Ibid., f. 135.
52 BArch, Reichskolonialamt R 1001, nr. 8503, Julius Kühn. Halle. a.s. Mitteilungen der Deutschen Landwirtschaftsgesellschaft. 21 jg. Berlin, den 30.06. 1906, f. 19.
53 Firma Thorer und Hollender, *350 Jahre Thorer*, 10.
54 Nauen, *Karakulzucht in Südwest-Afrika Und Die Firma Theodor Thorer [Karakul Teelt in Suidwes-Afrika En Die Firma van Theodor Thorer] Karakul Breeding in South West Africa and the House of Theodor Thorer*, 62.
55 BArch, Reichskolonialamt R 1001 nr. 8509, f. 39.
56 BArch, Reichskolonialamt R 1001, nr. 8509. Deutsches Generalkonsulat für Süd-Afrika an das Auswärtiges Amt. Pretoria, den 14.05.1924.
57 BArch, Reichskolonialamt R 1001, nr. 8509. Sitzung der Karakul-Interessenten am 14.07.1927.
58 Silvester, "Beasts, Boundaries and Buildings: The Survival of Pastoral Economies in Southern Namibia 1915–1935," 103.
59 StA-L, Dresdner Bank in Leipzig 21018, nr. 476. Bericht der Sächsischen Revisions und Treuhandgesellschaft AG. 31.12.1931. The herd consisted of 2,740 ewes, 354 young ewes, 192 "hammers," 422 ewe-lambs, 161 ram-lambs, 13 young lambs, 22 rams, and two pure Bukhara rams.
60 Grimm, *Gustav Voigts, ein leben in Deutsch-Südwest*, 43.
61 Ibid., 64.
62 Kürschnerzeitung, nr. 287. 01.10.1931. die Bedeutung der Sudwestafrikanischen Karakulzucht.
63 BArch, Reichskolonialamt R 1001, nr. 8509, ff. 168–74.
64 Spitzner, *Karakulzucht in Südwest-Afrika und die firma Theodor Thorer*, 15.
65 Nauen, *Karakulzucht in Südwest-Afrika Und Die Firma Theodor Thorer*, 64–5. The first "half-shared" flocks were established at Oruhungu (district of Windhoek) and Gamis (district of Maltahoehe) and then at Dickdorn (district of Gibeo), Osema (district of Windhoek), Rietfontein (district of Windhoek),

Dordabis (district of Rehoboth), Düdoabib (district of Rehoboth), and Gross-Nabas (district of Gibeon).
66 Silvester, "Beasts, Boundaries and Buildings," 114.
67 Kürschnerzeitung, nr. 27. 21.07.1931, f. 711. Die Edelpelztierhaltung im Deutschen Reiche 1931.
68 PA AA, Konsulat Windhuk, nr. 92. Ernste Lage der Karakul-Ausfuhr in SWA. 24.11.1934.
69 BArch, Reichskolonialamt R1001, nr. 8510, f. 180. SPVG, Kalkfeld. 06.06.1936.
70 BArch, Reichskolonialamt R 1001, nr. 8509, f. 352. SWA Karakul Central 1928 Ltd. 30.01.1935.

References

Arndt, Helmut, and Manfred Unger. *Leipzig in acht Jahrhunderten*. Leipzig: Bibliographisches Institut, 1965.
Bachrach, Max. *A Practical Treatise*. New York: Prentice-Hall; Bailey & Swinfen, 1953.
Barth, Boris. *Die deutsche Hochfinanz und die Imperialismen: Banken und Aussenpolitik vor 1914*. Stuttgart: Steiner, 1995.
Beckert, Sven. "Das Reich der Baumwolle. Eine globale Geschichte." In *Das Kaiserreich Transnational: Deutschland in Der Welt 1871–1914*, edited by Sebastian Conrad and Jürgen Osterhammel, 280–302. Göttingen: Vandenhoeck & Ruprecht, 2004.
Bley, Helmut. *Namibia under German Rule*. Hamburg; Windhoek, Namibia: Lit; Namibia Scientific Society, 1996.
Eckert, Andreas. "Germany and Africa in the Late Nineteenth and Twentieth Centuries: An Entangled History?" In *Comparative and Transnational History: Central European Approaches and New Perspectives*, edited by Heinz-Gerhard Haupt and Jürgen Kocka, 226–47. New York: Berghahn Books, 2012.
Firma Thorer und Hollender. *350 Jahre Thorer*. Frankfurt am Main: Thorer & Hollender, 1962.
Fränkel, Jury. *"Einbahnstraße" Bericht eines Lebens*. Murrhardt: Rifra-Verl., 1973.
Graichen, Gisela, and Horst Gründer. *Deutsche Kolonien: Traum und Trauma*. Berlin: Ullstein, 2005.
Grimm, Hans. *Gustav Voigts, ein leben in Deutsch-Südwest*. Gütersloh: C. Bertelsmann, 1942.
Hodge, Joseph Morgan. *Triumph of the Expert: Agrarian Doctrines of Development and the Legacies of British Colonialism*. Athens, OH: Ohio University Press, 2007.
Klemm, Volker. "Landbauwissenschaften und landwirtschaftliches Hochschulwesen in Preussen vom Beginn des 19 Jahrhunderts bis in das 20 Jahrhundert." In *Wirtschaft, Wissenschaft und Bildung in Preussen: zur Wirtschafts- und Sozialgeschichte Preussens vom 18. bis zum 20 Jahrhundert*, edited by Karl Heinrich Kaufhold and Bernd Sösemann, 17–35. Stuttgart: Franz Steiner Verlag, 1998.
Louis, William Roger. *Ends of British Imperialism: The Scramble for Empire, Suez, and Decolonization*. London: I.B. Tauris, 2006.
Matter, Hans Eberhard, Paul Schöps, and Richard Franke. *Breitschwanz-Karakul: Legende u. Wirklichkeit*. Murrhardt: Rifra-Verl., 1973.
Meissner, Boris, Helmut Neubauer, and Alfred Eisfeld. *Die Russlanddeutschen: Gestern und Heute*. Cologne: Markus Verlag, 1992.

Nauen, Otto. *Karakulzucht in Südwest-Afrika Und Die Firma Theodor Thorer-Karakul Teelt in Suidwes-Afrika En Die Firma van Theodor Thorer-Karakul Breeding in South West Africa and the House of Theodor Thorer*. Windhoek: Meinert Ltd, 1936.

Nyhart, Lynn K. *Modern Nature: The Rise of the Biological Perspective in Germany*. Chicago: University of Chicago Press, 2009.

Schrank, Gilbert I. "German South West Africa: Social and Economic Aspects of Its History, 1884–1915." University Microfilms International, 1981.

Silvester, Jeremy. "Beasts, Boundaries and Buildings: The Survival of Pastoral Economies in Southern Namibia 1915–1935." In *Namibia Under South African Rule: Mobility & Containment, 1915–46*, edited by Patricia Hayes, 117–49. London: James Currey Publishers, 1998.

Spitzner, Karl Walter. *Karakulzucht in Südwest-Afrika und die firma Theodor Thorer = [Karakul teelt in Suidwes-Afrika en die firma van Theodor Thorer = Karakul Breeding in Southwest Africa and the House of Theodor Thorer]*. S.l.: s.n. J. Meinert, 1936.

Zimmerman, Andrew. *Alabama in Africa: Booker T. Washington, the German Empire, and the Globalization of the New South*. Princeton, NJ: Princeton University Press, 2010.

5 Resource Substitution and World Market Isolation

The First World War as a Testing Field for Interfirm Cooperation (1914–1920)

Introduction

World War I is often identified as a watershed moment in the development of modern industry and business.[1] This was certainly so in Germany, where the need to develop alternative business practices and production methods because of shortages in raw materials, energy resources, and labour was comparatively much higher.[2] On the one hand, the war facilitated the renewal of business organisation through methods such as the substantiation of science-industry cooperation and the creation of new sources of resources based on substitution. Businesses also more rapidly introduced methods of mass production. On the other hand, the state interfered with the organisation of business in an unprecedented manner. The German state rearranged the organisation of business by establishing the so-called war corporations. These were overarching private-public partnerships run by state officials and businessmen that led the planning of production and the allocation of labour and resources.[3] Via these corporations, production quotas were forced on businesses, particularly those situated in strategic sectors. The priorities of the war administration had ramifications for the size of firms since planning and larger production orders favoured big business.[4] In raising wartime production, various industries, even those that were part of non-strategic sectors, were increasingly organised into corporations under stern state control.

However, accounts dealing with the development of business during World War I have systematically narrowed the focus of research on big business and the larger production units situated in strategic sectors. For instance, research on business and war is predominantly focused on big businesses in the chemical industry and steel industry. Businesses that procured, produced, and sold goods for consumption stand somewhat in the margins of this research trend. Michael Schäfer has emphasised that this bias has created a vacuum in our understanding of business and war in world market–oriented regions like Saxony.[5] Our general understanding of the impact on the war economy on Saxony is therefore limited to the obvious yet superficial observation that World War I was particularly unfavourable to the structure of the Saxon economy compared to other German regions, because it was characterised by a multitude of small to medium-sized enterprises that depended on world markets and producing consumer goods.[6] However, major shifts in the production and trade of consumer goods undoubtedly took place in these sectors and industries. According to Nancy Green, the war facilitated the introduction of techniques of mass production and had an impact on business organisation in the garment industry.[7] However, our understanding of how such businesses adapted to the exigencies of the war and its aftermath is limited. The same goes for the effects of the war upon the industrial district formation in the fur industry.

This chapter will pursue two main questions. How did new production processes or processes of resource substitution affect the fur industry in Leipzig? And what were the effects on the business organisation in the district? Did the war lead to the institutionalisation of new forms of local collaboration? This chapter will pay attention to both the patterns and impact of resource substitution and the restructuring of local business networks because of pressures of the state-led war economy. These developments are seminal since they affected the ability of the district to participate in world trade.

Rabbits, Leipzig, and the Creation of the War Fur Ltd (1914–1917)

With the invasion of Belgium on 4 August 1914, the German empire finally plunged into a war that many mistakenly believed would end in just a couple of months. Besides the impact of this widespread notion on military considerations, it had also frozen attempts to prepare the economy and businesses adequately for a lengthy struggle.[8] The result is well known: shortages of raw material jeopardised industrial output and faltering food supplies caused famine in Germany at an early stage in the war.[9] However, the establishment of the Raw Materials Section (*Kriegsrohstoffabteilung*) in August 1914 saved Germany from complete disaster. It was this institution that, to a large extent, designed Germany's wartime economy and organised the allocation of resources or their substitution.[10]

In the case of the fur industry, available resources finally ran dry in December 1915. An alternative resource was found rather quickly in the backyard of German households: rabbit furs. The advantages of rabbit keeping, both for skin production and nutrition, were fully recognised because of the shortage experience of World War I. As food shortages were endemic in Germany during the war, the German state promoted keeping small animals in German households.[11] In other countries, like in France and Belgium, however, household rabbit keeping as a source of nutrition and pelting was already a typical phenomenon in the nineteenth century. However, the belated introduction of rabbit keeping in Germany is more comparable to the situation in England, where the circumstances of the Great War likewise caused the practice to expand substantially.[12] Rabbit skin trading had existed in England and Wales since the 1860s, providing supplies for the wool and skin processing industry in London, although this trade was marginal in comparison with Belgium and France.[13]

Throughout the war, rabbit breeding in Germany gained momentum. By 1918, the practice of rabbit keeping inside Germany began to assume large proportions. Rabbit meat in particular was increasingly consumed and rabbit skins were an important product for household husbandry. The agricultural census of 2 September 1918 counted 14,012,618 rabbits in the German Reich, the majority of which were found in the Prussian provinces (8,524,568). Saxony as well had turned into an important region with about 1,152,636 rabbits; there were 366,534 rabbits in the city of Leipzig.[14] These statistics illuminate the fundamentals of the new rabbit fur industry. The increase was quite spectacular: in 1913 there were only 2.5 million rabbits in the German rabbit breeding industry.

German rabbit fanciers and the Leipzig fur industry encountered each other at a relatively late stage of the war as both had managed to delay incorporation into the state-led war economy until the final period of the conflict. It was as late as 1917 when the architects of the war economy fully realised the economic potential in utilising rabbit breeding as a source for the production of military garments. The fur industry, in turn, maintained a certain level of 'free trade' until the end of 1915. At the beginning of the war, the non-strategic fur industry was outside the scope of the KRA (*Kriegsrohstoffabteilung*) because their resources and industrial capacity were not of vital importance for the German war economy. Modest quantities of raw furs continued to find their way to Leipzig; they were mainly shipped in via neutral countries or drawn from stockpiled raw furs in Leipzig warehouses. In addition, private business often conducted profitable commerce with the army. For example, Theodor Thorer transformed his factory in Lindenau to process sheepskins for the army, which "successfully replaced the loss in his fur dyeing operations." The profit of Thorer in the second half of 1914, 870,000 marks, was substantially larger than the profit made before the outbreak of the war, which amounted only to 623,000 marks.[15] For certain firms, business during the war was thus not entirely unprofitable. David Kölner, a fur trader from the Brühl, sold his stock of sheep furs for more than 100,000 marks to the army, at a price that exceeded his personal expectations.[16]

The initial 'persistence' of the Saxon fur industry in the war economy should not be exaggerated. Unavoidably, the German wartime economic institutions severely damaged the fur market as time went on. First, factories and warehouses belonging to the fur industry were incorporated by the war administration in order to produce armaments needed for the war machine. Second, in order to keep the price levels of fur garments under control, the Prussian war administration decided to auction furs that were confiscated from occupied territories. State-led auctions meant loss of market control for the Leipzig firms.[17] Third, by early 1916, the stock in the Leipzig warehouses was nearly exhausted.[18] Thorer mentioned that he had difficulties in procuring new furs in 1915 and that commerce largely focused on liquidating the last stockpiled resources and manufactured goods.[19] Fourth, in January 1917, commercial possibilities with neutral countries were further exacerbated when the Reich declared that all import traffic required the permission of the government and prohibited the export of certain types of furs in order to control the strength of the mark.[20]

Furthermore, rabbit skins as resources increasingly entered onto the horizon of public authorities that saw the products as resources for the hide and fur industry. Due to the growing problems related to commerce with neutral countries, the Saxon government lobbied to transform Leipzig into the manufacturing centre of the new rabbit skin industry.[21] Both traders and manufacturers in Leipzig attempted to gain permission from the war administration to import rabbit skins directly from occupied Belgium. Simultaneously, however, the war administration of Prussia also began to see the potential in the growing number of rabbits kept by German households as resources for the leather goods needed by the army and navy. By early 1917, the Prussian war administration planned to establish a new war corporation in order to prepare for the registration and confiscation of rabbit skins.

The creation of a Leipzig-based war corporation now gained momentum. Worried by the prospect of a war corporation established outside Leipzig, representatives of the trade and dyeing industry in the city preferred to sacrifice their independent position in the war economy and therefore proposed a new war corporation for the procurement of rabbits firmly attached to the Brühl.[22] Supported by Saxon politicians, businessmen in Leipzig promised 1,500,000 marks for the foundation of the corporation.[23] The Saxon and Brühl initiatives eventually resulted in the creation of the "War Fur Ltd" (Kriegsfell AG) in March 1917 with its headquarters in Leipzig.[24] Through this decision, Saxony and the fur industry exerted control over the emerging domain of rabbit skin trade in Germany and avoided their businesses being rendered superfluous.

War corporations (*Kriegsgesellschaften*) were composed of business groups and were designed to raise wartime production through cooperation between the state and private business. In the first stage of the war, the government established war corporations with the aim of centralising all economic activities related to food production and the management of scarce resources needed for armament production. The corporations were often organised alongside internal industry associations with differing degrees of state control.[25] The Kriegsrohstoffabteilung (KRA), the raw materials division of the Prussian government led by Walther Rathenau, was the central organisation that supervised the activities of individual corporations.[26] Strategic resources like chemicals (Kriegschemikalien AG) and the production of metal (Kriegsmetall AG) were almost immediately put under state control. By the end of World War I, about 200 war corporations had been established. The advantage of this type of corporation was that the war administration could make use of the expertise of private industry (primarily big business) and thereby integrate them into the war economy rather than turning off private initiative completely in the enormous task of war production.[27]

War Fur Ltd, the war corporation that controlled the fur industry, was founded on 1 March 1917. It blended together state control and private initiative in a hybrid model akin to those corporations established in an earlier phase of the war. The Kriegsfell AG, created with the aim of supplying the army with garments and controlling the procuring of rabbit skin, was designed as a joint-stock company and many Leipzig fur firms participated in it. The Kriegsfell consisted of 25 shareholders from private industry who were predominantly fur firms from Leipzig. More than half of the shareholders came from Leipzig while about 10 participants operated in other German cities. Some of the lead firms in Leipzig were on the list such as Theodor Thorer and Friedrich Erler; the absence of larger Jewish trading firms like the Eitingons and the Ariowitsch firm is remarkable, but given their migration background perhaps not unaccountable.[28] In addition, it seems that most of the participating firms possessed some kind of manufacturing plant—the Jewish merchants predominantly focused on commerce. Profits also played a role, although they were directly limited since profiteering by means of the war economy was controversial. As such, the dividends from Kriegsfell AG profits were limited to a maximum of 5% interest on the shares.

How did the private-public partnership shape the inner structure of War Fur Ltd? The shareholders of the Kriegsfell AG elected a board of supervisors of three to eight persons; motions were decided by a majority vote. Leipzig's domination can be seen in the board of 1917: there were the Leipzig traders Paul Thorer, Alfred Nauman, Friedrich Dodel, and Richard Schmidt (the president of the Leipzig Chamber of Commerce), two government representatives (Gustav Stresemann and a spokesman for the Bavarian government), and two businessmen who came from outside Leipzig.[29] In possession of a veto, the voices of state delegates weighed much more than their private counterparts. Moreover, the KRA retained final control over the price-setting mechanisms on the new rabbit skin market. In other words, private actors had a large say but the final decision was always in the hands of state representatives.

Despite state control, the participation of the fur industry in War Fur Ltd offered a number of opportunities. Most importantly, the location of the war corporation in Saxony was crucial to the fur industry's continuation as one of the key sectors of the regional economy. The Saxon government was particularly pleased that Leipzig was chosen as the host city for War Fur Ltd: "Leipzig was chosen as the headquarters, in particular with regard to the fact that the eligible commercial and industrial sectors exist there, the Saxon government and industry have long promoted rabbit keeping, and the creation of a competitive system to process rabbit skins."[30] Together with the decision to place the corporation in Leipzig, the kingdom of Saxony was promised that the surplus rabbit skins would be distributed to fur firms based in the city. The Kriegsfell auctioned its first surplus of rabbit skins to the private fur industry in March 1918.[31] The auction meant the influx of 1,500,000 rabbit furs into private industry. The decision to locate War Fur Ltd in Leipzig, and ultimately to control the supply chains of rabbit skins, thus contributed significantly to the short-term survival of Saxony's fur industry and perhaps its existence in the 1920s.

In the Rabbit Warren? Science, Industry, and the Making of the Rabbit Industry (1917–1920)

Resource Substitution at Work

The War Fur Ltd in Leipzig was primarily created with the aim of organising the procurement, distribution, and production of rabbit skins. The transformation of rabbit skin producers into resource suppliers formed the main challenge. Procurement was chiefly organised via periodic confiscations that forced rabbit keepers to hand in skins. The War Fur Ltd reimbursed producers according to uniform price levels set by the Prussian war administration. However, confiscations and the price caps were highly controversial. According to War Fur Ltd officials, the number of rabbits kept in Germany was, in all likelihood, much greater than the number counted by the official census (14,012,618 rabbits in September 1918). German rabbit fanciers and keepers tended to under-register the number of rabbits in their possession since cloaking the existence of additional animals was held to be an effective way to avoid confiscation. Therefore the administration doubted the correctness of the census and claimed that about 20,000,000 rabbits existed in Germany.[32] As well as the notorious confiscations, rabbit keepers also had the opportunity to trade in skins to collection centres.[33] The procurement of rabbit skins required an extensive network of collection centres covering the entirety of the German Reich. In a short period of time, War Fur Ltd established 4,000 collection centres in about 2,800 localities; however, this was still considered insufficient.[34] From the individual collection centres, rabbit skins were transported to a large warehouse rented by War Fur Ltd in Leipzig, which was situated on Katzbach Street, close to the large central railway station in town. The main site of War Fur Ltd employed about 50 male and 70 female labourers. The workforce in the warehouse, who packed and graded thousands of rabbit skins, formed the backbone of this new domestic supply line.

Even though rabbit keeping spread rapidly across German cities during the war, expectations regarding the turnover of rabbits skins were somewhat disappointed. Lack of efficiency in particular was a deeply rooted problem. Between 1917 and 1918, breeders provided War Fur Ltd 12 million rabbit skins; only roughly 8 million of these could be used in the manufacture of garments. Inept treatment, decay, loss, and theft in the distribution centres wasted a staggering 33% of this yield.[35] On top of that, animal disease slowed down production. Rabbit breeding in Germany suffered badly from coccidiosis: it accounted for the death of about 90% of young rabbits. Moreover, rabbit production suffered from the same problems that plagued state-led efforts to incorporate agricultural production into the war economy. State dirigisme made household animal husbandry perform far below capacity.[36] The unpopular system of price caps and quantity regulations drove both rabbit breeders and German peasant farmers out of the market.

War Fur Ltd and Scientific Development

The creation of a rabbit skin industry was thus an enormous task, one that the Leipzig corporation wished to achieve in a relatively short period of time. War Fur Ltd strongly believed in the potential of the rabbit skin industry: it was held that rabbit production would reach 27 million skins in one or two years.[37]Aiming at both promoting as well as rationalising rabbit keeping, War Fur Ltd established a "department of education" (*Aufklärungsamt*). This department went on a propaganda offensive against both rabbit fanciers and the larger public by making itself more visible in the public sphere. Training of the rabbit breeder was seen as an important task. The information department of War Fur Ltd deployed 96 instructors that went around the country to generally promote rabbit keeping and hold lectures about the treatment of skins.

Aside from its propaganda department, War Fur Ltd relied on research and innovation in order to make the new production paradigm based on rabbit skins function. Unlike in other German industries, where the main scientific contributions derived from the implementation of resource substitutes, innovations in the fur industry were not to be found in improved production methods, since manufacturing procedures for rabbit skins already existed. As mentioned above, the main challenge of the rabbit supply line was to reduce waste that occurred at the start of the production process, namely in the rabbit pens. Solving this problem would require cooperation with experts in animal management and veterinary scientists. Modern animal management can be defined as the method that "integrates the proper feeding, breeding health care, housing, and handling of domestic animals to optimise their production"[38]; it seemed particularly important to professionalise this supply line that was largely organised by amateurs in the field of animal husbandry. Veterinary scientists focused on the more pressing task of relieving high mortality levels in the German rabbit colonies.

The war corporation was thus relevant for the fur industry as a whole because it constructed networks with university science departments on the one hand and agricultural expertise on the other. Empowered by the state, the fur industry had the capacity to establish and pursue these links. The board of War Fur Ltd called into being a scientific commission, which assembled a clutch of university professors and agricultural experts from various German universities and research institutes. In particular, professor G. Fröhlich of the Agricultural Institute of the Halle University and Hans Raebiger, the founder of the Bacteriological Institute and member of the Agricultural Chamber of Brandenburg (*Landwirtschaftskammer Brandenburg*), were commissioned by the Leipzig war corporation to reduce the impact of parasitic diseases.[39] The largest threat to the rapidly expanding German rabbit population was the parasitic disease coccidiosis, which threatened young rabbits between six and eight weeks old. Coccidiosis took on epidemic proportions from 1916 to 1917 and constituted the main threat to the ambitious plans of War Fur Ltd. Therefore, Raebiger had started research into the causes and treatment of rabbit coccidiosis by the end of the war.

Indeed, commissioned by the war corporation, Raebiger's research into coccidiosis challenged traditional veterinary policies and the attitude of agricultural authorities towards rabbit breeders. Raebiger tackled the lack of etiological understanding within circles of breeders and agricultural experts. In his view, agricultural education was biased towards recognising the symptoms of coccidiosis and devoted too little attention to preventing the spread of the disease. According to the Agricultural Chamber of Brandenburg, Raebiger's home institution, the spread of the disease was mainly caused by contact with contaminated excrement. This meant that the cause of disease was related to the poor hygiene in household rabbit keeping. Raebiger's assertion about the poor hygienic standards in German rabbit pens shifted the focus of agricultural policy onto breeders' ineptitude and amateurism.[40] The recommendations regarding hygiene and diet formed the linchpin of renewed veterinary policy towards domestic animal keeping. As such, like in the case of karakul farming, through scientific expertise the fur industry had an additional instrument to influence and control the supply chain. The fur industry thus found support for transforming rabbit breeders into producers amongst scientists like Raebiger, who attached more value to implementing practical solutions related to "sound and rational" animal management such as stricter sanitary conditions and proper nutrition.[41]

In sum, the work of Raebiger and others increasingly interfered with the social world of rabbit keeping. This trend continued to be central well after the war as scientists continued to expand their grip on the German rabbit fancier. In 1920, first, the leading genetic scientist Hans Nachtsheim of the Kaiser Wilhelm Institute for Genetic Science (*Kaiser Wilhelm Institut der Vererbungsforschung*) became the president of the Association of German Rabbit Breeders (*Verein Deutscher Kaninchenzuchter*), one of the largest rabbit breeding organisations. His central task was rationalising breeding methods in order to optimise rabbit skin production. Second, since state authorities had finally embraced the importance of rabbit keeping, disciplining the rabbit breeder according to the principles of animal management surfaced as a vital objective. In 1920, the Prussian ministry of agriculture proclaimed further rationalisation of rabbit breeding, mainly by educating the rabbit fancier on efficient breeding and ways to improve the exploitation of the animal. This new line of policy differed clearly from the *laissez-faire* attitude to rabbit breeding before the war when keepers were relatively independent and their requests for state assistance were usually denied. After the war, the pendulum had clearly swung in favour of intervention: "As a means of promotion, we recommend teaching through lectures, the organisation of training courses, instructions on how to rationally conduct farms, the establishment of facilities which enhance the breeding productions (fur value), the establishment of breeding centres with state support, and granting awards for outstanding achievements."[42] In addition, the Prussian agricultural authorities started to regulate the flourishing rabbit fairs and exhibitions. It saw in these exhibitions a threat to the economic exploitation of rabbit keeping since these shows promoted the keeping of special breeds that were useless for food and skin production. After the war, business, science, and industry had successfully intruded into the social world of rabbit keepers.

The Rabbit Skin Market in the Aftermath of the War

When the war ended, the war corporation lost the ability to conduct business or to steer production of skins for fur clothing production. Peace made the existence of the war corporation obsolete, even undesired. The forced cooperation between Leipzig firms and the state in the form of War Fur Ltd had, however, a lasting influence. First, rabbit skins acquired a prominent position within the Leipzig fur cluster. According to Hans von Nachtsheim, rabbit skins constituted 42% of the turnover in the German fur industry in 1924.[43] Keepers continued to make use, to a certain extent, of the infrastructure that had been created by War Fur Ltd, such as the local collection centres. Nevertheless, the organisation of the supply line of rabbit skins underwent several changes when War Fur Ltd was liquidated in July 1919, with a stronger position for breeders.[44] That being said, the War Fur Ltd had failed to create a self-sufficient supply of rabbit skins. In 1924, Germany imported 12,000,000 gold marks worth of rabbit skins. In 1927 imports almost doubled to 23,038,000 gold marks, which was equivalent to 18 million rabbit skins.[45] In the case of rabbit skins, thus, foreign trade remained seminal. Second, rabbit skins became the linchpin of trade and mass production in the fur industry.[46] Several of the largest firms in Saxony expanded because of the success of rabbit manufacturing: the Walter AG in Markrandstädt turned into the largest firm of the district, with 1,400 labourers in 1923, because of rabbit dyeing.[47] Rabbit dyeing was thus responsible for increased labour opportunities in the district, even though the arrival of an elephantine firm in the district disturbed size distribution. Mass production entered into the world of specialised businesses.

Other firms also continued improving the production process for manufacturing rabbit skins and this led to renewed forms of cooperation. In 1920, some Leipzig fur industrialists and traders (Theodor Thorer, Friedrich König, and Theodor Kniesche) established a joint venture, the *Vereinigte Rauch-waren Veredlungs Werke GmbH*, with the aim of improving the production processes. The common goal of the new joint venture was "perfection . . . by sharing our experience and technical knowledge and by putting aside our special interests. Next, we will cooperate to refine our previous methods and create new ones. The reputation and history of the individual companies guarantee performance and progress."[48] According to these industrialists, processing rabbit furs presented an opportunity for mutual learning: "For employers and dyers, the risk must be reduced in producing rabbit skins: we will therefore create a communal way of dressing rabbits. This common procedure will be suitable for all dyeing methods and our operations will run consistently and uniformly."[49] The process of resource substitution had been successfully incorporated into the Leipzig fur industry.

A third lasting influence of War Fur Ltd was the institutionalisation of scientific research at the service of the fur industry. In October 1918, the corporation entertained plans to centralise research in a permanent experimental research station. The economic and political stakeholders in Saxony that dominated the board of War Fur Ltd were able to make sure that the new experimental station would be established in the proximity of the fur cluster: "Saxony has the largest concentration of the fur trade, whose activity has rendered the main profits of the war fur corporation and promoted the breeding of rabbits during the war . . . this alone justifies that such an institute should be in Leipzig."[50] In July 1919, Kriegsfell AG spent 75,000 marks on installing a research institute in the buildings of the agricultural experimental institution in Leipzig-Möckern, one of the oldest in Germany. This was far less than 200,000 marks originally planned.[51] The Leipzig Fur Merchants Association offered 10,000 marks to the new research institute. Inspired by the needs of its sponsors, the institute was commissioned to study the nature and variables that determined the qualities of skin and hair: "Thorough and comprehensive scientific work is required in order to clarify the physiological and biological conditions of the most pertinent questions involving the skin and hair."[52] The research institute was also renowned for its research into animal nutrition theories. New research was therefore also directed at discovering the optimal nutrition patterns for rabbits and, more importantly, the influence of food on the quality of the skins, meat, and fat of the animal.[53] The funding of Leipzig-Möckern was an important development, as scientific research on animal breeding for the needs fur industry was now institutionalised in Leipzig. Eventually, the institutionalisation of the science-industry networks laid the groundwork for dealing with resource supply problems and world market dependency in the interwar period.

Restoring the Old Order? War, World Markets, and Local Cohesion

Thus far, this chapter has placed emphasis on War Fur Ltd and the impetus the war corporation gave to collaboration between agricultural science and the fur industry and to resource substitution. In the war corporation, fur industrialists were more or less forced to cooperate with one another and with actors outside the fur industry. Although some networks continued to exist, the war corporation never served as a basis for continued interfirm cooperation in Leipzig after its liquidation. Despite its control of the fur trade during the last stage of the war, the war corporation did not monopolise the collective action of the fur firms. On the contrary, it will be argued here that intensified cooperation between firms in Leipzig emerged in other contexts as well.

International Competition and the Birth of Interfirm Cooperation in Foreign Trade

As was the case for many other German industries, World War I separated the Leipzig fur firms from the world market. At the beginning of the war, with large parts of this industry still operating under quasi-free market conditions and the rest supplying the army, optimism about the future of the city was prevalent. However, such a sanguine attitude dwindled quickly.[54] The war created new dynamics in the international fur industry, making centres like New York and St Louis in America expand rapidly. For Leipzig, trade with neutral countries, mainly in Scandinavia, barely compensated for isolation. In fact, Scandinavian companies were increasingly competing with Leipzig rather than providing for it. As early as 1917, Danish and Swedish fur traders commenced dyeing and dressing of raw furs in several small-scale production units.[55] The attempts of Scandinavian trading companies to take over the 'Russian business' were very far along. For instance, during the course of the war, Swedish trading companies slowly expanded their trading activities in Siberia. In the summer of 1918, leading Danish fur merchants planned to establish a company "with the explicit aim of trading with Russia and Siberia, but also Northern America."[56] Nevertheless, the Danish plans caused great turmoil in Leipzig.

The longer the war lasted, the more the firms realised that collective action was required to maintain or reconstruct Leipzig as an international fur capital. In the beginning of 1916, a meeting held between the Leipzig Fur Merchants Association and Leipzig's city council centred on the way in which St Louis profited from the war in Europe.[57] The discussion chiefly focused on thwarting the development of alternative distribution centres like St Louis in order to prevent Leipzig from becoming a fringe player in peacetime. It was in this context that on old idea resurfaced: the Fur Merchants Association proposed that the city should finance the establishment of an independent auction company in Leipzig. Auctions constituted a market institution that was both disliked and admired in Leipzig. On the one hand, it was the chief market institution of the Anglo-American fur trade. Auction companies had not only laid the foundation of London as a fur centre but had also supported the growth of new primary markets in North America. Through auction companies, traders in St Louis and New York had achieved what

Leipzig wanted once the war ended. On the other hand, the auction as an instrument of competition was quite controversial in Leipzig. The British auctioneers and their rigid organisation had been particularly galling before the war and had sharpened the Anglo-German rivalry in this sector.[58]

The firm Heinrich Lomer had already untaken unsuccessful attempts in the 1870s to hold auctions in Leipzig in order to compete with London. The first auction to take place in Leipzig was organised by War Fur Ltd in March 1918 to sell the surplus of rabbit skins to private industry. Nonetheless, many considered the practice unfair. The trade journal *Der Rauchwarenmarkt* noted that "it is a known fact that when the competition is sitting side by side, as it is the case in the auction hall, prices are quite involuntarily sent high, although not to the insane height of the last August auction, and has a harmful effect on the entire market and thus destroys the free business in the rabbit skins that has recently developed."[59] The rabbit auction remained the only such experiment for years, as the city council refused to finance a Leipzig auctioneering company: the original plan of an internationally important auction company never materialised.[60] Yet the idea of creating auctions in Leipzig never really left the table. The appeal for auctions also demonstrates that the fur cluster believed that the strengthening of Leipzig as an international fur capital was an objective to be attained through collective action.

Secondly, the war also offered opportunities in terms of international trade, the pursuit of which entailed further cooperation between individual businesses. Opportunities for the German industry, especially for those businesses focussed on the Russian trade, emerged when the eastern front disintegrated. The time between the armistice and the treaty of Versailles was called the "transitory economy" (*Übergangswirtschaft*) in German business circles, a period in which businesses hoped to restore commercial relations with the Russians on favourable terms. The revival of economic relations with the East featured prominently in the German economic aspirations. According to Ritschl, the creation of a continental economic empire was one of the most significant aspects of the German wartime economy and it continued to frame post-war German economic policy and thought.[61]

By the same token, firms in Leipzig believed that the city could resume its former position as a depot between East and West. However, external circumstances forced Leipzig firms to cooperate in order to pursue Siberian business.[62] The German authorities especially encouraged interfirm cooperation in conducting trade after the treaty of Brest-Litovsk: "International negotiations with Ukraine and Austria-Hungary will limit the number of merchants and we do not even know if the governments of Ukraine and the new Great Russia will tolerate the activities of free traders."[63] The urgency of securing the old supply line and the inaccessibility of Russia further stimulated the need for stronger cooperation. In February 1918, the Leipzig fur industry jointly appointed Robert Ehrmann, a fur trader who was then in the service of the German army as an officer, as a trade diplomat, charged with starting the first negotiations with Russian fur traders.[64] In Moscow, Ehrmann started preparations for the establishment of a jointly organised "trade institution" (*Vermittlungsstelle*) that would be responsible for the purchase of Russian furs.[65] By March 1918, the aspiration to rebuild commerce along pre-war parameters had largely been replaced by plans to construct trade consortiums and jointly organised operations. War Fur Ltd also acquired a modest role: "A number of larger Leipzig fur firms will be taking part in the procurement of Russian furs. . . . These raw furs will be sent to War Fur Ltd, which will transmit the prime furs again to a consortium of fur traders and furriers in order to distribute them over the German market."[66] In May 1918, such a consortium was about to be established in Leipzig. However, because of the ongoing struggle between Bolsheviks and the Whites, the treaty of Brest-Litovsk remained a dead letter in terms of the much desired revival of the Russian trade.[67] Nonetheless, just as with the idea to establish auction companies, the collective action in the transitory economy had opened the door for further measures in this vein in regards to foreign trade. Collective action in the transitory phase would serve as a model for post-war trade relations between German business and Soviet channels.

The Importance of Trade Associations in the Wake of World War I

State intervention in business life also significantly contributed to the development of collective action in the district. Notwithstanding the fact that the Brühl agreed to its incorporation into War Fur Ltd in order to maintain Leipzig as the main German centre in the trade of skins and hides, the firms united against the disturbing impact of proliferating state regulations upon trade. The incorporation of fur firms into the war corporation did not manage to reduce these tensions. Collective action against state control surfaced more strongly once the war ended. Particularly unpalatable to the equilibrium in Leipzig was the perception that state institutions favoured particular businesses. As the Leipzig Chamber of Commerce protested, "It is not right that our state institutions favour one part of the Leipzig businesses. All firms should be treated equally by the state institutions that are involved in the import/export business (the Reichsbank, the Commission for Import and Export, and the Customs Office)."[68] In general, the Leipzig firms remained in favour of ending the disturbing state-led economy and restoring the free economy immediately after the war ended. Thus, trade associations became important in the battle against state interference.

In order to counter state interference, local institutions like the Chamber of Commerce and the Leipzig Fur Merchants Association, which united the standpoints of individual commercial firms, acquired a more prominent status in the city, especially during the post-war years of 1918–1922. The membership of the Merchants Association rose spectacularly in the aftermath of the war: from 131 in 1918 to 406 members in 1920, whereas there had been only 42 members in 1908.[69] The Fur Merchants Association appointed a prominent leader to defend the interest of the cluster in the person of Paul Hollender. After the death of his father-in-law Paul Thorer, Hollender had become the manager of the lead firm Theodor Thorer.[70] In 1921, he was elected as the president of the Leipzig Fur Merchants Association and remained so until the early 1930s. As such, the Thorer company acquired a leading position in terms of business organisation in the district. The Fur Merchants Association was not the only institution that defended the interest of the district. As mentioned in Chapter 2, representation followed the lines of specialisation in the district. The trade association for the industrial manufacturers, the so-called Association of German Fur Dressers and Dyers, was a strong association with headquarters in Leipzig. Amongst its members were 120 Leipzig firms and 90 firms outside the city.[71] Finally, the Association of German Furriers was a prominent association after World War I.

In the post-war years, the associations in Leipzig had to lobby because of the ongoing state interference in the management of the economy, which became particularly strong when battling the unstoppable inflation that raged until 1923.[72] The Fur Merchants Association continuously negotiated with the Ministries of Finance and Foreign Trade about the position of furs in Germany's international trade.[73] The bewildering number of import/ export restrictions, new taxes, and regulations often severely disturbed the business equilibrium in the district. They successfully lobbied against an export tariff of 20% on export of manufacturing rabbit skins, which was damaging to this new business. Furthermore, the Fur Merchants Association even managed to 'liberate' the fur industry from the stringent supervision of the Leather Trade Department in 1923.[74] Leipzig associations also lobbied against the luxury taxes imposed in the early Weimar Republic, which could add up to 15% on sales. In contrast to the battle against export tariffs, lobbying here meant a long-lasting effort: it took until 1924 for the government to reduce the luxury tax to 10%.[75] It was finally abolished on 1 April 1926. Business associations had become an indispensable form of safeguarding local interests. Especially the Leipzig Fur Merchants Association emerged as a powerful lobby in the early 1920s, and a facilitator of collective action, a status they would maintain throughout the interwar period.

Conclusion

The chapter has examined the Leipzig fur cluster during the First World War. In particular, emphasis has been placed on the ramifications of the war on local production regimes and business organisation. Firstly, the chapter has cast attention on the discovery of rabbit skins not only as a resource substitute for furs but also as an item that enabled mass production. Firms in Leipzig created dyeing processes on new resources that were produced *en masse* by German households. Rabbit skins continued to serve as an important resource for the Leipzig fur industry after the war whilst the industry was still isolated from the world market. Therefore the fur industry had expanded its possibilities significantly through the new production paradigm based on rabbit skins. Old and new factories in Leipzig focussed on the production of this new item.

The war intensified 'scientification' in light industries like the fur industry that were incorporated in the war machinery. The cooperation between science and industry was generated by the war corporation, which had united private and public interests. Once the war corporation was set up, linkages between science, experts, and the industry were more firmly established. In making use of applied agricultural and veterinary expertise to 'manage' the supply line of rabbit skins to Leipzig, the fur industry turned into a more science-based industry. The cooperation with agricultural scientists, Mendelian genetics, and veterinary science in the early twentieth century was one of the key steps in the development of the modern fur industry, which is almost entirely based on the supply of farmed pelts instead of hunted wildlife. The process of resource substitution was successfully completed after World War I, when several factories in Leipzig became specialised in the mass production of rabbit skin garments. The trading and manufacture of rabbit pelts remained an integral part of the district and alleviated pressures from the world market.

What we have learnt from studying the fur district is that although such processes of scientification were of great importance to small firms and industrial districts, they generated different effects in terms of business organisation. Unlike other industries, however, processes of scientification did not lead to in-house research departments inside individual firms. Instead, the fur industry created links with experts and university science in institutions external to the firms themselves. The cooperation with agricultural science was institutionalised in separate, collectively sponsored, and local research centres. This can be seen in the foundation of the agricultural research centre in Leipzig-Möckern. However, even though these institutions were external to the firm, the research was tailored to the needs of the fur industry.

Although the war corporation had facilitated business-science networks, War Fur Ltd never surfaced as a model for post-war collective action or public-private partnership. Collective action in post-war Leipzig rather focused on reversing the war economy headed by the state. The proliferation of new regulations that concerned trade and industry increased the importance of lobbying for the district firms. The growing importance of trade associations and interfirm cooperation was part of a wider development in Saxony. The region suffered more from state dirigisme and isolation because of its dependency on world trade. In danger of becoming a region in decline, institutions like the Association of Saxon Industrialists (*Verband Sächsischer Industrieller* or VSI) and the Leipzig Chamber of Commerce transformed into a bulwark of resistance against the multitude of social and political changes after the war.[76] The growing awareness that surfaced amongst Saxon entrepreneurs that their region was changing from a powerhouse into a problem region fortified the expansion of the trade associations.[77] The strengthening of trade associations in Saxony thus epitomised a growing regional self-consciousness and a proactive attitude towards external challenges. Likewise, the associations of the Leipzig fur industry entered more pronouncedly into the public arena, backed by unprecedented membership levels. Such institutions were able to address problems that were related to re-admission to the world market or state intervention slowing down foreign trade. The need for this kind of representation never ceased to exist in the interwar period.

Notes

1 Szöllösi-Janze, "Losing the War but Gaining Ground: The German Chemical Industry during World War I," 92.
2 Mommsen, "Deutschland," 225.
3 Stolleis, *A History of Public Law in Germany, 1914–1945*, 38.
4 van de Kerkhof, "Public-Private Partnership im Ersten Weltkrieg? Kriegsgesellschaften in der schwerindustriellen Kriegswirtschaft des Deutschen Reiches," 132.
5 Schäfer, *Familienunternehmen und Unternehmerfamilien*, 32.
6 Bramke, "Sachsens Industrie (gesellschaft) in der Weimarer Republik," 28.
7 Green, *Ready-to-Wear and Ready-to-Work*, 29.
8 Wehler, *Deutsche Gesellschaftsgeschichte 1914–1949*, 4:47.
9 Burchardt, "Eine Neue Quelle Zu Den Anfängen Der Kriegswirtschaft in Deutschland 1914," 72.
10 Feldman, *Army, Industry, and Labor in Germany, 1914–1918*, 45.
11 Alexander Von Schwerin, "Tierzucht, Strahlen und Pigmente," 56.
12 Marie, "For Science, Love and Money," 923.
13 Collins, *The Agrarian History of England and Wales*, 7, 2:1672.
14 For the figures of the rabbit census see: BArch, Kriegsfell AG R 8731, nr. 11. Anlage, 2.09.1918.
15 StA-L, Deutsche Bank, Filiale Leipzig 21017, nr. 550, f. 10.
16 StA-L, Deutsche Bank, Filiale Leipzig 21017, nr; 386, Bilanzakte D. Kölner, Leizpig, den 29.08.1914.
17 Sächs. HStA, Außenministerium 10717, nr. 2510. Handelskammer Leipzig an das Ministerium des Innern Dresden. 18.11.1915.
18 Stadtal, Messeamt Kap 66, nr. 18, p. 14. Leipziger Abendzeitung 15.01.1916.
19 StA-L, Deutsche Bank, Filiale Leipzig 21017, nr. 550, f. 11.
20 Sächs. HStA, Wirtschaftsministerium, nr. 226, f. 2.
21 Sächs. HStA, Aussenministerium 10717, nr. 2473, Durchslag. S.d.
22 Sächs. HStA, Aussenministerium 10717, nr. 2473. Königlich Sächsisches Ministerium des Innern, an das Königlich Preussische Kriegsministerium, Kriegsrohstoff-Abteilung, Dresden, den 8.02.1917.
23 Sächs. HStA, Aussenministerium 10717, nr. 2473. Ministerium des Innern an das Ministerium der auswärtigen Angelegenheiten. 01.02.1917.
24 BArch, Kriegsfell AG R 8731, nr.1. Notarielle Ausfertigung, Leipzig am 19 März 1917.
25 Stolleis, *A History of Public Law in Germany, 1914–1945*, 38–9.
26 Burchard, "Eine Neue Quelle Zu Den Anfangen Der Kriegswirtschaft in Deutschland 1914," 72.

27 Roth, *Staat und Wirtschaft im Ersten Weltkrieg*, 21.
28 BArch, Kriegsfell AG R 8731, nr. 1. Notarielle Ausfertigung. Leipzig, am 9 Marz 1917.
29 Ibid.
30 Sächs. HStA, Aussenministerium 10717, nr. 2473. Preussische (Kreuz)Zeitung no. 156. Vom 26.03.1917.
31 Von Schwerin, "Tierzucht, Strahlen Und Pigmente," 55.
32 BArch, Kriegsfell AG R 8731, nr. 10, Bericht 25.05.1918.
33 BArch, Kriegsfell AG R 8731, nr. 25, 08.03.1918.
34 BArch, Kriegsfell AG R 8731, nr. 11, f. 16. Sd (probably 1919)
35 BArch, Kriegsfell AG R 8731, nr. 10, Bericht, 25.05.1918.
36 Ritschl, "The Pity of Peace: Germany's Economy at War, 1914–1918 and beyond," 57.
37 Barch, Kriegsfell AG R 8731, nr. 10. Bericht 25.05.1918.
38 *The Canadian Encyclopedia*, 58.
39 BArch, Kriegsfell AG R 8731, nr. 10. Rapport Aufklärungsamt. s.d. see also in this file: Anlage 3.
40 BArch, Kriegsfell AG R 8731 Kriegsfell AG, nr. 11. Anlage 2. Abschrift. 21 Januar 1919.
41 BArch, R 8731 Kriegsfell AG, nr. 11. Anl. 2. S.d. Raebiger: *Kokzidiosis, das große sterben*.
42 GStA PK, I. HA REP 87 B. nr. 22137, Niederschrift über Massnahmen zur Hebung der Kaninchenzucht am 28 und 29. Januar 1920. Anschrift 1.
43 Schwerin von, *Experimentalisierung des Menschen*, 65.
44 BArch, Kriegsfell AG R 8731, nr. 2. The last meeting of the Kriegsfell to conclude its liquidation took place on 20.11.1920.
45 Salaschek, *Vom Notstandstier zum Wohlstandstier*, 50.
46 Nestler, *Rauchwaren- und Pelzhandel*, 46.
47 BArch, Zulassungsstelle an der Berliner Börse, R 3118, nr. 836, f. 89. In 1921, it had already 1150 workers, but in 1889, only 450.
48 Sächs. HStA, Wirtschaftsministerium 11168, nr. 216. Vereinigte Rauchwaren-veredlungswerke G.m.b.H. Leipzig. 01.01.1920.
49 Ibid.
50 Sächs. HStA, Aussenministerium 10717, nr. 6772. Abschrift Handelskammer Leipzig. 24.09.1918.
51 Sächs. HStA, Wirtschaftsministerium 11168, nr. 2999, f. 26. Satzung 18.07.1919.
52 Sächs. HStA, Außenministerium 10717, nr. 6772. Arbeitsministerium V. Hübel, an die Kriegsfell-AG, 15.11.1918.
53 Sächs. HStA, Wirtschaftsministerium 11168, nr. 2999, f. 51. Niederschrift. 12.05.1921.
54 Sächs HStA, Wirtschaftsministerium 11168, nr. 226, ff. 43–55.
55 Sächs HStA, Aussenministerium 10717, Nr. 2510. Die Handelskammer Leipzig an das das Königliche Ministerium des Innern. 23.08.1917.
56 Sächs. HStA, Aussenministerium 10717, nr. 6772. Abschrift. 2.10.1918.
57 StadtaL, Messeamt Kap 66, nr. 18, Verband der Leipziger Rauchwaren Firmen E.V. Leipzig 21.02.1916.
58 StadtaL, Messeamt Kap 66, nr. 18, Ernst Goldfreund: London, St. Louis oder Leipzig? (Deutsche) Tageszeitung 21.12.1915.
59 Der Rauchwarenmarkt 1919, nr. 6. 21.01.1919. p. 1. Die Jahrestätigkeit der Leipziger Handelskammer und die Kriegs-Fell-AG.
60 StadtAL, Messeamt Kap 66, nr. 18. Besprechung 13.03.1916.
61 Ritschl, "The Pity of Peace: Germany's Economy at War, 1914–1918 and beyond," 42.

62 Sächs. HStA, Aussenministerium 10717, nr. 2510. Über die Gestaltung des Rauchwarenhandels in der Übergangswirtschaft. 26.02.1918.
63 Ibid.
64 BArch, Reichswirtschaftsministerium R 3101, nr. 21167, f. 126.
65 BArch, Reichswirtschaftsministerium, R 3101, nr. 21168, f. 78.
66 Sächs. HStA, Aussenministerium 10717, nr. 2510. Durchslag. am 16.3.1918.
67 Ibid., ff. 1–13.
68 Sächs. HStA, Außenministerium 10717, nr. 2510. Leipzig, Die Handelskammer an das Königliche Ministerium des Innern 20.12.1917.
69 Kürschnerzeitung, 1930. Nr. 16. 1.06.1930, p. 542. Leipzig und der erste Welt-Pelz-Kongress.
70 Lübstorff, "Paul Hollender."
71 Rückert, *Leipziger Wirtschaft in Zahlen*, 888.
72 Ullmann, "Kriegswirtschaft," 231.
73 Barch, Reichswirtschaftsministerium R 3101, nr. 3540, f. 6.
74 Sächs HStA, Reichswirtschaftsministerium R 3101, nr. 3540, f. 13.
75 Brosig, *Die Entwicklung der Umsatzsteuer in Deutschland*, 7.
76 Adolph, "Die Wirtschaftspolitik des VSI 1928–1934," 158.
77 Volker, "Wirtschaftsraumliche Orientierung als Unternehmensstrategie. Das Beispiel der Leipziger Handelskammer während der Weimarer Republik," 91.

References

Adolph, Jens. "Die Wirtschaftspolitik des VSI 1928–1934." In *Wirtschaft und Gesellschaft in Sachsen im 20: Jahrhundert*, edited by Werner Bramke, 157–85. Leipzig: Leipziger Universitätsverlag, 1998.
Bramke, Werner. "Sachsens Industrie(gesellschaft) in der Weimarer Republik." In *Wirtschaft und Gesellschaft in Sachsen im 20: Jahrhundert*, edited by Werner Bramke, 27–53. Leipzig: Leipziger Universitätsverlag, 1998.
Brosig, Miriam. *Die Entwicklung der Umsatzsteuer in Deutschland: Vom Kaiserreich bis zur Gegenwart*. München: GRIN Verlag, 2008.
Burchard, Lothar. "Eine Neue Quelle Zu Den Anfangen Der Kriegswirtschaft in Deutschland 1914." *Zeitschrift Für Firmengeschichte Und Unternehmerbiographie* 16, no. 2 (1971): 72–7.
Collins, Edward. *The Agrarian History of England and Wales. 7: 1850–1914*. Vol. 2. Cambridge, UK: Cambridge University Press, 2000.
Feldman, Gerald D. *Army, Industry, and Labor in Germany, 1914–1918*. Princeton, NJ: Princeton University Press, 1966.
Green, Nancy L. *Ready-to-Wear and Ready-to-Work: A Century of Industry and Immigrants in Paris and New York*. Durham, NC: Duke University Press, 1997.
Kerkhof, Stefanie van de. "Public-Private Partnership im Ersten Weltkrieg? Kriegsgesellschaften in der schwerindustriellen Kriegswirtschaft des Deutschen Reiches." In *Wirtschaft im Zeitalter der Extreme: Beiträge zur Unternehmensgeschichte Deutschlands und Österreichs: im Gedenken an Gerald D. Feldman*, edited by Hartmut Berghoff, 106–34. München: C. H. Beck, 2010.
Lübstorff, Friedrich. "Paul Hollender." Accessed May 17, 2013. www.deutsche-biographie.de/sfz33496.html.
Marie, Jenny. "For Science, Love and Money: The Social Worlds of Poultry and Rabbit Breeding in Britain, 1900–1940." *Social Studies of Science* 38, no. 6 (December 1, 2008): 919–36.

Marsh, James. *The Canadian Encyclopedia.* Edmonton: Hurtig Publishers, 1985.

Mommsen, Wolfgang J. "Deutschland." In *Enzyklopädie Erster Weltkrieg,* edited by Gerhard Hirschfeld, Gerd Krumeich, and Irina Renz, 15–31. Paderborn: Schöningh, 2003.

Nestler, Kurt. *Rauchwaren- und Pelzhandel.* Leipzig: Dr. M. Jänecke, 1929.

Ritschl, Albrecht. "The Pity of Peace: Germany's Economy at War, 1914–1918 and Beyond." In *The Economics of World War I,* edited by Stephen Broadberry and Mark Harrison, 41–77. Cambridge, UK: Cambridge University Press, 2005.

Roth, Regina. *Staat und Wirtschaft im Ersten Weltkrieg: Kriegsgesellschaften als kriegswirtschaftliche Steuerungsinstrumente.* Berlin: Duncker & Humblot, 1997.

Rückert, Hans. *Leipziger Wirtschaft in Zahlen: Sammlung der Statistik aus dem Leipziger Wirtschafts-Handbuch.* Leipzig: Industrie- und Handelskammer Leipzig, 1930.

Salaschek, Irene. *Vom Notstandstier zum Wohlstandstier: Kaninchenhaltung in Deutschland Geschichte und Bedeutung für die Veterinärmedizin.* Bristol: Tenea, 2009.

Schäfer, Michael. *Familienunternehmen und Unternehmerfamilien: zur Sozial- und Wirtschaftsgeschichte der sächsischen Unternehmer, 1850–1940.* München: C. H. Beck, 2007.

Schwerin, Alexander von. *Experimentalisierung des Menschen: der Genetiker Hans Nachtsheim und die vergleichende Erbpathologie, 1920–1945.* Göttingen: Wallstein, 2004.

———. "Tierzucht, Strahlen Und Pigmente: Genetik und die Herstellung von Tiermodellen für die Humangenetik. Hans Nachtsheim und die Vergleichende und Experimentelle Erbpathologie in Deutschland 1920–1945." Berlin: Freie Universität Berlin, 2003.

Stolleis, Michael. *A History of Public Law in Germany, 1914–1945.* Oxford: Oxford University Press, 2004.

Szöllösi-Janze, Margit. "Losing the War but Gaining Ground: The German Chemical Industry during World War I." In *The German Chemical Industry in the Twentieth Century,* edited by John E. Lesch, 15–57. Dordrecht: Springer, 2000.

Ullmann, Hans-Peter. "Kriegswirtschaft." In *Enzyklopädie Erster Weltkrieg,* edited by Gerhard Hirschfeld, Gerd Krumeich, and Irina Renz, 220–233. Paderborn: Schöningh, 2003.

Volker, Titel. "Wirtschaftsraumliche Orientierung als Unternehmensstrategie: Das Beispiel der Leipziger Handelskammer während der Weimarer Republik." In *Unternehmen im regionalen und lokalen Raum: 1750–2000,* edited by Ulrich Hess, Petra Listewnik, and Michael Schäfer, 179–97. Leipzig: Leipziger Universitätsverlag, 2004.

Wehler, Hans Ulrich. *Deutsche Gesellschaftsgeschichte 1914–1949.* Vol. 4. München: C. H. Beck, 1987.

6 Fur Farming in the Interwar Period

A Source for World Market Retreat?

Introduction

Describing the role of the Leipzig industry in the creation of fur farming in the interwar period is the objective of this chapter. Resource substitution during World War I had opened the door for fur farming, which entered Germany at an almost unprecedented pace. Between 1921 and 1931, about 1,000 new fur farms were constructed across the country. By the end of the 1930s, fur farming, primarily centred on the production of silver fox skins, had transformed into an important wellspring of resources for the industry in Leipzig. The fur farming business did not emerge separately from the industrial district in Leipzig. On the contrary, it was the Leipzig industry that initiated the formation of the first experimental farms and firms continued to exert influence over farming well into the 1930s. The industry's support for fur farming ripened because of the post-war problems in international trade. Leipzig businesses encountered difficulties in supplying the district with resources, especially immediately after World War I.

An important dimension of fur farming was research and development. Fur farming was an innovation: it entailed the creation, distribution, and application of new knowledge. As such, the creation of a new production paradigm based on fur farming heralded a period of further entanglement between Leipzig business and science. The business-science nexus in the creation of fur farming in Germany runs parallel to the previous chapters on rabbit and karakul breeding. Fur farming was especially linked to breakthroughs in experimental and applied genetics, which increasingly unveiled their potential to the agricultural sciences and anthropology. Applied genetics involved the 'improvement' of animals, plants, and humans through artificial selection or sterilisation.[1] Applied genetic science was of paramount importance to the development of fur farming. Breeders used the rules of artificial selection in the production of rare and valuable colour variations such as the silver fox, a 'melanistic' mutation of the red fox.[2]

The literature affirms that one of the advantages of industrial district is that the need for innovation is more easily perceived and district firms are able to set in motion new innovation processes.[3] Indeed, as has been demonstrated in literature, business both in Germany and beyond became increasingly science-based at the beginning of the twentieth century, meaning that "scientific research and systematic applications thereof . . . turned into a routine activity of the company."[4] Nevertheless, the increasing historical importance of science and technology for businesses is often linked to bigger business and industrial corporations. In addition, surprisingly little is known about agricultural sciences in this process.[5] How did these smaller business communities organise scientific research and implement innovations in a field that was remote from their commercial activities? As briefly indicated in the previous chapter, the organisation of agricultural research in the context of an industrial district forces us to rethink the classic image of in-house industrial research departments or corporate laboratories. The chapter will therefore emphasise the alternative ways in which the district organised research on fur breeding and whether it was able to implement the findings of such research into the sourcing of new resources.

The examination of fur farming in connection to the Leipzig industry leads us into territory as yet unchartered by the research literature. The chapter is a pioneering contribution to the history of modern fur farming. We know surprisingly little about fur farming on the European continent and only slight more in regards to North America.[6] The creation of fur farming nevertheless constituted a major wider historical development in the conquest of nature and the zoological domestication of new types of animals. In 2007, about 88% of all furs consumed came from farms whereas hunting constituted the major source well into the 1930s.[7] Fur farming of the early twentieth century constituted a major transformation in ecological history: it alleviated the pressures on animal populations from fur trapping and hunting, which was a severe problem in North America and Siberia.[8] By placing the emergence of fur farming in Germany in this wider context, the chapter contributes to the historical understanding of one of the most controversial farming niches in contemporary society.

Fur Farming: A New Business?

The International Development of Fur Farming

Before turning to the developments in Germany, let us take a closer look at the emergence of fur farming as an international phenomenon. Fur farming started in a region that was already one of the largest fur producers in the world, Canada. Prince Edward Island in the Saint Lawrence gulf specifically formed the cradle of modern fur breeding. Fur breeding commenced on the island as early as 1887; apparently, a few pioneer farms had emerged by around 1894.[9] On the eve of World War I, 277 farms operated on the island. The practice accelerated after 1921 when Canada's conservationist environmental policy furthered the proliferation of small fur farmers at the local level.[10] As such, the total number of fur farms in Canada reached 1,240 units in 1923. Prince Edward Island remained the El Dorado of North American fur farming with 448 farms: 41% of Canadian ranched fur was produced on the island.[11] Monoculture was the norm. Only 61 farms reared animals other than silver foxes.[12]

By the beginning of the 1930s, fur farming formed a significant sector of the Canadian fur industry. The percentage of ranched furs increased from 3% in 1920–1921 to about 19% at the end of the decade. In the early 1930s, when the real value of the raw fur yield decreased, ranched furs represented about 30% of Canadian fur production.[13] This upward trend continued to characterise the Canadian fur trade at least until the beginning of World War II. By 1938, fur farming generated almost 50% of the total value of production. In addition, farming increasingly diversified when producing silver foxes on Canadian farms decreased.[14] In importance and magnitude, Canadian fur production on farms far exceeded that of countries on the European continent.

Similarly, the rearing of silver foxes had entered the US by the end of the nineteenth century. In 1922, the Biological Survey registered the presence of 500 breeders farming one or more species of furbearing animals.[15] Farmers in the United States also specialised in the silver fox, a mutant of the common fox, a popular item on the world market; they also bred raccoon and mink, although to a lesser extent.[16] By 1940, the US ranked 2,644 fox farmers.[17] The production of farmed silver fox skins in the US was larger than in Canada. Between 1931 and 1933, Canada produced 95,000 silver fox skins on average, whereas production in the US exceeded the 100,000 benchmark (110,000 skins in 1931, 130,000 in 1932, and 150,000 in 1933).[18] After 1940, however, the dictates of fashion required the furs of other animals like mink, which made fox farming steadily decrease in popularity. While taking these minor differences into account, both Canada and the US were leading countries in the production of farmed furs. The growing success of farming across the Atlantic inspired traders and farmers in Europe. The first fur farms in Europe were created in Scandinavia: in Norway (1913) and in Finland (1916). In the interwar period, Scandinavia emerged as the centre of European fur farming. Norway had around 20,000 relatively small fur farms prior to World War II.[19]

Fur Farming in Germany: The First Stages (1921–1925)

The first mention of fur breeding in Germany was made shortly after the end of the Great War and was inextricably connected to the name of the Munich professor of zoology, Reinhard Demoll (1882–1961).[20] Demoll's ideas concerning fur farming resonated strongly in Saxony, where it was enthusiastically portrayed as a promising venue to replace the destroyed supply routes from tsarist Russia.[21] Several Leipzig firms supported Demoll's plan to create an experimental farm and they formed a partnership with him. In 1921, a Leipzig business group established the Experimental Fur Breeding Farm

(*Versuchszüchterei Edler Pelztiere GmbH & Co*). The farm was located near Hirschegg-Riezlern in the Bavarian Alps and close to the border with Austria. The farm was a cooperative venture between several businessmen in Leipzig: Friedrich Erler & Co, Theodor Thorer, Heinrich Lomer, Emil Zahn, and A. Nathan & Co.[22] While Demoll headed the practical management of the farm, Walter Krausse, a manager of the Erler firm, was appointed as the head of the overarching project. The breeding on the experimental farm started at the end of 1922 with the introduction of four foxes purchased in Canada. In 1923, the first 'German' foxes were born in captivity.

In the wake of the Bavarian experimental farm and its expanding silver fox population, numerous farms were set up throughout Germany. Like in Bavaria, altitude was considered relevant for fur farming, in the belief that the environment there was better suited to animals used to a subarctic climate. The few farms founded in Saxony were therefore located in the mountains south of Dresden, the so-called "*Sächsische Schweiz.*"[23] Contemporary publications counted 56 fur farms in Germany in the summer of 1926, where the majority of farms were situated in Prussia (23) and Bavaria (21). These first farms mainly focused on the rearing of silver foxes (770 animals) and mink (270 animals). The development of fur farming in Saxony (only two farms), the heart of the German fur industry, was relatively small.

At this stage, however, farming as a new source of furs for the industry was still far off on the horizon. In this experimental and expansive phase, fur farmers were hardly concerned at all with pelting for the market in Leipzig: the sale of fur skins represented only a marginal share of the total supply. Contemporary sources mentioned the symbolic sale of 26 white fox skins to the fur industry in 1926: the 'best skins' were sold for 435 RM on average.[24] Most of the first farms in Germany concentrated at this stage on reselling foxes to provide breeding stock for other farmers. Only in a later stage, fur farming would gear up for market production.

Fur Industry and Science in the Late Weimar Period

After the mid-1920s, when fur farming emerged strongly in Germany, Leipzig firms endeavoured to transform the city into the capital for the development of fur farming. The most important development in this respect was the creation of the research centre, the Institute for Furbearing Animals and Fur Research (a rather unwieldy translation of *Reichszentrale für Pelztier und Rauchwarenforschung*, henceforth the Reichszentrale). Founded in 1926, the fur industry hoped to mould the fur breeding movement into an efficient supply source through this scientific institution.[25] The need to influence fur farming stemmed largely from the fresh experience during the war of the arduous attempts to rationalise rabbit keeping. Walter Stichel, a member of the Reichszentrale, wrote in 1926: "Fur farming falling on the same track as rabbit keeping must be avoided at all costs . . . the invested capital for fur farming is simply too high to allow for experimentation and imperfections."[26]

A central rationale behind the research centre was therefore not only the support of research but also the promotion of an attitude of professionalism in fur farming. For instance, in 1929, the director of the Reichszentrale Paul Schöps wrote pointedly in one of his many newspaper articles that "fur farming means work and not leisure."[27] Via the research centre, the Leipzig industry also controlled the Association for Silver Fox Breeding (*Verband für Silberfuchszucht*), which chiefly gathered fur farms in Saxony together and competed with other farmers organisations for control.

The organisational aspects of the research institution mirrored the collaborative networks between fur firms in Leipzig. It also revealed links between these firms and those political stakeholders of the region interested in strengthening the local economy. Regional public authorities in fact played a major role in the creation of the research institution. While the initial 20,000 RM budget of the Reichszentrale was rather modest, it is particularly striking that firms provided only 3,500 RM (the Fur Merchants Association 2,000 RM and various firms 1,500 RM). Regional governments and public institutions raised the remainder of the sum. Both the Chamber of Commerce in Leipzig and Saxony's Ministry of Economy donated 6,000 RM, making them the chief sponsors.[28] The balance between public and private funding did not change later. In 1927, the total budget was raised to 28,000 RM but funding from the fur industry only increased to 6,000 RM.[29]

Of course, the rather modest funding was reflected in the organisation of the Reichszentrale itself. The research centre was run by firm personnel and its offices were initially housed in one of the trading houses on the Brühl, the Friedrich Erler & Co firm, which specialised in the treatment and sale of fox skins. Paul Schöps, the appointed leader of the Reichszentrale, was a high-ranked official in the Erler firm. Schöps' appointment demonstrated the role of Erler as one of the lead firms of the district, especially in the field of innovation. I have alluded earlier to Erler's leading position in the development of the synthetic fur dyeing industry in Leipzig with the chemist Stieglitz. The Erler firm embodied a tradition of close cooperation between industry and science. Aside from the leading role of Erler, the meetings of the Reichszentrale were followed by entrepreneurs from the largest trading and dyeing businesses in Leipzig, like Arndt Thorer (Theodor Thorer), Richard König, and Walter Krausse (Friedrich Erler & Co).

The low budget and loose organisational structure of the Reichszentrale flies in the face of the classic image we have of research and development centres in industries at the beginning of the twentieth century. Rather than conducting research independently or within the walls of the business, the Reichszentrale was intended as the central node inside a *research network*. In other words, the institute was designed to assemble experts who worked on the scientific, economic, and practical underpinnings of fur breeding. The Reichszentrale generally eschewed participating in direct research, with the notable exception of an experimental farm that was set up in Connewitz, a town south of Leipzig.[30] The 500-square-metre experimental farm was situated in the local forest and its research focused largely on aspects of animal management like the study of nutrition patterns and finding suitable pens for different types of furbearers. The creation of the experimental farm coincided with a budget increase of the institute in 1928, which almost doubled to 41,976 RM. Almost half of the budget was spent on the infrastructure of the research institute while 14,736 RM was donated to associated professors and institutions.[31]

Aside from having its own experimental farm, the most important feat of the Reichszentrale was assembling an epistemic community of experts. The centre had a more or less permanent body of researchers at its disposal that formed a commission of experts. The commission advised on the main issues of contemporary fur breeding. These experts, 11 scientists from German-speaking academia, remained attached to their home institutions. The commission of experts was firmly rooted in Leipzig or its immediate surroundings. Five of the 11 experts worked in an academic institution in Leipzig or in one of its neighbouring cities. The fur industry especially profited from the expansion of Leipzig University, then the third largest in Germany, which opened a new veterinary and animal breeding faculty in 1923. The extended veterinary faculty became an important scientific advocate for the development of fur breeding. Members supported the research network and even incorporated fur farming into teaching activities for veterinary students.[32] Three scientists of the expert commission had been appointed at the new faculty of the university of Leipzig: Johannes Richter, Carl Scheunert, and Curt Sprehn. Sprehn and Scheunert worked as veterinary scientists at Leipzig University, though in different departments. Johannes Richter, a veterinary surgeon, was associated with the Leipzig Institute for Animal Breeding and Animal Obstetrics (*Institut für Tierzucht und Geburtskunde der Universität Leipzig*). Richter soon included the diseases furbearing animals suffered into his research.[33] Two scientists in the network were in the immediate vicinity of Leipzig; one of them was Gustav Fröhlich, who had headed the Institute for Animal Breeding and Dairy in the Halle University (*Institut für Tierzucht und Molkereiwesen der Universität Halle/Saale*) since 1915.[34] Another was Heinrich Prell of the Zoological Institute of Tharandt College (*Zoologisches Institut der Forstlichen Hochschule in Tharandt*), appointed rector in 1927.[35]

In addition to being strongly embedded within the region, the fur industry's research centre adorned the network with leading scientists throughout German-speaking academia. Two such scientists lived in Munich: Reinhard Demoll, and Heinrich Henseler, who was active in Halle between 1910 and 1920 and thereafter associated with the Munich University. Last but not least, there was the renowned genetic scientist Hans von Nachtsheim of the Kaiser Wilhelm Institute for Genetic Science (*Kaiser Wilhelm Institut für Vererbungsforschung*) in Berlin-Dahlem, whose scientific contribution to the development of animal breeding has been acknowledged in historical scholarship.[36] As a colleague of Erwin Baur, the most renowned genetic scientist in Germany, he ranked as one of the most influential members of the research network. The promotion of Mendelian genetics among amateur breeders was a major motivation for genetic scientists like von Nachtsheim.[37] Indeed in the 1920s, the institutionalisation of genetic science in Germany was still in a developing stage, especially when compared to the US.[38] Frustration at this state of affairs enhanced the willingness of genetic scientists like the prominent Hans von Nachtsheim to participate in new fields of agriculture like fur farming.

The Activities of the Reichszentrale (1926–1929)

Promotion of Research in Germany

The main activities of the Reichszentrale were the promotion of research into differing aspects of fur breeding and encouraging professionalisation among the numerous new amateur farmers. The latter was seen as an important task since it was the underlying aim of the fur industry to develop farming as a reliable resource supplier. Most scientists saw no harm in reconciling scientific research with commercial goals. Alexander Sokolowsky, a Hamburg professor who published through the Reichszentrale, defined the field of research as follows: "The domain of the study of furbearers is limited to the keeping and breeding of fur breeding animals and . . . the study of the fur coats of these creatures for the tasks of the fur trade."[39] Other scientists wanted to change practices of animal breeding rather than support the fur industry. The desire to instil an attitude of professionalism in the new farmers was shared by university scientists, mainly from the fear that amateurism would sabotage scientific advances. The practical knowledge of breeders was based on 'shared knowledge' derived from 'personal experience' with animal keeping rather than scientific principles or the insights of basic animal management.[40]

The Reichszentrale gave an impetus to this new field as the bulk of the expenditure went directly to research. In 1927, the Zoological Institute in Tharandt received 6,000 RM and director Prell got 1,200 RM for his research in America. The Reichszentrale did not pay wages but reimbursed travel costs (3,000 RM). Research was not limited to fur farming: dyeing received 2,000 RM and another 2,000 RM went to various other research projects.[41] So, with only a little spending, the Reichszentrale was able to set several research projects in motion. Curt Sprehn and his assistants at the Leipzig University performed dissections on 940 deceased animals on German fur farms to establish the main causes of death.[42] The Leipzig veterinary facility did not receive any funding for this research. Drawing on support and goodwill from associated academics, stimulating research with minimal investments was a strength of the Leipzig research network.

The role of the Reichszentrale as a facilitator of research can also be seen in its efforts to publish and circulate the research of scholars working on fur farming. These publications also reveal the kind of research being performed. The *Arbeiten der Reichszentrale*, a compilation of the 26 most important publications between 1926 and 1930, dealt with multifarious topics, although animal management clearly stood out as the most important. About 12 publications related to this subject and included reports on experiments into breeding new species and the acclimatisation of furbearing animals in Germany. About seven publications were devoted to aetiology of furbearers; this was the second-largest genre published in the compilation. Like the majority of scientific publications on rabbit breeding during World War I, such publications chiefly focused on the most common causes of death and on diseases or pathogens that affected the quality of the breeding stock. If these scientific publications are to be trusted, farmed animals suffered from parasites most of all and scabies to a lesser degree. Indeed, parasites were the largest cause of death among silver foxes. Twenty-three fox pups died in 1926 because of parasites; the overall total loss from that year was 72 foxes. This was a painful loss of production capital since a new fox would easily cost 3,000 marks.[43]

While the previous publications mainly served a public of peers interested in various aspects of fur farming, the results of scientific research were also popularised for laymen and amateur breeders. Leipzig published its own journal, *Die Pelztierzucht*, which had become one of the leading journals on fur farming in Germany since 1924. In addition, an important publication series were the so-called leaflets (*Merkblätter*) designed as instruction notes for fur breeders. They aimed at rationalising fur breeding by suppressing amateurish practices. One leaflet for example dealt with the slaughter methods. The leaflet argued against primitive methods like strangling in favour of chemicals and electrocution, which, most importantly, minimised the risk of damage to the skin.[44] Publications in *Die Pelztierzucht* conveyed similar information about the practices and methods of fur farming. Topics ranged from adequate nutrition patterns to the optimal size of animal pens.

Again, the research network did much more than research, and attempted to control and streamline this new supply chain of furs. Scientists saw an important task in limiting speculation. In the first stage of fur farming, the resale of furbearing animals generated most of the profits for pioneering breeders. Consequently, it prevented breeders from orienting their production to the market of Leipzig, the so-called pelting stage. This was a problem that also affected the Canadian and American fur farming businesses in the beginning years.[45] Von Nachtsheim, for instance, was particularly worried that unrealistic profit expectations would damage fur farming because of the appeal to fortune-seekers: "In several newspapers and journals, fox breeding has been represented as an industry for gold diggers, promising profits of 180% and more. . . ."[46] In 1927, the Reichszentrale warned animal traders about advertising unrealistic profit margins. The Reichszentrale reported that "if the prospects in fur farming for well-funded and experienced breeders are by no means unfavourable, these exaggerated descriptions on profitability contrasts the realistic circumstances of today."[47] The Reichs-centrale and by extension the industry focused on farms that would base profits on the production of skins.

In the fight against amateurism, academics and experts called for more official control over fur farms. Scientists inspected the farms that were asso-ciated with the Leipzig Association of Breeders. They were convinced of the benefits to be derived from expanding the system of control: "If it is possible to introduce strict measures and we manage to implement official controls, there will be no fear that the industry of fur animals will suffer from diseases like some other types of animal breeding, which lack uniform and strict supervision."[48] The associated scientists Heinrich Prell legitimised the inter-vention of experts and the state in fur farming by referring to the successes of the American government in planning fur farming.[49]

Attempts to install control and the fight against the speculative animal trade proved largely ineffective. The Reichszentrale's power was limited because of the decentralised organisation of fur farming in Germany and the state's refusal to set out a legal framework. Each competing farming association followed its own agenda. The main competing lobby group, the Union of German Fur Farmers' Associations in Munich (*Bund Deutscher Pelztierzüchter-Vereine*), was led by Reinhard Demoll, who formerly coop-erated with the Leipzig industry.[50] Whereas the Leipzig organisation was bent on integrating farming into the city's fur industry, Demoll's organisa-tion assumed the role of defender of the small farmers and breeders. The Demoll organisation was more successful in influencing government policy. In 1930 the Ministry of Health decided to impose stricter measures upon foreign imports of new breeding stock, which damaged the Reichscentrale's fight against speculation since it strengthened the position of domestic ani-mal traders and their sales policy.[51]

The Internationalisation of Autarky

Aside from the internal problems that the Reichszentrale suffered, the fur industry itself substantially revised its strategy for fur farming. The revival of the international trade in the second half of the 1920s refocused the inter-est of the fur industry in fur farming. Trade relations with the USSR were fully re-established after the treaty of Berlin in 1925. Whereas initial fur farming projects were clearly inspired by autarkic principles, the German advances in breeding were increasingly being used in the context of for-eign trade relations. In particular, the Leipzig experimental farm and several researchers of the network supported the development of fur farming in the Soviet Union.[52] The potential of farmed fur there was deemed much higher, as the Reichszentrale director Schöps wrote in 1928: "[Fur farm-ing] will have a totally different meaning for the Russian economy than it would for ours." In the same letter, he stated that fur farming in the Soviet Union should be supported: "It is after all pleasing to see Russia build its fur farming with the help of the Leipzig district."[53] As such, sourcing farmed furs in the USSR was seen as a viable alternative. This meant a major shift from the initial autarkic visions that had undergirded the participation of the industry in farming.

An important amount of resources and human capital of the Leipzig research network was indeed invested in the internationalisation of fur farming. The Reichszentrale held support to the USSR to be paramount since fur farming lagged far behind in Russia in comparison to other fur-producing countries. Earlier attempts to establish fur farming there had tragically failed. A single fur farm established on the eve of the First World War was inevitably lost in the quagmire of the civil war. In 1925, the Soviet trade agency Gostorg established a new fur farm on a small island on the Enissei River near Dudinka in northernmost Siberia. However, the farm was poorly equipped and later shut down.[54] It took until 1927 before the Soviet authorities finally decided to pursue a more energetic policy towards fur farming: importantly, they secured the help of the Leipzig associations, foremost the Reichszentrale. With the support of German shipping companies and the Leipzig research network, the Soiuzpushnina (the Soviet fur syndicate) arranged a Canadian animal transport and shipped about 100 silver foxes and 900 muskrats through Hamburg to Leningrad. The animals purchased from Canadian farms were selected by the Deutsche Versuchszüchterei edler Pelztiere GmbH, the firm that was in charge of the Leipzig fur farm in the Alps.[55]

The Leipzig farming association not only supported the organisation of animal transports but also provided assistance for the construction and supervision of new farms. In 1928, Fritz Schmidt, the manager of the above-mentioned Leipzig farm, left for the Soviet Union in order to support the establishment of a large farm near Archangelsk. After Archangelsk, Schmidt went to Pushkino (north of Moscow) where he was appointed scientific director at the Central Instructional Farm. There, he devoted himself to the study of Russian sables in captivity.[56] Schmidt stayed in Pushkino until 1934. Other experts travelled temporarily to the USSR: Curt Sprehn followed Schmidt to Pushkino to teach Russian biologists about animal diseases. Friedrich Joppich, a German expert on rabbit breeding, travelled to the Soviet Union as well. Instead of protecting its findings from foreign interests, the Leipzig research network shared them with the Soviets.

The helpfulness of the Leipzig network, however, failed to transform Soviet fur farming into a reliable source for the Leipzig industry.[57] As we will see later, the Soviets radically modified their foreign trade policy, abandoning the New Economic Policy (NEP) in favour of Stalin's ambitious five-year plan. Instead of focusing on the export of resources, the five-year plan shifted attention to the export of industrial goods. Consequently, the resource exports from the Soviet Union dramatically decreased. The Leipzigers' gamble to export expertise on autarkic fur farming to the USSR failed not only because of the collapse of the NEP; it was also due to the fact that the USSR failed to convert foreign expertise into practical full-scale fur farming.[58] Whereas the farming business in the Soviet Union reached levels in 1930 that were comparable to those in Germany in 1926 (738 silver foxes and 258 blue foxes), growth of fur farming largely stagnated afterwards.[59] In fact, fur farming in the USSR only acquired prominence after World War II. This is rather surprising given the larger agricultural potential and suitable climatic conditions for fur farming. This delay was partially connected to the Soviet Union's negative stance on genetic science, adhering to the neo-Lamarckian ideas proposed by the peasant plant-breeder Lysenko.[60] Only in the late 1950s did experiments with fur farming attain momentum again, with the revival of genetic science, and state fur farms continued to expand well into the 1980s. Again, however, the interest of the Reichszentrale in Soviet farming illustrates that the Leipzig firms had international ambitions with sourcing fur farming.

The Stabilisation of German Fur Farming and the Collapse of the Research Network, 1930–1939

In spite of domestic problems like speculation and the focus on foreign investments, fur farming in Germany grew spectacularly by the end of the 1920s (see Table 6.1). From 56 farms in 1926, the figure multiplied to an astounding 1,074 farms in 1931. Their geographical distribution remained largely unchanged. Bavaria and Prussia were still the central hubs of fur farming, although Prussia had clearly achieved predominance by this date.

The motley variety of furbearing animals on the German farms is a particularly striking post-1926 development. German farms domesticated up to six types of furbearing animals. However, most farms remained specialised in the rearing of silver foxes (8,593) and mink (7,019). Germany's silver fox farming was still dwarfed by Canada (58,000) and Norway (35,000). The popularity of silver fox breeding corresponded with changing patterns in the consumption in the interwar period, which favoured this variety of the

Table 6.1 German Fur Farms (1931)[61]

German States	Number of Farms
PRUSSIA	577
BAVARIA	254
SAXONY	41
WÜRTTEMBERG	74
BADEN	13
THÜRINGEN	26
HESSEN	29
OTHERS	60
TOTAL	1,074

Table 6.2 Species of Fur Animals Raised on German Farms (1931)[62]

Animal Species	Farms	Number of Animals
SILVER FOX	467	8,593
ARCTIC FOX	43	306
MINK	441	7,019
RACCOON	136	932
NUTRIA	179	1,926
KARAKULS	25	1,508

common fox.[63] Before the Great War, only about 3,000–4,000 silver foxes were sold annually on the world market: by 1931, turnover had climbed to an incredible 330,000.[64] World production of silver foxes continued to climb, reaching 400,000–500,000 skins in 1932, despite the economic crisis. Farming was an important part of the global silver fox industry. Between 1932 and 1933, about 40,000 silver foxes were traded on the autumn and winter auctions in Leipzig: 10,000 of the pelts originated in German farms and the rest came from Austria, America, and Scandinavia. By 1934, German fur farms had a breeding stock of 16,564 silver foxes.[65]

However, German fur farming's entrance onto the market coincided with the economic crisis of the early 1930s. This utterly shattered the high-profit expectations that many had seen in the business. In the first place, lower demand and significant overproduction created downward pressures on price levels. In the early 1930s, the Reichszentrale feared for the future of fur breeding in its current form and ceased to welcome newcomers into the industry: "A very large part of the German and other European fur farms operate today unprofitably. . . . the value of silver fox pelts has decreased so drastically that the majority of farms need to cover the cost of farming."[66] Good-quality pelts were still sold between 150 and 200 RM, but this was a massive decrease from pre-1930s levels when they were sold for over 1,000 RM. Furthermore, it was estimated that 150 RM was the cost of raising a fox and lower-graded pelts fell under this price level. This meant that many breeders were operating at a loss.[67]

Meanwhile, the research network suffered from the economic crisis. State funding, especially that from the City Council, the Leipzig Chamber of Commerce, the Saxon Government, and the Prussian Ministry of Agriculture, was severely curtailed.[68] By 1932, it was clear that the existence of a joint research network was no longer desirable. Hollender and Krausse tried to transfer the institution to Leipzig University, since it could no long afford to rent its location, let alone perform its basic tasks.[69] However, the university refused to house Reichszentrale within the university walls. The Reichszentrale thus remained independent but its role was marginal after 1932. Attempts to push the network towards research into synthetic dyeing were equally ineffective. In times of crisis, no firms or public institutions were willing to fund the research institute.

Perhaps the booming success of fur farming also played a role in the decline of the research network as farms no longer needed guidance. By 1934, the number of fur farms had doubled to 2,015 farms.[70] In contrast to the Weimar administration, the Nazis were sympathetic to the autarkic potential of small-scale animal breeding. Like many other groups of small animal breeders, the Reich Food Corporation (*Reichsnahrstand*) incorporated the fur farmers in an overarching institution, the Reich Professional Assocation of Fur Farmers (*Reichsfachgruppe Pelztierzüchter*). State dirigisme and the focus on self-sufficiency central to Nazi economic policy made farmed furs increasingly prominent at the Leipzig market. In 1935, the RAVAG, a Leipzig fur auction company, noted that German products acquired a larger role in the fur market: "Due to the expansion of fur farming in Germany, larger deliveries for auctions are to be expected in the near future."[71] In 1938, the RAVAG concluded an important deal with two fur farming cooperatives based in Berlin. The contract involved the sale of an unprecedented number of farmed skins, 14,000 silver fox and 25,000 mink.[72] In turn, the RAVAG granted a 300,000 RM advance to the farmers. It was therefore the first large contract between the German fur industry and the farming business. The contract adequately illuminates the progress of the German fur farming after 1935. The auction company generally sold around 30,000 silver fox skins and 5,000 mink skins annually in the period between 1934 and 1936.[73] In 1936, the RAVAG only sold 3,000 farmed fox skins in Germany but in 1938 they increased the number to 14,000. While firms had failed to establish Leipzig as a centre of expertise, fur farming was now an integral part of the economy of the Leipzig district on the eve of World War II.

Conclusion

The development of fur farming led to collective action in the industrial district. The result was the foundation of the Reichszentrale, whose function it was to create networks with scientists and experts. The institution was not a traditional research station that worked on behalf of a number of firms. It was never the intention of the industry to fund a fully equipped research centre; rather, it was intended to profit from the formation of an epistemic community of scientists. The structure and geography of the network resembled the way in which the district participants tried to profit from local resources and endowments. The large majority of researchers connected to the centre came from Leipzig or university towns nearby. The industry profited especially from the creation of a veterinary faculty at the Leipzig University. Aside from the two experimental farms in Leipzig and in the Alps, the institute had little infrastructure other than its bureaus in Leipzig. However, it made use of the infrastructure of adjacent research institutions like the Zoological Institute in Tharandt.

The examination of a small institution has shown that processes of scientification can take alternative shapes in the context of an industrial district.

Historical scholarship should continue to pay attention to alternatives to the classic models of in-house research, formalised partnerships between business and university, and public-private partnerships. Many processes of innovation were set in motion as a result of network activity. It should be stressed that the functioning of the network was not inimical to the development of fur farming. On the contrary, the network was able to generate research on various aspects of fur farming and its members did influence the farming business in terms of animal management and sanitation. Nonetheless, processes of innovation in the industrial district were messy; they were set up relatively easily but fell into inertia just as quickly since a common strategy for the implementation of innovation was absent. In addition, businesses never lost sight of the international dimension in developing what was an autarkic alternative to world trade, as the support for Soviet fur farming shows. The fur industry's primary concern remained the restoration of world trade, also in the 1920s, which is the subject of the next part.

Notes

1 Rader, "Scientific Animals: Reflections on the Laboratory and Its Human-Animal Relations, from Dba to Dolly and Beyond," 121.
2 Roth and Merz, *Wildlife Resources*, 203.
3 Porter, "Locations, Clusters, and Company Strategy," 262.
4 Marsch, *Zwischen Wissenschaft und Wirtschaft*, 23.
5 Szöllösi-Janze, "Institutionelle Umgestaltung Der Wissenschaftslandschaft Im Übergang Vom Späten Kaiserreich Zur Weimarer Republik," 70.
6 Roth and Merz, *Wildlife Resources*, 203.
7 Roots, *Domestication*, 127.
8 Delort, *L'Histoire de la fourrure de l'antiquité a` nos jours*, 275.
9 Clutton-Brock, *A Natural History of Domesticated Mammals*, 192.
10 Colpitts, *Game in the Garden*, 160.
11 TNA, HBCA, Public Record Office, (BH 2639), A92/17/102, f. 32.
12 Ibid.
13 LAC. URG 84 A-2-a. File no. U270, pt. 2 (ReeL T 12898), f. 1105. Fur Production of Canada, Season 1933–1934.
14 Ray, *The Canadian Fur Trade in the Industrial Age*, 119.
15 Ashbrook, "The Fur Trade and the Fur Supply," 6.
16 Ashbrook, *Fur Resources of the United States*, 9.
17 Clutton-Brock, *A Natural History of Domesticated Mammals*, 192.
18 Der Rauchwarenmarkt, 17.01.1936. Die Aussichten der Pelztierzucht.
19 *The Norway Year Book*.
20 Bosl, *Bosls Bayerische Biographie I*, 132.
21 Die Kürschnerzeitung, nr 9, 27.04.1919. Ein Forschungsinstitut für Pelztierzucht.
22 StA-L, Hermelin-Verlag 21098, nr. 644, private notes of Dr. Paul Schöps concerning the company history F. Erler, 30/01/1985.
23 Sächs. HStA, Wirtschaftsministerium 11168, nr. 1980, f. 188.
24 Sächs. HStA, Wirtschaftsministerium 11168, nr. 490, f. 15., Sonderdruck (. . .) Ernst Stakemann. pp. 614–15.
25 Sächs. HStA, Wirtschaftsministerium 11168, nr. 489, f. 32, Sitzung 8 Marz 1927.
26 Ibid., ff. 70–82, here 82.
27 Die Pelztierzucht, 1929, nr. 2, p. 175, 05.09.1929. Pelztierzucht und Viehseuchengesetz. von. Dr. P. Schöps. Leipzig.

28 Sächs. HStA, Wirtschaftsminsiteirum, nr. 489, f. 32. Protokoll. 08.03.1927.
29 Sächs. HStA, Wirtschaftsministerium 11168, nr. 489, f. 44.
30 Ibid., f. 110.
31 Ibid., f. 148.
32 Leipziger Universitätsarchiv, Phil. Fak B3/32.04, Bericht 17.06.1927.
33 Wolter, "Johannes Richter (1878–1943)—Leben Und Werk Eines Protagonisten Der Veteirnärgeburtshilfe.," 105.
34 "Gustav Frölich."
35 See: Nachlass Pr. Heinrich Prell. Archives of the University of Dresden.
36 Engel, "Hans Nachtsheim."
37 Schwerin von, *Experimentalisierung des Menschen*, 20.
38 Harwood, "National Styles in Science: Genetics in Germany and the United States between World Wars," 396.
39 Sokolowsky, "Pelztierforschung," 2.
40 Von Schwerin, *Experimentalisierung des Menschen*, 58. see p. 59.
41 Sächs. HStA, Wirtschaftsministerium 11168, nr. 489, f. 29.
42 Sächs. HStA, Wirtschaftsministerium 11168, nr. 490, f. 182.
43 Ibid., f. 15.
44 Ibid, f. 221.
45 Colpitts, "Conservation, Science and Canada's Fur Farming Industry, 1913–1945," 86.
46 BArch, Reichsgesundheidsamt R 86, nr. 3467. Teilabschrift 12.10.1925.
47 Sächs. HStA, Wirtschaftsministerium 11168, nr. 489, f. 39.
48 Sächs. HStA, Wirtschaftsministerium 11168, nr. 490, f. 70.
49 Prell, "Zur Frage Der Planmässigen Pelztierzucht."
50 BArch, Reichsgesundheidsamt R86, nr. 3467. Deutsche Landwirtschaft Gesellschaft. Aktenvermerk 5.02.1930.
51 BArch, Reichsgesundheitsamt R 86, nr. 4926. Abschrift. 8.08.1931.
52 Weiner, "The Canging Face of Soviet Conservation," 254.
53 Sächs. HStA, Wirtschaftsministerium 11168, nr. 489, f. 203.
54 PA AA, Botschaft Moskau, nr. 467. Durchschlag. 18.02.1926.
55 Die Pelztierzucht, 1927. Nr. 1. p. 17. Paul Schöps. Der Russische Pelztierzucht.
56 Sächs. HStA, Wirtschaftsministerium 11168, nr. 489, f. 193. Nachrichtlich. Oberregierungsrat. 26.10. 1928.
57 PA AA, Botschaft Moskau, nr. 467. Deutsch Russischer Verein zur Pflege und Förderung der gegenseitigen Handelsbeziehungen. an die Deutsche Botschaft Moskau.3.07.1926.
58 Roth and Merz, *Wildlife Resources*, 212.
59 Die Pelztierfarm, nr. 10, den 07.03.1931. Pelztierzucht in Russland (nach amtlichen Material).
60 Sakwa, *The Rise and Fall of the Soviet Union*, 276.
61 BArch, Reichsgesundheitsamt R 86, nr. 4926. Auszug aus "Vierteljahrshefte zur Statistik des Deutschen Reiches." 40 Jahrgang 1931, 3. Heft.
62 See: Der Kürschnerzeitung. Nr. 27. 21.09.1931. p. 711. Die Edelpelztierhaltung im Deutschen Reiche 1931.
63 Die Kürschnerzeitung, nr. 2, 19.01.1913., Die Weisse Pelzmode von Berlin.
64 BArch, Reichsgesundheitsamt R86, nr. 4926. Ausschnitt aus der Deutsche Tageszeitung, no. 46. 18.02.1932.
65 Sächs. HStA, Wirtschaftsministerium 11168, nr. 1979, f 55; f. 108.
66 Sächs. HStA, Wirtschaftsministerium 11168, nr. 490, ff. 162–6.
67 Ibid., ff. 173–4.
68 Stadt-AL, Kap 35, 1406, bd.1. Reichszentrale für Pelztier und Rauchwarenforschung, Leipzig, an den Rat der Stadt Leipzig, neues Rathaus, 17.09.1932.

69 Leipziger Universitätsarchiv. Rep II/I/LL bd. 1. 1932. Rat der Stadt Leipzig. Schuldamt. An se. Magnifizenz, den Herrn Rektor der Universität, Leipzig, 03.12.1932.
70 Vogelsang, "Die Tierzucht in Der Zeit Der Weimarer Republik Und Des Nationalsozialismus," 105.
71 StA-L, Commerzbank 21016, nr. 58, f. 75. RAVAG. Geschäftsbericht 1935.
72 StA-L, Commerzbank 21016, nr. 413, f. 153.
73 StA-L, Commerzbank 21016, nr. 58, f. 75. Geschäftsbericht 1934, f. 78, Geschäftsbericht 1935, f. 79. Geschäftsbericht 1936. Silver and blue fox skins sales amounted to 28,387 in 1934, 32,444 in 1935, and 34,006 in 1936. The sales of mink were 3,986 in 1934, 4,697 in 1935, and 6,265 in 1936.

References

Ashbrook, Frank. *Fur Resources of the United States*. Washington, DC: United States Government Printing Office, 1930.

———. "The Fur Trade and the Fur Supply." *Journal of Mammalogy* 3, no. 1 (February 1, 1922): 1–7.

Bosl, Karl, ed. *Bosls Bayerische Biographie*. Regensburg: Pustet, 1983.

Clutton-Brock, Juliet. *A Natural History of Domesticated Mammals*. Cambridge, UK: Cambridge University Press, 1999.

Colpitts, George. "Conservation, Science and Canada's Fur Farming Industry, 1913–1945." *Histoire Sociale / Social History* 30, no. 59 (May 1, 1997): 77–108.

———. *Game in the Garden: A Human History of Wildlife in Western Canada to 1940*. Vancouver: UBC Press, 2002.

Delort, Robert. *L'Histoire de la fourrure de l'antiquité à` nos jours*. Lausanne: Edita, 1986.

Engel, Michael. "Hans Nachtsheim." Accessed February 12, 2014. www.deutsche-biographie.de/sfz67745.html.

"Gustav Frölich." Accessed February 12, 2014. www.catalogus-professorum-halensis.de/froelichgustav.html.

Hammer, Simon. *The Norway Year Book*. Oslo: S. Mortensen, 1966.

Harwood, Jonathan. "National Styles in Science: Genetics in Germany and the United States Between World Wars." *Isis* 78, no. 3 (1987): 390–414.

Marsch, Ulrich. *Zwischen Wissenschaft und Wirtschaft: Industrieforschung in Deutschland und Grossbritannien 1880–1936*. Paderborn: Schöningh, 2000.

Porter, Michael E. "Locations, Clusters, and Company Strategy." In *The Oxford Handbook of Economic Geography*, edited by Gordon L. Clark, Maryann P. Feldman, and Meric S. Gertler, 253–75. Oxford: Oxford University Press, 2000.

Prell, Heinrich. "Zur Frage Der Planmässigen Pelztierzucht." *Sonderndruck Aus Der Zeitschrift Die Pelztierzucht* 2, no. 2 (n.d.): 5–8.

Rader, Kelly. "Scientific Animals: Reflections on the Laboratory and Its Human-Animal Relations, from Dba to Dolly and Beyond." In *A Cultural History of Animals in the Modern Age*, edited by Randy Malamud, 119–39. Oxford: Berg, 2011.

Ray, Arthur J. *The Canadian Fur Trade in the Industrial Age*. Toronto: University of Toronto Press, 1990.

Roots, Clive. *Domestication*. Westport: Greenwood Publishing Group, 2007.

Roth, Harald H., and Günter Merz. *Wildlife Resources: A Global Account of Economic Use*. Berlin: Springer, 1997.

Sakwa, Richard. *The Rise and Fall of the Soviet Union.* New York: Routledge, 2005.

Schwerin, Alexander von. *Experimentalisierung des Menschen: der Genetiker Hans Nachtsheim und die vergleichende Erbpathologie, 1920–1945.* Göttingen: Wallstein, 2004.

Sokolowsky, Alexander. "Pelztierforschung." *Pelztierforschung* 1, no. 6 (1926): 1–5.

Szöllösi-Janze, Margit. "Institutionelle Umgestaltung Der Wissenschaftslandschaft Im Übergang Vom Späten Kaiserreich Zur Weimarer Republik." In *Wissenschaften Und Wissenschaftspolitik: Bestandsaufnahmen Zu Formationen, Brüchen Und Kontinuitäten Im Deutschland Des 20. Jahrhunderts*, edited by Rüdiger Vom Bruch and Brigitte Kaderas, 60–74. Stuttgart: F. Steiner, 2002.

Vogelsang, Ingmar. "Die Tierzucht in Der Zeit Der Weimarer Republik Und Des Nationalsozialismus." Tierärztliche Hochschule Hannover, 2006.

Weiner, Douglas R. "The Canging Face of Soviet Conservation." In *The Ends of the Earth: Perspectives on Modern Environmental History*, edited by Donald Worster, 252–77. Cambridge, UK: Cambridge University Press, 1988.

Wolter, Franka. "Johannes Richter (1878–1943)–Leben Und Werk Eines Protagonisten Der Veteirnärgeburtshilfe." University of Leipzig, 2011.

Part III

World Market Restructuring and the Fur Capital (1920–1939)

7 Business as Usual? Adaptation to World Market Restructuring (1919–1925)

Introduction: A New Context for Internationalisation

During and after World War I, the international fur industry underwent considerable transformations. North American markets and manufacturing centres gained more prominence and the formation of the Soviet Union drastically changed the parameters that governed the trade in Siberian furs. The position of the Leipzig fur industry in the commodity chain was traditionally based on its historical favourable position in the East-West transit trade. Part III of the book is entirely devoted to the impact of world market restructuring on the industrial district of Leipzig. What was the future of Leipzig and its many SMEs in the post-war trade? How did firms react to the transformations in the world market? What were their effects on local embeddedness? As the title of this chapter indicates, patterns of continuity in both local arrangements and international trade will be stressed. These will show how the industrial district carved out a future in the new trade system. However, it is also impossible to ignore discontinuities like the formation of new economic institutions and the spatial developments that characterised the international fur trade after World War I. This chapter is therefore also devoted to examining the changing patterns of the world market and connecting them systematically with the industrial district in Leipzig.

One of the most radical transformations was the creation of the Soviet monopoly on foreign trade. In essence, its creation complicated the international commerce of private firms. Firstly, the firms that controlled the organisation of foreign trade lost their privileged access to raw materials. Secondly, the state monopoly limited the number of potential transactions. Russian private businesses and middlemen were replaced by a complex myriad of Soviet trade institutions. In particular, the trade delegations outside the USSR, primarily those in London (ARCOS), New York (Amtorg), and Berlin (Handelsvertretung der UdSSR), controlled most exports.[1] The Soviet Department of Trade determined the trade flows and controlled the currencies allocated to import and export.[2] Firms thereby lost control over various stages of the commodity chain and were forced to adjust to this new framework.[3] In sum, transactions no longer took place in a 'free' market system in the fairs inside and outside Russia and steered by tariffs, but were hosted by state agencies of various kinds and made subject to the domestic and international political considerations of the new communist state.

Despite the complexity surrounding the trade monopoly, it has often been argued that industrialists during the early years of the Weimar republic remained oriented towards trading with the East. The experiences of the profitable 'Russian trade' (*Russengeschäft*) before World War I were central for post-war trade revival; historian Pogge von Strandmann has called this the "pressure of continuity."[4] However, few attempts have been made to empirically study firms' strategies in the pursuit of the 'Soviet trade,' except for big businesses like Siemens, which managed to adapt their international business strategies to the framework of trade opportunities set out by the Soviet monopoly.[5] The narrow focus on big business has emphasised the formation of international cartels and close ties between businesses and government to revive Soviet trade.[6] Indeed, dealings with the Soviets seemed to favour increases in size. Smaller entities have largely been neglected in the so-called Russian business of the 1920s and processes of internationalisation. Does the "pressure of continuity" also apply to district participants with a similar track record of trading in Russia? Moreover, what strategies did firms follow to meet the conditions set out by the Soviet monopoly and to profit from opportunities in the changing nature of international trade?

In the introduction, I noted that reactions towards macroeconomic changes could entail two reactions in the district. On the one hand, lead firms, which acted as gatekeepers between the industrial district and the outside world, surfaced more strongly. On the other hand, the central assumption of this research is that exogenous challenges set in motion processes of collective action in the district. This third part of the book investigates both patterns in light of the changes in the commodity chain that occurred before the outbreak of the economic crisis in 1930. Although emphasis has been placed upon interfirm collaboration, the strategies of individual firms mattered, especially in the immediate aftermath of the war when the global economy of furs was being restructured and the new system of trade was still highly unpredictable. The chapter will examine the actions of the lead firms of the industrial district in the 1920s and question their role in the re-admission to the world market. In addition, I will also examine the extent to which the function of lead firms had ramifications on the social structure of the industrial district. The other two chapters of this section will then examine processes of interfirm cooperation in this period of world market restructuring.

Emerging Markets and Interfering States: The Transformation of International Fur Commerce in the 1920s

The Fur Industry and Trade in North America

An important development in the international commerce of furs was the growing importance of North America, not only in commerce and manufacturing but also in terms of consumption. Several cities across the Atlantic surfaced as leading manufacturing centres either before or during World War I, when warfare obstructed transatlantic trade with London and continental markets. North American cities emerged as new markets and were chiefly constructed around auction sales. A number of New York fur firms established the New York Fur Auction Sales Corporation in 1916.[7] The foundation of the New York Fur Auction had a surprising connection to the fur business in Leipzig. Many merchants of German or Jewish descent who were involved in the new auction house had ties to the business world in Leipzig. St Louis established itself as a centre earlier than New York; both auction centres replaced sales of particular types of furs in London and kept profits in America. In Canada, Montreal came to play an important role in terms of trade and manufacturing; it was joined by Toronto and Winnepeg.[8] Montreal transformed into a prominent fur auction centre when Canadian fur dealers established the Canadian Fur Auction Sales Company in 1920.[9] At the first auction, the company sold 949,565 pelts valued at $5,037,114 USD.

The development of new buying structures across the Atlantic meant heavy competition for London as a market for international furs. Before World War I, London dominated the organisation of Canadian fur sales. Of the $5,100,000 of undressed furs destined for the US and Great Britain, $3,000,000 went to the latter. Between 1915 and 1930, most of the shipped Canadian raw furs were sent to the United States. At that time, 20–40% of the Canadian fur exports went to Great Britain on average. Particularly revealing are the Canadian export figures of 1923: the British market absorbed $4,473,968 of the $16,206,225 total while the American merchants purchased most of the rest.[10] However, in the long run, the market share of London was gradually restored and balanced with North American markets. In the early 1930s, the London market once again dominated the trade of Canadian undressed furs. Between 1932 and 1934, London's share in the sale of Canadian raw furs fluctuated at around 64%, and it continued with a share of over 50% in the following years.[11] Nevertheless, the commodity chain in American furs had changed; it was increasingly characterised by prominent new markets, foremost New York and Montreal.

The Soviet Foreign Trade Monopoly in the Fur Trade (1921–1925)

In the commodity chain of Siberian furs, changes were more far-reaching. On 22 April 1918, Lenin's decree "On the Nationalisation of Foreign Trade" began an earthquake in international trade. It stipulated that foreign trade was to be conducted by official institutions of the Soviet Union. Therefore, foreign firms that imported or traded with the Soviet Union were forced to deal with the state agencies that replaced Russian traders and foreign firms.[12] The monopolisation of trade by the state theoretically ended the privileged access of foreign firms to fur resources and the organisation of exports.[13] Foreign trade with the USSR was, however, not evident in the immediate after-war period. Trade relations only normalised slightly when the Soviets signed a temporary trade agreement, negotiated by Leonid Krasin, with Great Britain in 1921. As a result, the Soviets established a trade delegation in London, the All Russian Cooperative Society (ARCOS).[14] Although the temporary agreement signified both a commercial and diplomatic breakthrough, it failed to produce a ratchet effect on the USSR's foreign trade. Western businesses and government representatives remained highly sceptical of the Soviet experiment. Trade relations further 'normalised' in favour of the Soviets in the wake of the failure of the Genoa conference in 1922. The Soviets and the Germans signed a separate agreement in Rapallo as an alternative to Genoa; this further disrupted attempts to adopt a unified trade policy towards the Soviet Union and opened the door for international competition over the export of Russian commodities.[15]

For the USSR, the trade monopoly and the search for foreign trade partners were of crucial importance since foreign trade was paramount for economic recovery. The idea was to stimulate the export business in order to gain the currency necessary to import the machinery and goods needed for the construction of an industrial infrastructure.[16] Lacking alternatives, export schemes centred on a surge in the export of agricultural commodities and resources. However, due to the assault on 'kulak' landownership, grain production slowed and failed to meet the export quotas designed by Soviet planners. However, the share of oil products, flax, and furs in the structure of trade increased spectacularly, largely because of underachievement in the production of agricultural commodities. Due to these factors, the fur trade acquired a prominent position within the overall trade structure. In fact, furs came to serve as one of the strategic pillars of the Soviet foreign trade in the 1920s, creating a relative export value that floated around 10% (see Table 7.1). The strategic role of furs (and not only during the NEP) in the economic consolidation of the Soviet Union is largely overlooked in Soviet economic history.

Table 7.1 USSR Export Value of Furs (1921–1926)[17]

	FURS IN USSR EXPORT
1913	0.43%
1921/22	3.49%
1922/23	3.79%
1923/24	4.97%
1924/25	11.65%
1925/26	9.85%

The comeback of furs as a revenue pump in the economic transition of the early Soviet Union was uncannily redolent of pre-Petrine times, when they had been one of the key commodities of the Muscovite tsardom. Furs had lost their strategic value in the long interlude. Whereas export of furs before 1914 represented no more than 1%, the Gosplan gave the Russian fur trade a larger role after 1921: it accounted for up to 5.5% of the Soviet Union's predicted exports. Indeed, between 1923 and 1927, the Russian fur trade exceeded the prospects set out by Gosplan as it contributed an astonishing 10.7% of the actual exports on average. At that time, only grain exports exceeded the value of furs.[18] The strategic value of furs is an aspect to keep in mind while considering the position of Leipzig in the interwar international fur business. The Soviet Union needed foreign sales markets for this strategic resource. This created both opportunities and pitfalls for foreign firms, also for the Leipzig firms.

How did furs become so important to the Soviets? Firstly, the strategic importance was owned to the comparatively rapid resumption of fur procurement. Expressed in quantities, Soviet fur exports had already reached 70% of pre-war levels in the 1922–1923 season, whereas fur procurement was only at 28% in 1921.[19] In comparison, foreign trade in its totality only reached 38% of pre-war levels in 1926. The gap in fur procurement between 1912 and 1924 narrowed because of the ending of the civil war—Siberia had been one of the central stages of the fighting. Secondly, it is possible that the standstill in the Russian fur trade during the war reversed the exhaustion of wildlife in the Siberian woodlands. Unfortunately, this interesting environmental dimension cannot be pursued here due to the lack of source material. In any case, the resumption of fur procurement once again came at the expense of wildlife. The priority given to the export plans overruled the implementation of environmental regulations and the desire to create a sustainable fur trade in several Soviet economic circles.[20] In 1924 and 1925, reports warned about the serious depletion of furbearing animals. The 10% export level reached at that time was therefore an almost absolute boundary imposed by ecology. Thirdly and finally, the Soviets profited from price upswings determined by the world market, which largely had their source in the growing demand for furs in the US. Pelts attained prices on the postwar market that were, on average, 259.9% higher than in 1913.[21] These were the three defining features that made the fur trade paramount within the Soviet monopoly.

The Foreign Markets for Siberian Furs, 1921–1925

Despite the 'bureaucratisation' of foreign trade, commerce with the Soviets was certainly not impossible. Foreign trade, and therefore connections to trade partners, ranked high among the priorities of the economically troubled USSR. The monopoly was exploited in order to level the balance-of-payments, which was running a problematic deficit. As such, the need for foreign currencies was highly pressing in the USSR; this stimulated the resumption of exports. As a result, the Soviet export trade continued to place the obtainment of credits and advance payments central in foreign trade relations, just like in the tsarist era.[22] It is important to note that fur firms oriented themselves towards both opportunities and the impositions of the trade monopoly.

Who were the main partners of the new Soviet fur monopoly in furs? Initially, the Soviet government saw Great Britain as its main trade partner, given the establishment of the London trade agency ARCOS in 1921. Great Britain therefore emerged as the principal customer of Russian fur exports in the first half of the 1920s, as can be clearly seen in Table 7.2.[23] Germany took a secondary role, with import levels that were much lower than the years leading up to World War I when German traders imported on average 60–80% of Russian furs. The efforts of Leipzig firms to re-enter the Russian business, which will be discussed later, only yielded a modest result. The exception was the 1922–1923 season when Germany attracted 30% of the Soviet exports. Thus, as Table 7.2 demonstrates, London temporarily turned into the main trade hub for Siberian furs.

These observations on the fur trade dovetail with Soviet-German economic relationships in the interwar period, which were only restored systematically in the second half of the 1920s. Initially, the Rapallo treaty between Germany and the USSR, which involved the most favoured nation principle, led to heightened economic activity in 1923 between the two countries.[24] However, economic and political relationships reversed during the next few years. Firstly, after the withdrawal of Belgium-French troops from the Rhine area, Germany followed a course of reconciliation with Western powers that deprioritised efforts centred on the Soviet trade. In addition, other countries also established trade relations with the Soviets out of fear that Germany would dominate trade with the USSR.[25] Second, German relations with the Soviet Union were not good, despite the rapprochement in Rapallo. Germany refused to grant the Soviet trade agency in Berlin (established in 1921) extraterritorial rights. A police raid on the agency in 1924 (it was accused of financing communist activities) and Soviet support for communist uprisings further disrupted trade relations between the two.[26]

Table 7.2 Soviet Fur Exports to Germany, Great Britain, and the US (1921–1926)[27]

	GERMANY	*GREAT BRITAIN*	*US*
1921/22		10%	
1922/23	30%	11%	4%
1923/24	19%	32%	25%
1924/25	12%	52%	23%
1925/26	18%	45%	17%

Furthermore, domestic developments in the Weimar Republic, inflation in particular, had soured the reputation and position of German traders in international trade.[28] Imports were more expensive due to the inflation and had a ratchet effect on the export of manufactured furs.[29]

The result of these developments was that the British market became the principal supplier for the German fur trade. Particularly in the early 1920s, the prominent position of Britain (which it probably owed to the export of Russian furs) is clearly visible (see Figure 7.1).

However, the leading position of Great Britain was maintained only for a short period of time. The trade statistics of Germany reveal a continuing preference for trading with the Soviet Union, which manifested itself strongly in the second half of the 1920s. In terms of quantity, Great Britain became the largest supplier. However, in terms of value, Siberian furs represented a larger share after 1925. This suggested that raw furs from Siberian formed a relatively large share of imports to Germany in the second half of the 1920s. Thus, after 1925, the Soviet Union was the main provider of furs for Germany, especially in terms of value. Indeed, after the treaty of Berlin between the USSR and Germany in 1926, the commercial intentions of the Rapallo treaty were finally put into practice. With a subsequent credit arrangement of 300,000,000 RM for exports, bilateral trade flows significantly improved. Consequently, fur exports to Germany followed the same upward trend. It took the German fur trade until the second half of the 1920s to restore its pre-war market share (Figure 7.3). Initially, volumes of imported furs were much lower than pre-war levels. In 1921 and 1922, Germany imported raw furs at levels that were only 25% of those in 1913.

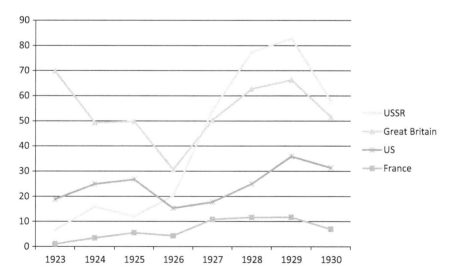

Figure 7.1 Suppliers of Raw Furs to Germany (1923–1930) in millions of marks

Table 7.3 German Import of Raw Furs and Export of Manufactured Furs (in thousand RM)[30]

	IMPORT (RAW FURS)	EXPORT (MANUFACTURED FURS)
1923	151,580	109,665
1924	126,561	126,956
1925	124,795	147,340
1926	102,486	154,970
1927	185,323	226,389
1928	235,526	305,255

In 1924, still facing the after-effects of hyperinflation, import quantities stabilised at 50% of the 1913 level. Only after 1925 did imports reach pre-war levels once again and the level of exports soared, largely because of the stabilisation of bilateral trade relations with the Soviet Union.

The framework sketched out above allows us to examine the actions and strategies of individual fur businesses during this time. From the trade figures analysed, we have learnt that the German fur trade was progressively restored in the 1920s and that the Soviet fur trade assumed an ever-increasing role in this comeback.[31] International political economy established the framework for trade, but how did businesses adapt to the new framework? In the first place, we are interested in trade networks with the East. Given the position of Leipzig in the pre-war Russian fur trade and the resumption of the Soviet-German fur trade after 1925, it is reasonable to expect a similar orientation and "pressures of continuity."[32] Indeed, prominent actors in the fur cluster had high hopes for the 'Russian trade' in the reconstruction of Leipzig's fur market. The Leipzig Fur Merchants Association, the most important one in the city, stated in one of its 1921 general meetings that "if the Leipzig traders serve themselves from the old sources in Russia, pay for large quantities of Russian and Siberian staple goods in marks, and bring them to Leipzig to be manufactured again and exported, only then Leipzig will fully regain its old place in the world trade of furs."[33] The idea that Leipzig should link up to the Russian trade was prevalent among businessmen.

The Leipzig Fur Capital and the Trade Monopoly

This section will analyse the way in which Leipzig firms were able to reconnect with the Soviet foreign trade institutions. In particular, we are interested in how individual (lead) firms re-assumed their role in forging links between the district and the outside world. An important observation is that many of the same businesses in Leipzig, that were active in prewar international trade, played a leading role in restoring trade relations with the USSR. Later, the impact of the lead firms' activities on the structure of the business cluster will be addressed. Amongst the most prominent businesses active in the Soviet fur trade were the businesses created around the Eitingon, Biedermann, Thorer, and Ariowitsch families. Indeed, the trade conditions of the monopoly (bigger contracts and payment in advance) favoured these larger businesses in Leipzig. However, the degree of continuity was not solely based on the size of the firm. As I will try to demonstrate, networks and connections, often based on pre-war business contacts in the Soviet Union, played a more prominent role as a pattern of continuity than has been hitherto assumed.

The Eitingon firm in particular had good connections with the London ARCOS export agency that exported approximately 70% of the furs procured in the Soviet Union between 1920 and 1923. The first fur contract issued by the ARCOS was granted to the "Eitingon-Schild holding," for the sum of $1,750,000.[34] The value of this contract cannot be underestimated: it was the first million-dollar deal between the Soviets and a Western firm and was heralded as a breakthrough in international fur commerce. However, the ARCOS deal also reveals a 'locational' power shift within the Eitingon firm. The deal with the Soviets coincided with the ascent of Matwey Isakovitsch Eitingon, nephew and son-in-law of the founder Chaim Eitingon, in New York. After the war, Matwey Eitingon returned from Moscow to the US to work in the New York branch led by Waldemar Eitingon, the oldest son of Chaim.[35] When Waldemar died in June 1920, the leadership of the New York business was taken over by the ambitious Matwey, who preferred to call himself "Motty," a less Russian-sounding name for American ears.[36] It was through his personal networks in Moscow that Motty Eitingon won the first contract in Siberian furs issued by ARCOS. In addition, Monya Eitingon, a cousin of Motty and his former trustee in the Moscow branch, became the head of the important London branch. With Motty as director of the New York branch and mastermind behind the first Soviet fur contract, the centre of power in the Eitingon family however moved from Leipzig to New York.

However, Motty Eitingon's fur deals with the Soviets show a rather unexpected continuity on the personal level. It is well known that the USSR incorporated a large group of former private entrepreneurs, traders, manufacturers, and artisans in order to speed up the process of economic recovery in the context of the NEP.[37] The historian Alan Ball described these businessmen and traders as "NEPmen" or, more thoughtfully, as "Russia's last capitalists" (since his book on the NEPmen was published before the collapse of the USSR). These NEPmen were tolerated by the Soviet authorities so that they could conduct trade and business in a semi-private fashion while their businesses were integrated into trusts or subordinated to state agencies.[38] They also played a leading role in trade agencies and foreign commerce as the need to set up export trade (foreign trade was seminal in economic

recovery) forced the Soviets to make use of the expertise of private businessmen. Lenin, for one, realised that the Foreign Trade Commissariat was
inefficient because of its inexperienced personnel.[39] Persons with important
business functions before the war therefore reappeared both in the lower
and higher echelons of the USSR's trade organisation. For instance, both
Leonid Krasin, the minister of foreign trade after 1920, and Boris Stomo-
niakov, the leader of the Soviet delegation in Berlin, were former employees
of the Siemens-Schuckert company in Germany and Moscow.[40] By the same
token, former private fur dealers were integrated into the state agencies that
ran the fur trade, especially since furs played a prominent role in Soviet
foreign commerce.

A systematic account on NEPmen in the Soviet fur trade is unfortunately
not available, but several sources do affirm their infiltration of the new
economic institutions. Their presence is to be found at every link in the
fur chain: NEPmen acted as hunters, the middlemen of procurement agencies, and agents in foreign trade bureaus. According to Douglas Weiner, the
implementation of hunting regulations in the USSR was heavily obstructed
by "formerly independent fur traders and middlemen who brought not only
their expertise but also their ethics to their Soviet positions."[41] Western fur
dealers also described the infiltration of NEPmen in the Soviet agencies,
often without revealing their names or the institutions they worked for. The
Russian commissioner who organised the abovementioned contract between
Eitingon and the Soviets in London was said to be a "former Siberian agent
of the Eitingon corporation."[42] Eitingon had friends in higher places as
well. Alexander Tyranovskii, a tsarist fur dealer and acquaintance of Motty,
became the leader of one of the Soviet state agencies that procured furs.[43]

Continuity in the Siberian trade meant the continuity of old friendships
and personal business relations. The personal connections with ARCOS in
London gave Motty Eitingon a tremendous competitive advantage and it
formed the basis for subsequent contracts. In 1923, another large share of
the Russian raw fur export through London was transferred to Eitingon
Schild & Co. The new contract involved the Eitigons paying $3,000,000
to ARCOS. The Deutsche Bank in Leipzig, an important creditor for the
Leipzig fur industry, noted in 1923 that "this contract caused a sensation
in the fur trade because the already powerful position of Eitingon is further strengthened and the outlook of their situation is the most promising
because of their connection to ARCOS."[44]

Another very specific advantage in the early Soviet business, and in international trade more generally, was based on advantages derived from citizenship: many Jewish entrepreneurs in Leipzig with a migration background
profited from this. Again the Leipzig cluster profited from the presence of
Jewish entrepreneurs, especially those with a migration background. The Eitingons, originating from Skhlov in Belarus, could travel more freely than
their German counterparts in a world that was still inhospitable towards former enemies. Motty and Chaim travelled with their Russian passports after

the war.[45] It is important to note that Russian Jews profited from their citizenship in another remarkable way. Despite a military law that ordered citizens of enemy nationalities to leave the city of Leipzig, the law was never strictly enforced against those of vital economic importance. In other words, Russian fur traders were allowed to stay in Leipzig throughout the war.[46] In addition, a special law in Leipzig prevented their possessions from being seen as enemy assets. Clearly, the local government was aware that strict implementation of the laws against enemy citizens would severely damage local business. As such, Jewish entrepreneurs in Leipzig could re-assume their role of connecting the Leipzig industry to the outside world. It was a specific advantage the district had in comparison to other German business clusters.

The Russian Jewish entrepreneur David Biedermann profited from the same nationality advantage. Biedermann was one of the few fur firms with connections to Leipzig that simply continued the Russian business during the war. When the war broke out, most of the firm's goods were still stockpiled in Russia but, unlike the Eitingons' Russian belongings, they were not sequestered. David Biedermann was therefore able to sell this stock in Britain and America. Furthermore, Biedermann's brother, residing on the other side of the eastern front, continued trading activities and visited the fairs in Nizhnii Novgorod on behalf of the Biedermann firm. Profits reached 1,000,000 roubles in the fur business and 1,400,000 roubles in the wool and animal hair trade between 1914 and 1917.[47] Many of Biedermann's factories and trade posts in in Manchuria and Mongolia remained operational long after the war. Biedermann's representatives continued to launch caravans into central Asia to barter for furs with local tribes. In the Far East trade, it was said that "Biedermann dominated the fur trade conducted at the Russian-Chinese border and even the Eitingon Schild concern remains of secondary importance over there."[48] This system remained operational until 1924.

The connections between other firms and Soviet foreign trade agencies largely followed the same pattern. The Ariowitsch firm in Leipzig, for instance, resumed trade with the Russians during the early 1920s in roughly the same conditions. It was said that this firm profited from associations with NEPmen as well: "Ariowitsch . . . has the best possible dealings with Moscow . . . and a former employee of the Ariowitsch branch in Moscow has now been appointed in the Soviet fur trade."[49] Owing to the family fortune, the Ariowitsch firm was able to finance the large contracts almost entirely out of its own means. In 1926, it was "making the largest business on the Brühl after the Eitingon family."[50]

While many entrepreneurs with a Russian Jewish background escaped the restrictions imposed upon German citizens and therefore resumed trade much earlier, German fur firms were able to strike similar deals with the USSR at the beginning of the 1920s. In 1922, Arndt Thorer purchased furs firsthand in the Soviet Union, mainly the skins of karakul and astrakhan sheep in which his firm specialised. In 1923, Thorer's quota of imported sheepskins grew from 185,000 to 205,000, thereby reaching pre-war import levels.[51] With the dyeing factory running at full speed again, Arndt Thorer and Paul Hollender resumed serving customers in Italy, France, and the US; thus Thorer regained his status as a leading firm in this market sector.

Inside the Thorer business, they were aware of the importance of the "personal continuity" in the organisation of Soviet fur sales. Arndt Thorer mentioned in 1921 that "according to our information in Moscow, the Soviets established a consortium that consists mostly of former fur traders, who managed to get a concession from the government to procure furs in Northern Europe, Siberia, and later also from Central Asia."[52] The Thorer firm easily established connections with the new trade institutions crowded with former Russian fur dealers. Thorer reported on one of Hollender's first journeys in 1923: "The travel of Herr Hollender to Russia in the summer of 1923 was accompanied by good fortune, because significant quantities of karakuls could be acquired at first hand. The transactions with the Russian authorities and the semi state-owned organisations in Moscow were carried out very smoothly and much to my satisfaction."[53] As such, even though Russian-German trade had its troubles, individual Leipzig fur firms paved the way for restoring the eastern supply chain. Gradually, Leipzig re-emerged as a centre of fur trading with the East.

Leipzig as a Gateway to the East?

Adding to the personal connections individual Leipzig firms entertained in Russia, information and intelligence were of strategic importance in the fur business of the 1920s. In contrast to the trade under the Romanovs that had been organised by foreign merchants, only scant information was available on procurement in Siberia and the size and composition of future yields. Due to the elimination of foreign firms in the Soviet Union, Siberia was a blind spot on the maps of Western businesses. Nonetheless, since the fur trade was still a highly speculative business, the need to have an overview of Siberian production was a necessity. An important development that supported the German-Leipzig fur industry was marked by the restoration of consular representation in the USSR. The German consulate in Novosibirsk (the former Novonikolaievsk) re-opened in 1923 and became an important institution for trade information.[54] Headed by consul-general Georg Wilhelm Grosskopf, it was one of the first foreign consulates to re-open in the USSR, and certainly in Siberia. Diplomats replaced, albeit to a lesser extent, the traders and German middlemen who had delivered insights about trade developments prior to World War I.

The reports of the Siberian consulate provided key information on Soviet fur procurement and business opportunities. Firstly, the Germans gained a precise insight into the drop in the absolute number of fur exports. The German Fur Trade Association in Leipzig positively received the reports drafted by consul Grosskopf in Novosibirsk: "If every German representative conveyed such good and well oriented reports as consul Grosskopf, then the German export trade and industry would have a safe guide to evaluate foreign markets and also a valuable aid in the extremely severe competition."[55] Reports were often published by subsidised newspapers like the *Ostexpress* and the *Ostwirtschaft*, the latter of which existed between 1911 and 1944. These newspapers depended upon novel sources of newsgathering like consular reports. Yet investigations into the Siberian fur market were not a straightforward enterprise and the Soviets disliked the consulate's reports gaining publicity. Grosskopf reported to Berlin: "I beg you to ensure that the reports are treated confidentially: they are certainly not to be published in the *Ostwirtschaft*, as occurred before. Because of the publication of these reports, damage has been done to the consulate, which up until now has been difficult to remedy."[56] Foreign consulates and their information-gathering diplomats were carefully monitored by the Soviet secret police.[57] The impact of information structures and newsgathering on the political economy of the early twentieth century should not be underestimated. Indeed, as has recently been demonstrated, the involvement of global newsgathering was one of the principal elements of German globalisation that survived World War I and continued to render political and economic advantages.[58]

Deficiencies in the economic organisation of the Soviet Union created new dynamics in the international fur business. The consulate rightly foresaw the growing importance of China in the legal and illegal transit trade of Siberian furs.[59] Indeed, throughout the 1920s, many international fur dealers opened branches in Manchuria and in the city of Harbin, close to the smuggling areas. Harbin was not just a depot in the illegal fur trade: the border south of Siberia was inhabited by valuable furbearing animals like the expensive and rare sable and the mid-priced *solongoi* and foxes. Jewish refugees who had fled Russia after the revolution and settled in China organised this irregular commerce in furs. Besides Harbin, Jewish traders settled in the city of Taijin, which exerted a similar function in the irregular commerce in furs. Over 100 Jewish fur firms were domiciled in this city.[60]

Firms sent agents en masse to China, many of them from Leipzig. Ariowitsch and Bromberg in particular participated in a Chinese division, the Siberian Fur Trading company; they jointly invested 2,000,000 RM.[61] As mentioned above, Biedermann remained active in this border zone. It may come as no surprise that Eitingon opened a subsidiary office in China during the 1920s. A report of Martin Lentschner, the German manager of the Eitingon-Schild corporation and an expert on the Soviet trade, reported on smuggling in 1924: "I do not want to leave unmentioned that the smuggling trade is lively this year. Especially at the Chinese and Mongolian border, but also at the Finnish, Latvian, and Polish borders, one finds a flourishing smuggling trade where traders are willing to pay higher prices for the furs [than Soviet agencies]. Similar things are happening during the procurement season in Bukhara."[62] The area bordering China "where procurements are virtually non-existent and where the hunters mainly sell their furs to

Chinese smugglers" remained a loophole in the Soviet fur trade well into the late 1920s.[63] The trade in Siberian furs was thus more international than official channels would lead us to believe. Intelligence became highly important if one wanted to profit from such international dynamics.

High-quality information and business connections with the trade monopoly fortified Leipzig's position in more ways than just informing companies as to the availability of opportunities. It also strengthened Leipzig as a centre of trade with the East. This can be seen in the fact that several foreign companies decided to re-establish a presence in Saxony's commercial hub. As early as March 1921, the Hudson's Bay Company appointed the German-Russian trader Sascha Hopfenkopf, a former agent of the British auction company A&W Nesbitt in Moscow, as a correspondent in Leipzig. Representation on the Brühl was required in order to keep up with the market in Soviet furs. Hopfenkopf was charged with the task of "keeping in touch with the developments of the Russian fur trade and proceed to Moscow if and when circumstances allowed."[64] In addition, he was allowed to conduct consignment trade, possessing a budget of £100,000. During the period of inflation, the HBC refused to withdraw him and stated that representation in Leipzig had become indispensable since "Leipzig had become far too important a fur trade centre."[65] Once trade with the Soviets further expanded, many more firms followed. Frederik Huth & Co, heirs of the German immigrant Frederik Huth who had opened a merchant bank in London in 1809 and were active in the fur trade from 1912, opened a branch in Leipzig in 1927. The Dresdner Bank estimated the capital basis of Huth's division in Leipzig to amount to £500,000.[66] The renewed interest of several major international fur firms in settling in Leipzig reveals that the city still played an important role in the international trade.

Internationalisation and Embeddedness

While foreign trade was one of the pillars of the success of the industrial district prior to World War I, it is questionable whether the industrial district as a whole benefited from patterns of internationalisation pursued by individual firms. In this period of time, the entire German fur trade was at a low ebb. Exports and imports had stabilised but at levels much lower than prior to 1914. However, several Leipzig firms did play an important role in the international fur trade; Jewish entrepreneurs especially followed an expansive policy profiting from advantages set out above. Did Leipzig firms evolve into more international entities so as to avoid regional and local problems? What was the relationship between new patterns of internationalisation and embeddedness? The question is an important one. A drain on business and human capital is commonly identified as one of the largest threats to decentralised business systems in a changing macroeconomic environment. Having suggested that many firms profited from their international organisation, this section will investigate whether the industrial district as a whole profited or lost from new processes of internationalisation and how new patterns of international business activity affected embeddedness.

Finding the Epicentre of the Eitingon Business (1919–1928)

The most complex case of an increasingly international Leipzig firm, seemingly outgrowing local business standards, was the Eitingon firm. The Eitingons changed the focus of their business both according to geopolitical transformations and changes in the family. This was already the case before the Great War, when business activities were spatially divided between Moscow, Leipzig, and New York. The Moscow-Leipzig axis was at that time central to the Eitingon business structure. Chaim Eitingon was one of the few Jewish merchants that the tsar allowed to stay in Moscow after the pogroms in 1882; as a transnational entrepreneur, he divided his time between Leipzig and Moscow. In 1914, Chaim Eitingon finally moved to Leipzig and lived there until his death in 1932. The Chaim Eitingon business was one of the largest firms in Leipzig, running on a business volume of 5 million marks, a size comparable to that of the Thorer firm. The New York business was arguably of minor importance in the pre-war trade, since it was only established in 1912. In 1919, power shifted to Motty Eitingon. Hereafter, the New York branch transformed rapidly into the main part of the Eitingon business and growth was expansive.

When the firm closed its million-dollar deals with ARCOS in and after 1921, the Eitingons gained a clear edge over their competitors. The initially strong position of the company in terms of the import of Russian furs provided the Eitingon-Schild holding with an average annual profit of $1,454,982 in the years between 1923 and 1925.[67] Profits continued to be staggeringly high later, amounting to $1,827,268 in 1926 and $1,912,310 in 1927. In 1925, the Eitingon family business was transformed into a holding, the Eitingon-Schild group. However, business remained principally a family matter, since 80% of the Eitingon shares were in the hands of the family.[68] The assets of Eitingon-Schild were estimated to amount to more than 17 million dollars after 1925. Profits were reinvested in such a way that allowed the Eitingon family to transform their firm into an international business empire. The pre-war axis between Leipzig and Moscow was expanded into a larger network of about 17 branches and agents over the world, with New York as the central node. Motty followed a policy of expansion in the US by acquiring important rival trading houses. Notable were the acquisitions of Funston Bros. & Co and Fouke Fur Co, which operated on the market of St Louis.[69]

Within the international and American expansion of the business empire, the Chaim Eitingon AG in Leipzig represented, in official terms, a separate entity within the Eitingon Schild holdings; its function in the business structure was described as a "commissioner."[70] While the Eitingon firm had undoubtedly become more multinational after the First World War, local stakeholders in Leipzig, not in the least the commercial banks and his competitors, still perceived of Chaim Eitingon as the centre of the Eitingon business empire. The Dresdner Bank described the link between the Eitingon family and businesses as "very close." The Leipzig division was said to profit from "the American business and its close contacts with the Soviets, as Chaim Eitingon was able to draw on large supplies at profitable conditions from the holding."[71]

It is, however, a difficult task to gain an accurate insight into the flow of goods and capital between the different branches of the Eitingon concern. Certainly, once trade relations between Germany and the USSR stabilised, the trade of the Eitingon concern through Leipzig division became more important. The contract of 1928 is one of the few that offers us some insight into the division of furs between the subsidiaries of the Eitingon concern. In June 1928, the Eitingon concern concluded a 12 million dollar deal with the Soviet trade department in Berlin—50% was paid for in advance. Accordingly, Motty Eitingon purchased raw furs for $12,000,000, $5,000,000 (or 22,000,000 RM) of which were destined for sale in Leipzig; these resources were "consumed by local traders and the Leipzig fur dressing and dyeing industry."[72] However, the remaining $7,000,000 of which were sold elsewhere. This example shows that the Leipzig division was not unimportant in the multinational structure. But there is no evidence to suggest whether this 1928 deal reveals a recurrent pattern or merely an incidental sales strategy. What we do know is that the Eitingon's business volume in Leipzig still ranked among the most prominent: it fluctuated between 1926 and 1928 at around 25 million RM, twice the volume of the Thorer firm.[73]

The fact of the matter is that Motty Eitingon followed an independent course in New York, but the success of the Eitingon empire enabled Chaim to do the same. As long as founding father Chaim lived, the Leipzig division remained an important part of the Eitingon empire. Indeed, Chaim's activism meant that the Eitingon branch in Leipzig remained an active participant in the local economy. In 1920, for instance, valuables of the Eitingon family in bank safes included 2,000,000 marks worth of securities. These assets reveal investments made in various German firms, including several regional companies: Seidel & Naumann (sewing machines, Dresden), Schubert & Salzer (textile machine construction, Chemnitz), and Hansa Lloyd (car construction, Bremen).[74] Of course, businessmen like Chaim, who had access to foreign currency, were in an advantageous situation when it came to buying assets in Germany.[75] The family also invested in real estate in Leipzig and, to a lesser extent, in Berlin according to the same principles.

More important were investments related to the local fur industry. In 1920, the Eitingon family financed the factory Walter AG, a fur dressing and dyeing company in Markränstadt, close to Leipzig. Walter AG was one of the largest factories in the wider Leipzig fur district: it employed about 1,400 labourers and 100 white-collar workers in April 1923.[76] It was also the only joint-stock company in the Germany fur industry. In 1921, the

Eitingon family owned about a third of its shares. In addition, the investment granted Chaim and Martin Lentschner, the manager of Chaim Eitingon AG, places on the factory's board. The Eitingon firm invested in the dyeing factory at a point when the exchange rate between dollar and the mark continued to widen.[77]

Later the Eitingons entertained the idea of founding their own dressing factory in Taucha (a town in the vicinity of Leipzig). The construction of the factory started in 1927. The factory in Taucha meant an additional 1,000,000 RM investment.[78] Chaim also invested in developing auction sales companies, several of which emerged in Leipzig during the 1920s. Eitingon joined one particular auction company, the RAVAG. Finally, Chaim Eitingon's interest in Leipzig went beyond business and industry. He was also one of the leading figures of the Jewish society in Leipzig. In 1922, he established and solely financed the Ez-Chaim-Synagogue, the largest orthodox synagogue in Saxony with space for 2,000 visitors. Six years later, he opened (with the support of Motty) the so-called "Eitingon Clinic" (*Israelitische Krankenhaus-Eitingon-Stiftung*), which also treated gentile patients (an explicit demand of its founders).[79] Even if the epicentre of the business undoubtedly moved across the Atlantic, the Eitingons did not disconnect from the Leipzig cluster and the family was not invisible in the social fabric of the city and in its religious community. The many investments in the local industry, as well as in the local (Jewish) community nuances the picture of the Eitingon firm as a multinational business empire increasingly detached from the district. The Eitingon remained a family enterprise with a multipolar power structure, with Leipzig occupying an important part.

The Robustness of Embeddedness: Examples From Other Firms

The same can be said of other firms in Leipzig: multinational business organisation took more important proportions throughout the interwar period while leaving local embeddedness intact. Ariowitsch established branches in Paris (Société d'Importation de Pelleteries, Paris), London (Ariowitsch & Jacop Fur Co Ltd), and Stockholm (Svenska-Norska Pälsvaru-Actiebolaget).[80] However, these branches were mainly used to further interests in Leipzig. Only when the Nazis' ascent to power curtailed Jewish entrepreneurship did Max Ariowitsch gradually turn his London division into the firm's headquarters.[81] Ariowitsch also opened a New York division between 1910 and 1914. Thus, it is somewhat surprising that Ariowitsch remained absent from the American market immediately after the war. Ariowitsch re-entered the American market only at the beginning of the 1930s with the *Anglo-American Fur Merchants Corp*. The embeddedness of the firm in Leipzig was also associated with the roots of the Ariowitsch family in the local Jewish community. In 1916, they converted one of their buildings in the Färberstrasse into the Beth-Jehuda synagogue.[82] The strong religious community in Leipzig was thus a motive for Jewish entrepreneurs in retaining business activities in Leipzig.

In the case of the Thorer firm, the balance between internationalism and embeddedness was clearly in favour of the latter. Despite the limited value of the New York branch of the Thorer firm before the war (see Chapter 2), the American branch did gain a more prominent position within the Thorer business empire after the conflict. During the war, Speer, the American manager of the branch, took over business entirely, transforming it into the Speer Fur Corporation. Paul Hollender reclaimed control over the Speer division in 1923.[83] As with the other examples considered, the internationalisation of the Thorer firm did not run counter to district participation. In fact, the New York division played an important part in the recovery of the Leipzig headquarters since the lion's share of the processed furs (garments made from karakul and Astrakhan skins) flowed to the North American market.[84] To give an impression of the importance of the American market, the turnover accounts of 1928 indicate that of the 11,191,000 RM total volume, 4,562,000 RM came from sales made to the New York branch.[85]

Thorer combined international trading activities with manufacturing in Leipzig. His factory remained a typical Saxon firm, dependent upon the world market for the import of raw material and the export of processed consumer goods. The factory in Leipzig-Lindenau, which was a source of employment for over 500 workers, remained central as it connected the supply routes of Siberia and Central Asia to consumer markets in Western Europe and across the Atlantic. Furthermore, the Thorer family continued investing in the local fur district. In 1924, just when the hyperinflation had hit the fur industry hard, Thorer expanded his operations in the dyeing industry by taking over Karl Adolf Schneider AG, which specialised in rabbit skin dyeing.[86] A final point to note is that the Thorer firm was traditionally successful in creating new links between the industrial district and the outside world. Before the war, Paul Thorer had established links with the sheepskin market of Bukhara. The Thorer business remained internationally oriented as it managed to establish good relations with the Afghan court, a growing exporter of karakul and Astrakhan skin. These good relations translated into increased commercial activities. Afghanistan increased its karakul farming exports from 100,000 to 150,000 skins per year to about 700,000–800,000 pieces in 1927. In March 1928, the Afghan king Aman Ullah, also known as the "reformer king," visited Leipzig and the dyeing factory of Theodor Thorer, the principal consumer of Afghan karakul skins. It was noted that Leipzig promised the Afghan king "to expand the trade relations between the Afghan skin trade and the city of Leipzig."[87] Even though the king Ullah was removed from power in 1929, his visit epitomises the importance of the Leipzig fur industry for the growing German commercial influence in Afghanistan after 1923.[88]

Conclusion

Despite the major changes in international fur trade set out above, there were patterns of continuity that enabled district firms to participate in international trade. Firstly, many of the traditional firms active in the pre-war Russia trade were able to restore commercial ties in the trade of Siberian furs relatively quickly. The fact that the Soviets favoured 'familiar' trade partners was not a coincidence. With the pressing aim of generating foreign currency, the Soviets incorporated former fur merchants into the institutions that conducted foreign trade and organised procurement. In addition, the bumpy transition to the Soviet trade monopoly had left several personal networks between private Russian fur traders and German businesses intact. Second, local businesses profited from a well-structured intelligence and trade information network that was seminally important in the re-creation of Leipzig as a commercial junction. Both aspects formed important elements in the recovery of the industrial district in the early 1920s.

The local embeddedness of the lead firms, both German as well as Jewish, remained robust even while they expanded their multinational business activities and while they became more important in terms of linking the district to the outside world. Internationalism did not weaken the industrial district in the way that macroeconomic developments did. In other words, even though internationalisation was an important feature of the fur trade in the 1920s, it is inaccurate to state that firms expanded internationally at the expense of investments in Leipzig. Rather, they did both. In addition, the dynamism of individual firms as players in the world market is but one of the explanations for the recovery of the trade. In order to fully grasp the recovery of the 1920s, we need to examine processes of interfirm cooperation as well. This will be the subject of the next chapter.

Notes

1 Quigley, *The Soviet Foreign Trade Monopoly; Institutions and Laws*, 35.
2 Lewis, "Foreign Economic Relations," 202.
3 Dohan, "Soviet Foreign Trade in the NEP Economy and Soviet Industrialization Strategy," 151. See FN 96.
4 Strandmann, "Großindustrie Und Rapallopolitik. Deutsch-Sowjetische Handelsbeziehungen in Der Weimarer Republik," 269.
5 Lutz, *Siemens Im Sowjetgeschäft. Eine Institutionengeschichte Der Deutsch-Sowjetischen Beziehungen 1917–1933*.
6 Schröter, "Europe in the Strategies of Germany's Electrical Engineering and Chemical Trusts, 1919–1929," 42.
7 Tough, *As Their Natural Resources Fail*, 258.
8 Sangster, "Making a Fur Coat," 255.
9 Ray, *The Canadian Fur Trade in the Industrial Age*, 101.
10 TNA, HBCA, Public Record Office, BH 2639, A92/17/102 Canada Dominion Bureau of Statistics, Fur Production of Canada, Season 1922–23.
11 LAC, RG84-A-2-a, File no. U270, f. 824.
12 McCauley, *The Longman Companion to Russia Since 1914*, 88.
13 Gatrell, "Poor Russia, Poor Show: Mobilising a Backward Economy for War, 1914–1917," 271.
14 Glenny, "The Anglo-Soviet Trade Agreement, March 1921," 80–1.
15 Quigley, *The Soviet Foreign Trade Monopoly; Institutions and Laws*, 20–3.
16 Dohan, "Soviet Foreign Trade in the NEP Economy and Soviet Industrialization Strategy," 241.

17 *Vneshnaya torgovlya CCCP za 1918–1940 gg.* (Statisticheskiy obzor), chast 1, p. 55, 80, 106. Export value of furs in 1913.
18 Dohan, "Soviet Foreign Trade in the NEP Economy and Soviet Industrialization Strategy," 205.
19 *Vneshnyaya torgovlya CCCP za 1918–1940 gg.* (Statisticheskiy obzor), chast 1. Quantities next to the relative value are an indication of fur procurement efficiency, since the prices had gone up considerably during the 1920s.
20 Weiner, *Models of Nature*, 39–40.
21 Ibid., 42. See in particular FN 12.
22 Pohl, *Die Finanzierung der Russengeschäfte zwischen den beiden Weltkriegen.*
23 Glenny, "The Anglo-Soviet Trade Agreement, March 1921."
24 Taylor, *Inflation der Untergang des Geldes in der Weimarer Republik und die Geburt eines deutschen Traumas*, 190.
25 Moss, *A History of Russia Volume 2*, 280.
26 Müller, *Das Tor zur Weltmacht*, 84.
27 *Vneshnyaya torgovlya CCCP za 1918–1940 gg.* (Statisticheskiy obzor), chast euvropa, 423–562, Germaniya, pp. 520–1. Chast 1 Evropa, p. 449. Chast strani severnoy ameriki; p. 1045.
28 Gross, "Selling Germany in South-Eastern Europe," 28.
29 Taylor, *Inflation der Untergang des Geldes in der Weimarer Republik und die Geburt eines deutschen Traumas*, 176–7.
30 Statistisches Jahrbuch für das Deutsches Reich, volumes: 1929, 1927, 1924. The values were recalculated retrospectively in the statistical yearbooks from the old paper mark in the new currency, the Reichsmark.
31 Strandmann, "Großindustrie und Rapallopolitik. Deutsch-Sowjetische Handelsbeziehungen in der Weimarer Republik," 274.
32 Ibid., 275.
33 Malbin, *Der internationale rauchwarenhandel vor und nach dem Weltkriege unter besonderer berücksichtigung Leipzigs*, 35.
34 StA-L, Deutsche Bank, Filiale Leipzig 21017, nr. 309. Filiale Leipzig an Deutsche Bank Filialbüro. 27.12.1921.
35 New York Times, Bolsheviki Held Eitingon Family, 25.05.1919.
36 Wilmers, *The Eitingons*. In terms of his name, he is referred to as Motty Eitingon in almost all correspondence, so we will henceforth do the same.
37 Ball, *Russia's Last Capitalists*, xvi.
38 Ball, "Building a New State and Society: NEP, 1921–1928," 169.
39 Quigley, *The Soviet Foreign Trade Monopoly: Institutions and Laws*, 30.
40 Strandmann, "Großindustrie Und Rapallopolitik. Deutsch-Sowjetische Handelsbeziehungen in Der Weimarer Republik," 276.
41 Weiner, *Models of Nature*, 42.
42 Sta-L, Deutsche Bank, Filiale Leipzig 21017, nr. 309, Deutsche Bank Filiale Leipzig an Deutsche Bank Filialbüro Berlin, 29.12.1921.
43 Wilmers, *The Eitingons*.
44 StA-L, Deutsche Bank, Filiale Leipzig 21017, Nr. 309. Abschrift 07.11.1923.
45 Unger, *Judaica Lipsiensia: Zur Geschichte Der Juden in Leipzig*, 270–1.
46 Simonsen, "Perfect Targets—Antisemitism and Eastern Jews in Leipzig, 1919–1923," 12.
47 StA-L, Deutsche Bank, Filiale Leipzig 21017, nr. 257, f. 41.
48 Ibid., f. 80, Firma D. Biedermann, 16.09.1924.
49 StA-L, Deutsche Bank in Leipzig 21017, Nr. 207, f. 14. Kreditakte, J. Ariowitsch Leipzig, 03.03.1928.
50 StA-L, Deutsche Bank in Leipzig, 210171, Nr. 207, f.185.
51 StA-L, Dresdner Bank in Leipzig 21018, nr.477, f. 64.

52 BArch, Reichswirtschaftsministerium R 3101, nr. 3638, f. 142. 11.11.1921.
53 StA-L, Dresdner Bank in Leipzig 21018, Nr.477, f. 64.
54 Belkovets, Belkovets, and Bonwetsch, *Gescheiterte Hoffnungen.*
55 PA AA, Botschaft Moskau, nr. 467, Abschrift Reichsverband der deutschen Rauchwarenfirmen 26.06.1926.
56 PA AA, Botschaft Moskau, nr. 467. Durchschlag. Nowosibirisk, den 12.02. 1926.
57 Kuromiya, *The Voices of the Dead,* 162.
58 Tworek, "Magic Connections: German News Agencies and Global News Networks, 1905–1945."
59 Skrivan, "On the Foreign Economic Relations of China in the Interwar Era," 80. Skrivan mentions the visible increase of furs, hides, and leather in the trade structure of China after World War I.
60 Ember, Ember, and Skoggard, *Encyclopedia of Diasporas,* 160.
61 StA-L, Deutsche Bank, Filiale Leipzig 21017, nr. 207. Kreditakte, J. Ariowitsch Leipzig. 3.07.1930.
62 Sächs. HStA, Aussenministerium 10717, Nr. 6772. Martin Lentschner (Leipzig) an Herrn Ministerialrat Wielisch, im Sächsischen Ministerium für Auswärtige Angelegenheiten.19.02.1925.
63 Küschnerzeitung, nr. 6. 21.02.1929. p. 1895. Vom sibirisch. Rauchwarenmarkt.
64 TNA, HBCA, Public Record Office, BH 2734, A 92/71/20, fo. V.
65 TNA, HBCA. Public Record Office, BH 2734, A 92/71/21, fo. 57. Memorandum with reference to fur intelligence. Mr. S. Hopfenkopf. 26.09.1925.
66 StA-L, Dresdner Bank in Leipzig 21018, nr. 79, f. 34.
67 New York Times, 7.12.1925. "New Issue: Eitingon Schild Co. Inc.
68 StA-L, Dresdner Bank in Leipzig 21018, nr. 268, Eitingon. 11.11.1927.
69 StA-L, Deutsche Bank, Filiale Leipzig 21017, nr. 309, Lt. Wirtschaftsblatt der neuen Leipziger Zeitung (nr. 8) vom 8.01.1926.
70 StA-L, Deutsche Bank Filiale Leipzig 21017, Nr. 309. Leipzig Aktennotiz, Eitingon Schild Co, 11.02.1922.
71 StA-L, Dresdner Bank in Leipzig, nr. 268. LNN. 6.11.1930.
72 Sta-L, Deutsche Bank, Filiale Leipzig 21017, nr. 309. Vertraulich 11.06.1928.
73 "Eitingon, Chaim Mordechow."
74 StA-L, Deutsche Bank, Filiale Leipzig 21017, nr. 309, f. 8.
75 Taylor, *Inflation der Untergang des Geldes in der Weimarer Republik und die Geburt eines deutschen Traumas,* 183.
76 BArch, Zulassungstelle an der Berliner Borse R 3118, nr. 836, f. 89. 16.04.1923.
77 StA-L, Deutsche Bank, Filiale Leipzig 21017, nr. 309. Filiale Leipzig an Deutsche Bank, Filialbüro, 5.06.1920.
78 StA-L, Dresdner Bank in Leipzig 21018, nr. 268, Ch. Eitingon AG. den 29.12.1927.
79 Unger, *Judaica Lipsiensia,* 271. The first Jewish clinic in Saxony had 79 beds.
80 StA-L, Deutsche Bank, Filiale Leipzig 21017, Nr. 207, f. 223.
81 Unger, *Judaica Lipsiensia,* 269.
82 Diamant, *Chronik der Juden in Leipzig,* 182.
83 StA-L, Dresdner Bank in Leipzig 21017, Nr. 477, f. 64.
84 Ibid, f. 64.
85 StA-L, Dresdner Bank in Leipzig 21017, Nr. 477, f. 56.
86 StA-L, Dresdner Bank in Leipzig 21018, nr. 476. Thorer Karl Adolf Schneider AG an die Dresdner Bank in Leipzig, Leipzig, den 6.09.1924.
87 StA-L, Dresdner Bank in Leipzig 21018, nr. 477, f. 54. L.N.N. 7.3.1928.
88 Mokhtarzada, *Entstehung und Entwicklung der deutsch-afghanischen Beziehungen,* 58.

References

Ball, Alan M. "Building a New State and Society: NEP, 1921–1928." In *The Cambridge History of Russia: The Twentieth Century*, edited by Ronald Suny, 168–92. Cambridge, UK: University of Cambridge Press, 2006.

———. *Russia's Last Capitalists: The Nepmen, 1921–1929*. Berkley: University of California Press, 1990.

Belkovets, Larissa P., Sergei Vladimirovich Belkovets, and Bernd Bonwetsch. *Gescheiterte Hoffnungen: das deutsche Konsulat in Sibirien 1923–1938*. Essen: Klartext, 2004.

Diamant, Adolf. *Chronik der Juden in Leipzig*. Chemnitz-Leipzig: Verlag Heimatland Sachsen, 1993.

Dohan, Michael Repplier. "Soviet Foreign Trade in the NEP Economy and Soviet Industrialization Strategy." Cambridge, MA: MIT Press, 1969.

Ember, Carol R., Melvin Ember, and Ian Skoggard. *Encyclopedia of Diasporas: Immigrant and Refugee Cultures Around the World. Volume I: Overviews and Topics; Volume II: Diaspora Communities*. New York: Springer, 2005.

"Eitingon, Chaim Mordechow." *Juden in Sachsen*, n.d. juden-in-sachsen.de/leipzig/personen/EitingonChaimMordechow.html.

Gatrell, Peter. "Poor Russia, Poor Show: Mobilising a Backward Economy for War, 1914–1917." In *The Economics of World War I*, edited by Stephen Broadberry and Mark Harrison, 235–76. Cambridge, UK: Cambridge University Press, 2005.

Glenny, Michael V. "The Anglo-Soviet Trade Agreement, March 1921." *Journal of Contemporary History* 5, no. 2 (January 1, 1970): 63–82.

Gross, Stephen. "Selling Germany in South-Eastern Europe: Economic Uncertainty, Commercial Information and the Leipzig Trade Fair 1920–40." *Contemporary European History* 21, no. 1 (2012): 19–39.

Kuromiya, Hiroaki. *The Voices of the Dead: Stalin's Great Terror in the 1930s*. New Haven, CT: Yale University Press, 2007.

Lewis, Robert. "Foreign Economic Relations." In *The Economic Transformation of the Soviet Union, 1913–1945*, edited by Robert William Davies, Mark Harrison, and Stephen G. Wheatcroft, 198–216. Cambridge, UK: Cambridge University Press, 1994.

Lutz, Martin. *Siemens Im Sowjetgeschäft: Eine Institutionengeschichte Der Deutsch-Sowjetischen Beziehungen 1917–1933*. Stuttgart: Franz Steiner Verlag, 2011.

Malbin, Max. *Der internationale rauchwarenhandel vor und nach dem Weltkriege unter besonderer berücksichtigung Leipzigs*. Oschatz: F. Oldecops erben (C. Morgner), 1927.

McCauley, Martin. *The Longman Companion to Russia Since 1914*. London: Longman, 1998.

Mokhtarzada, Mohammed Taufiq. "Entstehung und Entwicklung der deutsch-afghanischen Beziehungen: unter besonderer Berücksichtigung der Entwicklungshilfe der Bundesrepublik Deutschland für Afghanistan während der ersten Entwicklungsdekade." Freie Universität Berlin, 1972.

Moss, Walter G. *A History of Russia Volume 2: Since 1855*. London: Anthem Press, 2004.

Müller, Rolf-Dieter. *Das Tor zur Weltmacht: die Bedeutung der Sowjetunion für die deutsche Wirtschafts- und Rüstungspolitik zwischen den Weltkriegen*. Boppard am Rhein: H. Boldt, 1984.

Pohl, Manfred. *Die Finanzierung der Russengeschäfte zwischen den beiden Welt-kriegen: d. Entwicklung d. 12 grossen Russlandkonsortien.* Frankfurt am Main: Knapp, 1975.

Quigley, John B. *The Soviet Foreign Trade Monopoly; Institutions and Laws.* Columbus, OH: Ohio State University Press, 1974.

Ray, Arthur J. *The Canadian Fur Trade in the Industrial Age.* Toronto: University of Toronto Press, 1990.

Sangster, Joan. "Making a Fur Coat: Women, the Labouring Body, and Working-Class History." *International Review of Social History* 52, no. 2 (2007): 241–70.

Schröter, Harm G. "Europe in the Strategies of Germany's Electrical Engineering and Chemical Trusts, 1919–1929." In *Quest for Economic Empire: The European Strategies of German Big Business in the Twentieth Century*, edited by Volker R. Berghahn, 35–55. Providence, RI: Berghahn Books, 1996.

Simonsen, Jon Gunnar Molstre. "Perfect Targets–Antisemitism and Eastern Jews in Leipzig, 1919–1923." *Leo Baeck Institute Year Book* 51 (January 2006): 79–101.

Skrivan, Ales. "On the Foreign Economic Relations of China in the Interwar Era." *West Bohemian Historical Review* 2, no. 2 (2012): 73–86.

Strandmann, Hartmut Pogge Von. "Großindustrie Und Rapallopolitik. Deutsch-Sowjetische Handelsbeziehungen in Der Weimarer Republik." *Historische Zeitschrift* 222, no. 2 (April 1, 1976): 265–341.

Taylor, Frederick. *Inflation der Untergang des Geldes in der Weimarer Republik und die Geburt eines deutschen Traumas.* München: Siedler, 2013.

Tough, Frank. *As Their Natural Resources Fail: Native Peoples and the Economic History of Northern Manitoba, 1870–1930.* Vancouver: UBC Press, 2011.

Tworek, Heidi. "Magic Connections: German News Agencies and Global News Networks, 1905–1945." Harvard University, 2012.

Unger, Manfred, ed. *Judaica Lipsiensia: Zur Geschichte Der Juden in Leipzig.* Leipzig: Edition Leipzig, 1994.

Weiner, Douglas R. *Models of Nature.* Pittsburgh, PA: University of Pittsburgh Press, 2000.

Wilmers, Mary-Kay. *The Eitingons: A Twentieth Century Story.* New York: Verso Books, 2012.

8 Market Engineering as a Collective Enterprise (1921–1930)

Introduction

The period from hyperinflation to the crisis of 1929 could be described as the comeback of the Leipzig fur industry. The number of labourers and firms around 1925 had never been higher in the fur cluster: around 11,000 labourers worked permanently in the industry.[1] The growth of the local fur industry was largely due to its reintegration into the world market. As mentioned above, fur firms preferred to be oriented towards the world market rather than investing in autarkic alternatives. Moreover, overall economic parameters had gradually improved. The German economy was characterised by an upward trend in this period, especially after the Dawes plan had resolved inflation and restructured German debts.[2] Furthermore, the treaty of Berlin allowed German firms to resume dealings with the Soviet Union at levels that were reminiscent of pre-war standards. However, the Leipzig 'comeback' cannot solely be explained by pointing to the more favourable economic climate. We have already established the importance of Leipzig as a gateway to the East and also pointed to the successful international activities of individual Leipzig-based firms. Nonetheless, the transitions of the international economy were a source of collective action and interfirm cooperation as well. This chapter considers two main themes: bank-business relationships in the 1920s and the interfirm cooperation that led to the creation of joint-venture auction companies in Leipzig.

Auction companies had a long pedigree in the international fur trade. Auction sales formed the foundation stone of the fur trade in London and in new markets like New York and Montreal. Between 1874 and 1878, some Leipzig firms (Joseph Ullmann, Heinrich Lomer, Dodel, and Joseph Finkelstein) had already attempted to form auction sales in Leipzig.[3] While such attempts were unsuccessful, the idea revived in the 1920s against a background of world market restructuring. Auction companies in Leipzig will be presented as economic institutions that renewed the way in which market transactions were organised locally in order to converge with a world market that was increasingly organised by auction sales. The chapter will examine how auction companies were formed in Leipzig and in what ways they contributed to the international position of Leipzig as a capital in the fur industry.

The symbiosis between banking and the fur industry is a thornier issue. As we have seen, the cross-fertilisation between the competitive bank system in the local economy and the fur industry was one of the major pillars in the foreign trade of the fur district prior to 1914. What shape did this fruitful alliance assume in the 1920s? Academic debates on the role of German banks in the recovery of trade and industry in the interwar period have failed to advance an unequivocal answer. Many have questioned the existence of a symbiotic relationship between finance and industry and have stressed that firms were forced to find alternative sources of credit.[4] It is certain that monetary instability of the early 1920s, with the hyperinflation of 1923 as its nadir, deeply eroded the ability of the banking system to act as a financer of industry and trade. The relatively prosperous golden years that followed were not sufficient to build up substantial reserves or to restore the troubled banking system.[5] Nevertheless, few would disagree that unstable economic parameters automatically result in conservative banking policies. For instance, the financial historian Harold James noted thoughtfully that "the German banks, weakened because of the standstill of the inflation years, were not able to finance according to pre-war standards, but also took irresponsibly high risks to compensate."[6] Depending on the perspective from which one views the problem, the relationship between banking and business in interwar Germany remains a multifaceted puzzle. However, the problem of banking behaviour and its relationship with German economic recovery only interests us to the extent that it reveals collaborative patterns between economic agents in the industrial district.

Financing the Fur Capital

Banking and the Fur Industry in the Aftermath of the War

While the position of German banking as a financer of industry and commerce in the interwar period is not unequivocally established, I will attempt to examine the embeddedness of the banks in the district and their role as financers for the fur industry in the 1920s. Did banks in Leipzig redefine lending conditions and their favourable policy to the fur trade? What was the relationship between banking and district participants? An important first observation is that Leipzig remained the largest financial centre of Saxony after World War I, larger then Dresden and any neighbouring cities. In 1927, Leipzig housed 69 bank divisions, 22 of which were joint-stock banks possessing a capital of 55,099,000 RM, much higher than that held by the banks in Dresden.[7] The Leipzig credit market remained thus comparatively large. Secondly, there was the continuity of personal connections, especially between the fur industry and the two largest joint-stock banks, the Deutsche Bank and the Dresdner Bank. Eugen Naumann remained director of the Deutsche Bank and von Klemperer headed the Dresdner Bank until the banking crisis of the early 1930s. As discussed in Chapter 2, these men had fortified the new bank branches on the pre-war local market by primarily investing in clustered sectors like the fur industry.

Banks tried to adapt to the changing nature of the international fur trade, in particular by connecting to the lead firms that booked early international successes. The sudden expansion of the Eitingon holding in particular allowed Naumann to compete with the Dresdner Bank, the latter being the exclusive creditor of the Chaim Eitingon holding until 1920. After establishing informal contacts with Motty Eitingon and Martin Lentschner, a highly ranked official of the Eitingon holdings in Leipzig, the Deutsche Bank in Leipzig offered Eitingon a credit line of about 15,000,000 marks.[8] Additionally, Naumann offered the company an extra $250,000 in order to support its foreign trade. Naumann's competitive strategy failed only because the Berlin office of the Deutsche Bank interfered. Berlin feared the return of a highly competitive situation comparable to that before World War I. After contact with the Dresdner Bank, the head office noted: "The Dresdner Bank cherished . . . the wish that at least the neighbouring banks will not allow themselves to become the victims of an unhealthy competitive struggle and to enter into an extensive exchange of views on the limits of lending in general and in individual cases."[9] After the reprimand from Berlin, the Deutsche and Dresdner Banks jointly provided 15,000,000 marks. Thus, the Deutsche Bank barely prevented Naumann from increasing banking competition in Leipzig even further.

The David Biedermann merchant house forms an additional example of rapidly resumed bank investments in the post-war fur trade. Parallels in the relationship between the Deutsche Bank and Biedermann can easily be drawn with the bank's relationship with the Eitingons: both had maintained business in Russia and Great Britain during and after the war. Before 1914, Biedermann was already one of the largest accounts of the Deutsch Bank; they shared it with the Bankhaus Meyer & Co, a private bank, and the Bank für Handel und Industrie. Yet the Deutsche Bank was the chief financer. Naumann was impressed by Biedermann's business and expected the firm to become a major player after the war: "Biedermann maintains the Russian business to the broadest extent and can thus achieve higher profits than ever possible during peace time. After the war, Biedermann will be a customer who will bring us great benefits."[10] In line with these growing expectations, the Deutsche Bank in Leipzig granted an unsecured credit line for 2,000,000 marks in 1920— it had previously been restricted to 400,000 marks.[11] After hyperinflation ended, Naumann restricted the credits to a mere 100,000 RM.

The allocation of credit was not solely confined to the success stories of Jewish fur business. The Deutsche Bank, for instance, increased its commitment towards the Theodor Thorer firm as well. In 1919, Hollender asked the banks to double credit so that his firm could resume international trade. Particularly revealing was the strong position of the Thorer firm in negotiating the lending terms. Hollender, the leader of the Thorer firm, refused to put up additional collateral for the extra credit. The Berlin head office of the Deutsche Bank realised the powerlessness of the banks towards the Thorer firm: "We assume that the other banks did not receive cover for the doubled credits, so our situation is not much better than theirs. The tremendous increase in value of fur products renders the desire for the improvement of financial freedom of the firm more understandable, even though it is not pleasant to see that so much money is used for luxury products. . . . However . . . significant amounts seem to be destined for exports again and therefore a corresponding portion of foreign currencies will become available."[12] Again, competition between banks gave way to the softening of lending conditions. Only two of the smaller Leipzig banks refused Thorer's proposition for unsecured credit. With the support of the Deutsche Bank, the Dresdner Bank, and others, Thorer attained 4,600,000 marks worth of credit. As such, the banks resumed their role of benevolent creditors towards the local fur industry in the early 1920s.

The Short-Term Credit Market and Foreign Operations

The banks not only allowed larger businesses to resume trade by expanding credit lines: the fur industry was probably the principal recipient for medium- and short-term credits issued by the Leipzig banks. The 1924 cashbook of the Dresdner Bank in Leipzig illustrates that the vast majority of short-term acceptance credit flowed to the fur industry. The register mentions the grant of acceptance credit to about 103 firms in that year, 45 of which were fur firms. Many district firms consumed such short-term loans, as it constitutes an important instrument for the organisation of transborder trade. For example, most of the acceptance credit granted to the fur industry was issued in pounds sterling, presumably in order to allow for a visit to the auctions in London. Acceptance credit to the fur industry from the Dresdner Bank in Leipzig amounted to £394,600, which represented 66% of the total credit issued. Credit to individual firms ranged from £5,000 to £30,000 on average. The largest sum (£35,000) granted went to Mihran Allalmedjian, a somewhat unknown trader, while Thorer was granted £25,000.[13]

Although we lack an exhaustive overview, the Deutsche Bank similarly enabled Leipzig firms to visit the London auctions by issuing short-term acceptance credit. In 1921, Biedermann, one of the first firms to resume trade in Britain, received short-term loans of £10,000 in May and £30,000 in July on the occasion of a London auction. For the May auctions in London in the following year, the Deutsche Bank granted acceptance credit to Biedermann (£20,000), David Dubiner (£20,000), Silberkweit & Goldberg (£15,000), and Adolf Schlesinger Nachf (£10,000).[14] The support for Biedermann is surprising, since it was one of the few Leipzig firms still in the possession of a branch in London. For the winter auctions in 1922, the Deutsche Bank provided Reichenstein, Goldstaub, Dubiner, David Biedermann, and Theodor Thorer the sum of £62,000 between them.[15]

During the years of inflation, the provision of foreign credit was expensive for the German banks and meant a considerable effort. The availability of foreign currencies was of the utmost importance for the fur firms, especially in the first half of the 1920s, when London dominated the trade in Siberian furs. In the provision of pounds, the Deutsche Bank profited from its connections to the merchant bank J. Henry Schröders, one of the leading London bank houses in the beginning of the twentieth century; through this connection, it was able to provide money for fur firms trading in London.[16] Such credit enabled firms to operate on the London market and provide Leipzig with furs at a time when the raw fur market in Leipzig was at a low ebb.

We should also take into account that most of the Leipzig firms profited from multiple bank connections for short-term loans, general banking affairs, and acceptance credits. By early 1926, Thorer made use of acceptance credits in pound sterling sourced from no less than four German banks in Leipzig (ADCA £25,000, Dresdner Bank £25,000, Meyer & Co £10,000, and Reichskredit AG £25,000), while two other banks provided dollars (Darmstädter und Nationalbank $100,000 and the Stadtbank $75,000). Despite the fact that Thorer possessed a branch in London, they mainly relied on the neighbouring bank offices in Leipzig for the provision of pounds. In fact, the head office of Thorer in Germany obtained more credit in foreign currencies than the branch of the firm in London. Only two London banks provided credit to Thorer's London division for the auctions (Japhet £25,000 and Goschens and Cunliffe £20,000).[17] Furthermore, Thorer's bank partners domiciled in London's financial district also had German roots. First, Goschens and Cunliffe was the result of a 1920 merger between the bank Fruhling and Goschen and the Cunliffe Brothers. The Fruhling bank was established in 1814 by German merchants whilst the Cunliffe Brothers was a product of British bankers. Secondly, Japhet & Co was established by Saemy Japhet, a Jewish banker from Frankfurt, in 1895.[18] Larger businesses like Thorer obviously profited from multiple bank connections, both regional and international. Nevertheless, it is clear that banking affairs were centred on Leipzig.

Furs and Bank Competition in Leipzig (1920–1929)

The Eitingon firm undoubtedly gathered the highest number of credit lines from various banks. It may very well have been the largest firm account in Leipzig's financial world. By 1929, the Eitingon concern enjoyed a 2 million dollar credit line (or 8,400,000 RM) with the Dresdner Bank, substantially more than that of the Deutsche Bank, the ADCA (both $1,200,000), and the Commerzbank ($750,000).[19] In fact, the Eitingon family, in particular

Martin Lentschner, had refined the art of playing rival Leipzig banks against each other. In 1927, the head office of the Deutsche Bank wrote to the Leipzig office: "The Eitingons declared to you that they have been served by other banks more accommodatingly. We cannot help but notice that this is a deliberate strategy . . . to exert pressure on us so as to indulge their wishes and in all likelihood they employ this strategy towards other banks as well."[20] The success story of the Eitingons and their ability to profit from many bank connections substantially expanded the firm's role as a consumer on the local lending market.

Nonetheless, less powerful medium-sized businesses also used more than one bank, albeit usually not more than two. David Kölner, a fur trading business that had a trade volume of almost 2,000,000 RM in 1926, received auction credits from both the Deutsche and the Dresdner Banks.[21] The same went for Semi Goldstaub, a Jewish fur trader who divided his bank affairs between the two largest competitors on the Leipzig bank market. Thus, businesses like Goldstaub also made clever use of the competition between the largest joint-stock banks. Goldstaub wrote in 1927 that he opened a credit line with the Dresdner Bank simply because the Deutsche Bank refused to extend his credits; however, "he was willing to withdraw his affairs from the Dresdner Bank if the Deutsche Bank granted him an extra credit of 200,000RM."[22] Goldstaub nevertheless kept both his bank accounts. Additionally, both banks offered him acceptance credit (unsecured by the Dresdner Bank and partially secured by the Deutsche Bank) to a maximum of £30,000 for the London sales in 1929.[23]

Just as before 1914, the competition in the lending market put strains on the relations between the bank branches in Leipzig and the head offices in Berlin. This was particularly so in the case of the Deutsche Bank. In December 1921, the head office asked Naumann to reconsider the "liberal" agreement with the Eitingon family. According to Berlin, the Eitingon multinational mainly used the credits to ship raw furs directly to New York. Therefore, the impact on trade and industry in Leipzig was smaller than expected: "The gentlemen [of the board] agreed upon the fact that it cannot be the task of a German bank to lend dollars to an 'American firm.' We gladly support needs in Germany with our currency but we have to abstain from lending our scant currencies to foreign firms."[24] It should be noted that conflicts between the head office and regional offices were not exceptional in the history of the Deutsche Bank. The conflict between the local directors, prone to grant credits to local firms and befriended industrialists, and the bank leaders in Berlin, who were worried about lenient credit conditions, loomed large throughout the 1920s.[25] Here, the flexible lending behaviour of the Leipzig bank division was however deeply coloured by its position as an actor within the district economy. Furthermore, the bank clearly suffered from competition with the other joint-stock banks in the district.

In contrast to the board in Berlin, local bank officers did not feel uncomfortable with the fur firm's strong position on the lending market. On the contrary, it could be argued that the bank division identified itself strongly with the fate of the local industry and endeavoured to be a reliable partner. Bank directors and fur businessmen were on a good footing with each other. Banks and businesses were practically neighbours in downtown Leipzig. The building of the Deutsche Bank at the Rathausring was within walking distance of the Brühl.[26] Perhaps more important was a shared view on local affairs. Similar to the fur magnates themselves, the director of the Deutsche Bank in Leipzig saw the international activities of successful fur concerns as the launch pad for trade revival in Leipzig. International operations were seen as an absolute necessity for the survival of the fur district. Naumann, for instance, wrote to justify the credit for the Eitingon firm in the early 1920s: "The credit is justified from our point of view because the fur trade is essentially international and it fertilises the dressing industry in Leipzig, where the German fur industry is concentrated."[27] Naumann personally trusted the fur businessmen, including the America-oriented Motty Eitingon: "Motty Eitingon is an ingenious, and rarely clever man in his best years" and his firm is a "world firm."[28] The same admiration applied to the Biedermann business. Naumann wrote that the "Russian enterprises of the Biedermann concern, which continued commerce with England and the US during the war, achieved fabulous profits and nowadays ranks amongst the largest and most well-funded fur firms."[29] It was his personal conviction that an association with these firms would not only increase bank profits but also re-animate Leipzig's fur agglomeration. Demands for credit were therefore easily permitted, even when the head office in Berlin tried to restrict the link with the fur industry.

The lenient policy of the Deutsche Bank was not altogether different from other local Leipzig bank divisions. The Commerzbank and the ADCA had a large number of customers in the fur industry as well, although they focussed on smaller businesses. The local office of the Dresdner bank was widely known for its lenient lending policy towards the fur industry, especially the larger firms. The difference was that Dresdner Bank's head office seemed less concerned by the activities of its local branch vis-à-vis the Leipzig fur industry. Was the local division of the Dresdner Bank simply more independent than the Deutsche Bank? A clear answer cannot easily be established. In any case, it should be noted that the Dresdner Bank in Leipzig did not simply throw money at the fur industry but rather employed an assessment system of the firms to which it granted credit. However, the rating system was not very sophisticated: lending conditions were determined by personal networks and subjective assessments. The assessment not only took trade volume and the nature of business into account, but also considered the personal characteristics of the entrepreneur and the relationship between the bank director and business leaders.

The Dresdner Bank did impose restrictions once it found that entrepreneurs were taking too many risks or when doubts were raised about the personal capabilities of the entrepreneur. Leopold Apfel, a fur trader, was graded as "very decent but stupid" and therefore "credit for him is now not in order."[30] Positive traits were not always a guarantee of favourable credit conditions. Ephaim Kirschner was highly esteemed but his commerce was seen as too risky: he was forced "to show the annual trade balance until 1930" and "no unsecured credit was allowed."[31] Again, personal friendships and relations played a considerable role. The traders of Wachtel & Eskreis were seen as "very cultivated and a solid firm" and "should be treated very well."[32] The Dresdner Bank characterised the fur dealer David Chardack as a "trustee" of the bank: "He can acquire any credit he wants; he is very careful and has good customers."[33] The members of the Fein family—"a solid Jewish family"—were equally considered as "old friends of the Dresdner Bank," even though they maintained connections to the rival Danat and Commerzbank. The relationship between the bank and its fur customers was therefore highly subjective and reputational. Personal connections and impressions about the character of the entrepreneurs mattered in shaping the local lending market.

It should be stressed that the entanglement between the fur trade and banks was also the result of exogenous developments. The importance of London for the international fur market in the immediate post-war years gave impetus to the short-term lending market in Leipzig. In addition, the dealings with the Soviets were one of the main causes for the growing involvement of the financial sector in the fur trade. Even for a firm like Ariowitsch that operated relatively independently, the credit preferences of the Soviets and the large contracts were a challenge: "The firm J. Ariowitsch represents one of the soundest and strongest fur firms. The firm is . . . able to finance its imports to a large extent autonomously and therefore only seldom makes use of its rather small bank credit. . . . The nature of Russian affairs forces the firm to appeal to a larger amount of bank credit. . . ."[34] However, the ever-expanding involvement of the banks in the foreign affairs of the fur firms only added to the troubled relations between the local bank and the head office of the Deutsche Bank. Berlin presaged deficiencies in the trade with the Soviets: "If Mr. Ariowitsch indicates that he was able to gain special advantages in dealings with the Soviet Russian authorities because of his relations with those officials, we believe indeed that he will make large profits. But the question arises, how much longer? An old proverb says: the pitcher goes so often to the well that it finally breaks. If something should go differently than expected, it could be possible that the good relations of A[riowitsch] with certain Soviets will turn into the opposite and could lead to large losses for your customers."[35] The head office in Berlin believed that Leipzig was taking enormous risks through its indirect participation in foreign trade while local bankers considered it a necessity. In Leipzig, however, foreign trade was the compound of business-bank relationships.

Interfirm Cooperation and the Creation of New Market Institutions

Trade Consortia

Having established the important link between banking and the fur industry, let us now turn to collaborative networks between individual fur firms initiated by the need to restore foreign trade. A less successful example of interfirm cooperation in this field was trade consortia. Under Thorer's leadership, a number of traders in Leipzig planned to form a temporary trade consortium in 1920. The consortium was set up with the aim of establishing trade relations between the Soviet Union and Leipzig. In particular, use was made of Thorer's remaining personal connections in the USSR. The consortium appointed Strauven, an employee of the former German firm Dürrschmidt in Tashkent, as a trade representative of the consortium in Moscow. Strauven was an important representative of the Thorer firm in Russia and Central Asia well before the war: he played a crucial role in moving karakul herds from Central Asia to German South West Africa (see Chapter 4).

Arndt Thorer, who had just succeeded his deceased father in 1920 as owner of the Thorer firm, made his network resources available to a wider set of local firms. Importantly, he did so because he believed that the restoration of trade networks went beyond the individual interest of the firm he headed. Instead, Thorer believed himself to be part of a broader agenda, one that burdened him with responsibility towards Leipzig. He wrote in 1921 that "it has to be prevented that new Russian exports are sold in England or the US . . . These exports belong to our trade and dressing industry and will contribute to the recovery of Leipzig's old reputation in the international fur trade."[36] Such motives indicate that a lead firm like Thorer adhered to the wider goal of restoring Leipzig as an international marketplace. In other words, strengthening the 'local' was an important motive for firm strategies and stimulated processes of amalgamation into interfirm collaborative structures.

Nevertheless, the trade consortium failed to make a deal in Moscow. In November 1921, the government curtailed the actions of the consortium since it feared that sending Strauven to Moscow at this stage might inflict damage on the still fragile diplomatic relations with the Russian trade representation.[37] The early attempts of the Leipzig district to collectively gain concessions inside Russia were a failure. Failure was thus the fate of the consortia, despite the fact that it was a common practice by which German businesses organised foreign trade in the period between the wars.[38] Nevertheless, the trade consortium reveals once more the predisposition towards interfirm cooperation in the district.

Auction Companies as Interfirm Cooperation

Whereas consortia were a common practice for German businesses in the interwar period, auction houses in Germany were something of a novelty.

The formation of auction companies in Leipzig directly followed from the successes of various fur auctions in Leipzig that were organised independently by the Soviet government. The first Soviet fur auction, organised by the Soviet trade representation in Berlin, took place in Leipzig on 28 September 1921. In terms of their re-admission to the world market, the symbolic value of the auction for both the Soviets and the Germans cannot be underestimated. The visit of 500 merchants, 57 of whom were from France, reveals a large international interest in the sale of Siberian furs.[39] In the first auction sale, the Soviet government sold furs with the total value of 250,000 goldmarks.[40] Although further information on the first auction sales is scarce, the auctions were said to approach world market prices.[41] The next Soviet auction in March 1922 achieved sales worth $1,000,000.

The symbolic value notwithstanding, the independent Soviet auctions, organised by the Soviet state agency in Berlin, were a particular disadvantage for the district as they put pressure on the trading firm as the traditional intermediary between Russia and the Leipzig industry. A quote of Arndt Thorer in 1921 captures the stalemate: "When the Russians organise auctions, the foreigners buy directly in Leipzig and ignore the German fur trade completely. Nevertheless, we want to be, once again, the supplier of the other countries for Russian, Siberian, and Central Asian skins and this way will recoup foreign currencies."[42] The connection between trade and industry was indeed a salient aspect of the Leipzig fur district. In order to safeguard trade interests, six self-organised auction companies were formed as a solution to this problem in the early 1920s: the RAVAG, the Rauchwaren-Lagerhaus GmbH, Geverko, Mucrena, Ramico, and Norsia (Nordische Silberfuchs Auktion). In 1920, the Mucrena was the first auction company established in Leipzig, as one of its advertisements mentioned: "In 1920, the need was felt to provide the German and foreign fur trades with new provisions of raw furs."[43] However, the Mucrena was not a company established by Leipzig fur dealers; rather, it was a division of a hide and skin dealing firm in Berlin.

In contrast, the new companies Rauchwaren Lagerhaus GmbH and the RAVAG were the result of interfirm collaboration in the district. The Lagerhaus (established in 1922) in particular significantly extended the horizon of interfirm cooperation in Leipzig. No less than 39 firms participated in the new auction company, providing capital of 300,000 marks in 1922. The firm Gaudig & Blum provided the largest sum, 60,000 marks, followed by 20,000 marks from Theodor Thorer and 15,000 marks from Friedrich Erler.[44] The fact that these firms in particular played a leading role in the new auction company reveals an important transnational dimension in the formation of auction companies. Both Thorer and Gaudig & Blum had ties to the new auction business in New York, The New York Fur Auction Sales, established in 1916. Charles S. Porter, the representative of Gaudig & Blum in New York, was appointed president of the New York Fur Auction Sales in 1916. Similarly, Edward Speer, head of New York branch of Thorer, was named treasurer of the same company.[45] It is likely that these businesses' involvement in New York partly explains the foundation of an auction company in Leipzig. The joint venture model was also inspired by the same example, since the New York auction was based upon the participation of many firms. The successes of New York auctions in competing with British auction houses were undoubtedly appealing as well.

Thus, the unifying and participative model was effectively copied. Aside from the three firms listed above, capital investment divided relatively equally between the remaining 36 firms: 11 firms provided 10,000 marks, 10 firms provided 5,000 marks, and the remaining 15 firms provided 3,000 marks each. Over the course of the years, however, a smaller number of firms came to form the core of the auction company. A milestone in the development of the Lagerhaus took place in 1926, when it was transformed into a joint-stock company. This allowed larger firms to assume a more prominent role. By the early 1930s, Theodor Thorer owned 35% of the shares.[46] The firm Friedrich Erler and other trading companies of the Brühl (M. Bromberg & Co, Eisenbach & Stern, and Fein & Co) owned the remainder of the company shares. Initially, the firm epitomised an unprecedented scale of interfirm cooperation within the district but ultimately it came into the hands of a smaller circle of firms.

The other new auction company besides the Lagerhaus, the RAVAG (or Rauchwarenversteigerungs AG), was established slightly later, in March 1923. In contrast to the Lagerhaus, it was formed by only six firms from the Brühl.[47] These were Eisenbach & Stern, Max Feiler Gmbh, Rosenfelder & Sohn, Wienwurzel & Lorch, Ferdinand Salm, and Kurt Wachtel. An additional shareholder of this auction company was the Commerzbank in Leipzig, which illustrates the interest of the banks in processes of interfirm cooperation. The RAVAG gained additional eminence when Chaim Eitingon joined the firm as an expert "in the grading of the furs" and as a shareholder. Martin Lentschner was appointed as an additional member of the board. Again, it is important that the participation of larger firms like Theodor Thorer and Chaim Eitingon in interfirm cooperation reveals that business strategies of larger firms were not restricted to individual trade with the Soviets. This means an additional argument against the alleged 'rootless' business strategy in the early 1920s, especially of the Eitingons. Quite the contrary, these firms had appropriated the goal of strengthening commercial activity within the city through collective action.

The Activities of the Auction Companies

Let us examine the activities of the auction companies more closely. To begin with, both auction sales were organised according to the same principles. The Leipzig fur auctions were organised as 'English auctions,' which were characterised by selling via ascending bids. Second, the Leipzig auction companies issued advance payments relative to the value of furs put for auction sales. The auction company graded the value of the goods and then paid advances to suppliers.[48] Firms, foreign trade agencies, and farmers could entrust their goods to a wider arena of buyers and diminish the risk of losses. The practice of advance payment naturally attracted trading firms, fur farmers, and the Soviet trade agencies in need of money. The RAVAG, for instance, granted advances to firms and agencies that were interested in placing their furs on auction for about six weeks and for 50–60% of its expected value.[49] The Lagerhaus similarly granted "transport credit" (or Lombard credit) to the Soviets and other suppliers with the furs acting as the collateral. In this respect, the auction company corresponded to the development of ascending world market prices and to what could be called a 'financialisation' of the fur trade.

It should be underscored that the new market institution had to win over the trust of both buyers and sellers. To begin with, the RAVAG appointed an independent auction leader, Büttner, who was 'sworn' into office.[50] The practice of auctions was alienating for several observers. A journalist of the newspaper *Leipziger Neueste Nachrichten* visited a Mucrena auction in 1929 and wrote about auctions as if they were something from another world.[51] The journalist acquired the impression that the auction was something for insiders: "Members of the Brühl" dominated the auction room, often by using "secret non-verbal language" and rapid bidding; "The settlement of the auction appears to be mysterious for laymen. Nonetheless, it has the advantage that sales proceeds more rapidly and the swift decisiveness resembles business conduct on the Brühl, from where most of this auction participants come. And as on the Brühl, everything is treated confidentially as possible, so you will also not let the competition know what and how you bought. Hence the secret signs and body language."[52] The journalist concluded that the auctioneer must know every participant personally, since this mode of sale would otherwise be impossible. Despite being a borrowed market institution, auctions were relatively easily accepted by the Leipzig fur industry. Auctions were not an alien practice for them or remote from their experiences.

Importantly, competition between the auction companies, especially the Lagerhaus and RAVAG, was kept at bay. Two factors explain the lack of competition. Firstly, the Jewish firm Eisenbach & Stern, the only business with an interest in both auction companies, made good relations between the two auction houses possible. On the advice of Eisenbach & Stern, the Lagerhaus opened its warehouses and storerooms in 1923 to the recently established RAVAG.[53] The warehouses of the Lagerhaus were located in the north of Leipzig, a few blocks away from the main railway station. Later, the RAVAG rented a depot inside the freight train station. As such, both auction houses were strategically located close to the railway hub. Secondly, both companies focused on different market sectors. The Lagerhaus was arguably much more internationally oriented, in particular to the trade with the Soviet Union. The auctions of the Lagerhaus primarily brought commodities on behalf of the Soviet trade representation to the Leipzig fur market. On the other hand, the RAVAG predominantly, albeit not exclusively, organised the sales of farmed furs, like rabbits and other furbearing animals that were increasingly being bred in Germany as well as in neighbouring countries.

The Lagerhaus was created with the aim of taking over the independently organised Soviet auctions but it also organised the sales of fur trading companies. The Rauchwaren-Lagerhaus commenced auctioning furs in a commission for the Soviet trade agencies as early as 1922.[54] The first auction of the Lagerhaus took place in the prestigious Krystallpalast in Leipzig, an epicentre of the urban bourgeoisie with salons, meeting rooms, and a theatre. Later auctions of the Lagerhaus were held in the Neue Handelsbörse, a large building in the northwest of Leipzig that also housed the Chamber of Commerce.[55] Soviet auctions organised by the Lagerhaus were held every six months between 1922 and 1926.[56] The auction sales of the Lagerhaus supplied Leipzig factories and international customers with a variety of prime furs. Take the offering from September 1923 for instance. At this sale, 171,611 grey squirrels, 32,572 ermines, 13,912 karakuls, and almost 1,000 high-value Russian sables were sold.[57]

Equally, auction companies tapped into the booming, albeit less international, circuit of farmed furs or subprime furs (foremost rabbits) produced by small-scale husbandry in Germany and neighbouring countries. The auction company Mucrena in particular continued selling *Landwaren*, skins produced domestically, a legacy of the wartime economy. Foremost, this concerned the sale of rabbit skins in bulk. Mucrena procured furs not only from German farmers and animal keepers but also functioned as a European sales agency, dealing with suppliers from the Balkans, France, and Switzerland. In addition, its auctions were not only important for fur traders but also for shoemakers, leather traders, and hat manufacturers, who all bought raw material from these sales.[58] The RAVAG combined the sales of domestic fur skins with those that were imported. The RAVAG mostly dealt in rabbit skins, 1,952,737 of which were sold at the 1924 sales. Nevertheless, the RAVAG offered significant quantities of imported prime furs as well, like 37,366 foxes and 36,675 skunks and prime furs in very low quantities (like otter skins), ranging from 2,000 to 3,000 items.[59] All these types were sold during a number of irregular auctions throughout the year. For instance, in 1924, the RAVAG managed to hold 10 auctions, in which it sold almost double the quantity from 1923, when seven auctions were held.[60]

Since auction companies financed suppliers in advance, the participation of the local bank system is not surprising. The financial demands of the Soviets in particular warranted cooperation that went beyond the limits of interfirm cooperation in the fur sector. In fact, the banks became influential shareholders of the Leipzig auction companies. In the RAVAG, credit was provided by the Commerzbank, which also acted as a shareholder.[61] A new release of shares in 1928 made the Commerzbank the largest shareholder of the auction company.[62] The Dresdner Bank surfaced as the main financial force behind the Lagerhaus, especially after 1926.

In the spirit of restrained competition between the Leipzig auction houses, the practice of auctioning was neatly divided between the offices of the Dresdner and Commerzbank in Leipzig. The Dresdner Bank supported the Lagerhaus, while the Commerzbank did the same for the RAVAG. The Deutsche Bank, somewhat surprisingly given its interest in the district economy, refrained from participating in the auction hype. However, competition over the auction companies did surface when the Dresdner Bank attempted to establish connections with the RAVAG in 1929. Indeed, several businessmen involved in the RAVAG advocated a second credit line with the Dresdner Bank. However, Georg Kosterlitz, the director of the Commerzbank and representative on the board of the RAVAG, prevented this from happening. Nonetheless, bank competition produced beneficial effects on lending conditions. The Commerzbank offered unsecured credit. The Dresdner Bank refrained from demanding extra securities in their offer to the RAVAG, which consisted of credit to the limit of 400,000 RM: "The Commerzbank issues loans in unsecured form, so we will give loans according to the same conditions."[63] Aside from individual links with fur businesses, the role of local banks was of seminal importance in processes of interfirm cooperation as well.

Photograph 8.1 A Fur Auction in Interwar Leipzig. Reproduced with the permission of the Stadtarchiv Leipzig. (BA 1978.4824)

Auction Companies and Market Engineering

An important dimension of auctions was their ability to compete with rival fur centres. The implementation of this market institution therewith reflected the long-standing desire of local firms to maintain and reconstruct Leipzig as a fur capital, capable of competing with other centres. In Leipzig, auctions were thereby a clear rupture with the tradition of selling furs at the fairs and the organisation of foreign trade by individual businesses. The Leipzig trade fairs had become increasingly less important for the international fur trade, a trend that was already noticeable prior to World War I. Owing to the format of the sample fair that was introduced in 1895, the fairs were more important for the retailing sector than for wholesaling. The decline of the fairs diverged remarkably with the situation of wholesalers and smaller firms in many other industries; for them, the Leipzig trade fair remained a robust 'umbrella institution' for international trade throughout the interwar period.[64] The need to rely on a new umbrella institution like the auction company for the fur industry thus also had its roots in the decline of the fairs. Established as a new market institution, the foundation of auction companies stood central in processes of (international) market engineering by district firms. Walter Leiske of the Leipzig city administration stated in 1928 that auctions were a more important phenomenon for the fur trade than the fairs in terms of international commerce.[65]

Enabling Foreign Trade

Indeed, auction companies (especially the Lagerhaus and, to a lesser extent, the RAVAG) deliberately followed an international course. Once the practice of auction sales was firmly established in Leipzig, the RAVAG pursued a more aggressive policy on foreign markets. In 1928, the RAVAG forged plans to overtake the sale of Australian rabbits, which at that moment was in the hands of the British auction company Anning & Cobb.[66] The RAVAG managed to secure support from several Leipzig banks and auctioned 650,000 Australian rabbits in the following winter. In the early 1930s, the RAVAG became the principal partner of a German farmers' cooperative in Kalkfeld (South West Africa), on whose behalf they sold karakul skins and competed with the Thorer firm.

The international policy of the RAVAG also aimed to make Leipzig the centre for furs that were produced and procured in European countries.[67] The RAVAG focused on rabbit-skin producing countries like Belgium and the Nordic countries, where fur farming was developing at a much more rapid pace than in Germany. This internationalisation strategy, a trend of regionalisation expressed by the geography of fur farming, was conducted with the support of the Commerzbank, the main shareholder. By the early 1930s, the RAVAG managed to organise the sale of fox skins farmed in Sweden and Norway. Indeed, the sale of farmed furs from Germany and neighbouring countries would become the core business of the RAVAG (see Chapter 6).

The Lagerhaus focused on an entirely different market sector, that of the business of Siberian furs. The Lagerhaus was able to exploit the opportunities in the Soviet business available at that time.[68] I have already mentioned that the fur trade benefited from the treaty of Berlin (1925), which tremendously improved bilateral trade relations between Germany and Soviet Union. In addition, improved German-Soviet relations occurred simultaneously with a diplomatic crisis between Great Britain and the Soviet Union, namely the raiding of the ARCOS headquarters in London.[69] Irritated by the actions of the British police, the Soviets immediately reconsidered the role of London in the organisation of foreign trade.[70] Indeed one can see the shift in exports after 1927 in favour of Germany.

Between 1925 and 1933, German fur merchants and companies assumed more of a leading role in the Soviet fur trade (as seen in Table 8.1). However, unlike pre-war trade, domination never tipped into monopolisation. Britain and the US remained vital customers, dividing between them 30–50% of Soviet fur exports. Nevertheless, the shift of the Soviet trade towards Germany coincided with a general rise in the export value of furs. Export values of furs almost doubled from 1925 until 1927. In 1925–1926, Soviet fur exports totalled 241 million roubles; this jumped to 415 million roubles in 1927–1928. Only four years before, the total export of Russian furs was worth no more than 17 million roubles. In 1921, the quantity of the fur exports represented 835 tons (7,709,000 roubles), whereas in 1927 the Soviets managed to export 3,423 tons (211,124,000 roubles). Put differently, the value of Soviet fur exports increased exponentially (multiplied by 27) whereas quantity only quadrupled. The discrepancy between value and quantity further signalled ascending world market prices. Throughout

Table 8.1 Soviet Fur Export to Germany, Great Britain, and the US (1925–1933) in thousand roubles[71]

	GERMANY	GREAT BRITAIN %	US %
1925/26	18%	45%	17%
1926/27	42%	34%	10%
1927/28	51%	23%	8%
1928	51%	27%	6%
1929	50%	28%	11%
1930	51%	29%	7%
1931	43%	41%	2%
1932	43%	34%	6%
1933	53%	19%	9%

the interwar period, fur exports from the USSR never achieved levels higher than those between 1927 and 1928.

Auction companies in Leipzig played an important role in the Soviet trade revival after 1926, owing to their financial capabilities and strong bank connections. In early 1926, the Leipzig office of the Dresdner Bank acted as a financial intermediary between the Lagerhaus and the Soviet trade agencies. Direct associations were made not only with the Berlin trade representation (the German counterpart of the ARCOS) and the Selskosoiuz GmbH in Berlin, but also with the Moscow Narodny Bank Ltd in London. The branch reported in October 1926 that "the relationship [with the Berlin trade representation] has existed since early 1926 and has now expanded considerably, rendering high profits to our branch."[72] The activities of the Dresdner Bank in Leipzig differ from the general image of the role of German banks in the Soviet trade during the Weimar Republic, which existed in the provision of export credit that allowed the Soviets to pay for German imports.[73] In contrast, the Dresdner Bank in Leipzig issued 'import credit' in order to attract raw furs for auctioning.

In October 1926, the Dresdner Bank granted a Lombard credit of 1 million dollars (or 4,200,000 RM) directly to the Soviet trade representation in Berlin (Handelsvertretung der UdSSR). The Lagerhaus pawned furs from the Soviets in exchange for credits. The Dresdner Bank thereby expanded its role in the fur trade by functioning as a financial intermediary. Given its financial investments, the Dresdner Bank even hired extra experts to grade the pawned furs that were stored in the Lagerhaus in Leipzig.[74] As a rule, 25% of the value of the Siberian furs acted as a collateral in advance loans to the Soviets. The Soviets repaid the loans with earnings made on the auctioned furs. The system of trade relied entirely on Soviet credit requirements. Advances or loans were issued to the Soviets on almost all transactions. Kleiber, the leader of the fur department of the Soviet trade delegation, noted the chief importance of the export of furs: "Russia needs money, it needs advance payment for its exports so it can pay for its imports."[75] The main challenge for the Leipzig trade thus lay in financing the Russians, a problem which they had solved by partnering their auction companies with the local banks.

The Dresdner Bank further expanded its activities as a financial intermediary when it concluded a trade deal with the USSR State Bank in 1927, which exported furs along with the Soviet trade representation in Berlin. The USSR State Bank obtained $2,500,000 worth of acceptance credit from the Dresdner Bank for sending furs to Leipzig.[76] The new credit was managed by the head office in Berlin but the goods arrived in Leipzig and were inspected by the officials of the bank in the city. Later, the Dresdner Bank divided credit between the USSR State Bank, the Garantie und Kredit-bank für den Osten (or Garkrebo, a German bank specialised in trade with the Soviet Union), and the Moscow Narodny Bank Ltd. By 1927, the USSR State Bank made use of $2,000,000 of acceptance credit, the Garkrebo $1,780,000, and the Moscow Narodny Bank $1,700,000.[77] All these institutions delivered furs to be auctioned in Leipzig in exchange for credit. In turn, the Dresdner Bank in Leipzig opened new sources of credit in order to finance in the influx of furs. The bank received $1,000,000 of credit from the National Bank of Commerce in New York, while the head office in Berlin granted $2,000,000 to their Leipzig branch.[78]

The expanding role of the Dresdner Bank in financing Soviet trade agencies on behalf of the Lagerhaus had a ratchet effect on the importance of auction sales as a gateway for foreign trade. The sales of the auctions held by the Lagerhaus were worth roughly $3,000,000 on average.[79] In the spring auction of 1927, the Lagerhaus auctioned raw furs for a total value of about $2,000,000.[80] During the September auctions of the same year, the value of the total furs almost doubled to about $3.7 million—most of the goods were sold to Leipzig firms.[81] According to observers, this was one of the largest auctions ever held in Leipzig. These two auctions roughly accounted for 10% of the total furs imported to Germany from the Soviet Union in 1927. Seen from a regional perspective, auctions were even more important. The Dresdner Bank estimated that the value of $2,500,000 imported in furs represented 20–25% of all Soviet fur supplies to the Leipzig district. Auctions continued to deal in large values: $4,700,000 in September 1928 (7% of all German imports) and $4,200,000 in the spring auctions of 1929 (or 6.7% of the total German fur imports).[82]

It should be noted that the figures for 1928 and 1929 are incomplete and the imports through Soviet auctions must have been much higher. Nevertheless, with the creation of auctions as an umbrella institution, the Leipzig fur district clearly reinforced its position as a marketplace in the trade of Siberian furs. Auctions supplied many Leipzig firms and factories and also attracted an international pack of fur dealers. Leipzig firms profited indirectly from these sales: "The sales go, directly or through Leipzig firms, to North American, South American, English, French, Belgian, and Austrian fur traders."[83] The auction company brought a relative, if temporary, stability to the dealings with the Soviets. In addition, the local industry profited strongly and managed to export the manufactured furs to the growing market in the US. In 1928, the US consulate in Leipzig calculated that the Leipzig fur industry exported 71 million RM worth of furs, which climbed to a staggering 86 million RM in 1929. Leipzig furs were by far the largest export product from Saxony that reached the internal market in the US. In 1928, furs constituted 34% of all Saxon-made exports towards the US, and in 1929 even 40% of all Saxon exports.[84] The auctions attracted international customers and allowed Leipzig firms to supply local factories with raw material, who again produced for the world market.

Auctions at the Service of the Capital

The auction companies should be seen as one of the most important umbrella institutions for the facilitation of international trade in Leipzig since the fairs. Auctions were engineered in order to attract trade to the city. These commercial spillover effects were central; business profits came only second. The auction companies never became a big revenue pump for the participating firms. Rather, they served as an umbrella institution for the supply of the fur industry. Despite the enormous amounts of furs that were sold under the hammer of the auctioneer, the RAVAG's annual profits between 1924 and 1929 never exceeded the sum of 70,000 RM, even when business volume expanded rapidly. Although the profit levels of the RAVAG were stable and increased until 1929, they were much lower than individual profit levels of the larger or even medium-sized firms in the Leipzig district.

Profit levels of the Lagerhaus were generally higher, although they fluctuated more. In 1926, a record profit amounted to 124,543 RM. In comparison, David Kölner, a typical small-sized firm, attained a profit of 154,305 RM in the same year. Thus, even the internationally oriented Lagerhaus never managed to achieve profit levels approaching those of the lead firms in the district. The modest profit level was primarily caused by the nature of the auction sales. First, the auction house acted as an intermediary between sellers and buyer, conveying bulks of furs that belonged to a number of sellers to a sizeable arena of buyers. It only derived revenue from auction fees and commission percentages. Second, the RAVAG and the Lagerhaus chiefly relied on their bank connections, and not on the firm capital, to provide loans and advances to suppliers. It is likely that a large amount of the profits made on advances and credit flowed directly to the banks. They claimed a large share of the profits by issuing credit and arranging payment traffic on the auction. In 1929, for instance, the Dresdner Bank made a profit of $31,000 (130,200 RM) and an additional $9,000 (37,800 RM) through simply granting credit to the Russian state bank in exchange for furs.[85] By participating in the auction company, banks wielded substantial influence over the fur business. Whereas the first part of this chapter showed how local traders manipulated competition between banks, banks in turn assumed a strong position on the local market in furs and upon processes of interfirm cooperation. Thus, the observation that fur firms set the terms of commercial banking is nuanced when taking into account the influential role banks played in auction companies and thereby in the local fur trade.

Table 8.2 Profits and Business Volume of the RAVAG (1923–1929) in RM

	Profits	*Business Volume*
1924	29,732	165,992
1925	15,790	288,630
1926	46,057	454,621
1927	64,899	654,591
1928	69,711	727,200
1929	50,517	608,576

The Leipzig Auctions and the Magnitude of the Soviet Fur Trade

To conclude this section, I would like to point again to the international dimension of auctions in Leipzig and to the worldwide dynamics produced by this economic institution more generally. Firstly, it should be stressed that the fur trade was a cornerstone in the revival of Soviet-German commerce. The exports of furs to Germany played a huge role in the balance of trade. In fact, the revival of the German-Russian fur commerce noticeably disrupted the trade balance of Germany with its eastern trading partner. After 1926, Germany ran a trade deficit of 36.8 million RM, as opposed to the surplus of 55 million RM in 1925. As imports like furs increased in value, the bilateral trade balance in 1927 registered a deficit of 103.2 million RM in 1927.[86] As the following table indicates (Table 8.3), the imports of the German fur trade were to a large extent responsible for this bilateral trade deficit. Fur imports from the Soviet Union burdened the trade balance significantly more after 1925: proportions reached 14% of total imports in 1927 and furs represented one-quarter of all German imports from the USSR in 1928.[87] As such, furs were big business in terms of bilateral Soviet-German economic relationship, a dimension that is often overlooked. Moreover, the strategic magnitude of furs increasingly impacted upon the local Leipzig fur industry, especially in the 1930s.

Secondly, the growing importance of auctions was very much a transnational process. Auctions were being successfully used to transform cities into fur trading markets, especially in North America.[88] Similarly, the Leipzig auctions allowed firms to resume the trade of Siberian furs and tap into the growing market of subprime and farmed furs in Europe. International markets in the fur industry thus increasingly converged in terms of organisation. Auction sales surfaced as the principal mode of transaction and as the ruling market convention in the wholesale trade for both farmed and hunted furs. Furthermore, auctions commanded new dynamics in terms of governance of the commodity chain. Economic actors around the globe increasingly

Table 8.3 German Imports from the Soviet Union

	PERCENTAGE OF TOTAL IMPORTS	NOMINAL VALUE (MILLION RM)
1923	7%	6
1924	13%	15
1925	5%	14.5
1926	6%	23.3
1927	14%	64.9
1928	24%	92.1
1929	23%	100
1930	18%	80.2

saw auctions as a key institution in redefining their position in world trade. Auctions diminished the distance between resource producers, markets, and manufacturing. The Soviets were also not blind to the advantages of auction sales. They perceived auctions to be a more modern and advanced business practice than the system of trading through fairs, which had epitomised pre-war penetration of foreign capital into the Russian fur trade.[89] This was not only beneficial to the Leipzig auctions. In 1926, the Soviets also realised that auctions could be instrumental in transforming Russian cities into fur centres. In Soviet trade agencies, Leningrad was increasingly seen as the future centre of the Russian fur trade.

The Soviet desire to decrease dependency upon foreign fur trade centres also has to be seen in the context of the strategic importance of furs in the Soviet economy. By 1925–1926, exports of furs destined for the international fur market represented over 10% of the total Soviet export structure. However, the Soviets were well aware that earnings through foreign trade greatly relied on the export of furs. *Isvestiia* reported in 1929 that furs represented 15% of the Soviet export value.[90] The Soviet economists realised that foreign trade was based on a few strategic resources like fur and was therefore vulnerable to shifts in global demands. For that reason, the Soviets entertained plans to modify trade institutions even further: "Precisely because of the boom, they fear fluctuations in the world market even more, as this will cause severe losses and the collapse of their own foreign trade."[91] So the fur trade boom in Leipzig during the late 1920s was not without its problems. The strategic importance of furs played to the disadvantage of the industry in Leipzig. Trade with the USSR would therefore never regain its pre-war stability and predictability, despite the flexibility of the new economic institutions and cooperation between actors in the district.

Conclusion

In this chapter, it was shown how the Leipzig fur industry managed to coordinate local mechanisms of collaboration towards the changing structures of the world market. Two main areas of cooperation between economic actors have been discussed in depth. One domain of cooperation, that between single businesses and banks, links up to existing pre-war collaboration patterns, whereas the other one, the creation of auction firms by local firms and banks, signalled a breach with trade conventions in the Leipzig district.

The re-admission of the Leipzig fur industry onto the world market was to a large extent based on the availability of local financial resources. The conditions of the lending market were set in by fur firms, which allowed them to play a leading role in foreign trade. The local banks were of key importance to the re-admission of Leipzig firms onto the world market, not only by providing credit to individual firms but also because of their involvement in mutually led auction companies. These auction companies were not only unprecedented in scope, but also changed the way in which market transactions were organised. Auction companies pooled together the capital of a number of firms and they were run by a few entrepreneurs who headed fur firms in the district. The joint venture model enabled economic actors to tap into the new markets that defined the international fur industry of the 1920s, namely that of farmed furs and furs sold through the Soviet monopoly. Auction companies were thus a vehicle to establish Leipzig as a sales market in farmed furs, a key component of the modern fur industry. In that sense, joint venture auctions companies were important instruments in creating links between the industrial district and the new geographies of world trade.

Successful re-admission to the world market after World War I was not something that made Leipzig exceptional as a business cluster in Germany. Other German business clusters with a similar decentralised composition, like the Solingen steel industry, were equally successful in reclaiming pre-war market shares and business contacts, but, however, it is not known if this resulted from deliberate strategies, both on the level of the firm or in function of interfirm cooperation.[92] Auctions serve as a good example for market engineering, as they have been successfully introduced by other clusters in the past, the most well-known and best-researched example being the FloraHolland auctions of the Dutch Flower Cluster. In Holland, the auction were created as a response to external circumstances (economic crisis of 1880) and its creators worked for over 30 years to make all growers members of the auction.[93] It was mentioned that the auction served as a core value–adding activity, being shaped and modified deliberately so as to strengthen the global competitiveness of business clusters. As such, this chapter further attests to the ability of firms in clusters to co-create new related institutions with the purpose of strengthening the global competitive abilities of the cluster as a whole.

Notes

1 Fellmann, *Der Leipziger Brühl*, 116.
2 Boelcke, *Deutschland als Welthandelsmacht*, 14–15.
3 Fellmann, "Schlaufüchse und Blaufüchse vom Brühl," 441.
4 Balderston, "German Banking between the Wars," 605.
5 Simpson and Government, *War Crimes of the Deutsche Bank and the Dresdner Bank*, 258.
6 James, "The 1931 Central European Banking Crisis Revisited," 123.
7 Leiske, *Leipzig und Mitteldeutschland*, 212. In the capital of Saxony, there were 54 bank divisions (24 of which were joint-stock banks) with a capital of 44,386,000 RM.
8 StA-L, Deutsche Bank, Filiale Leipzig 21017, nr. 309 Filiale Leipzig an Deutsche Bank, Filialbüro, 5.06.1920.
9 StA-L, Deutsche Bank, Filiale Leipzig 21017, Nr. 309. Berlin Filialbüro an Leipzig, 28.06.1920.
10 StA-L, Deutsche Bank, Filiale Leipzig 21017, nr. 257, f. 41. Leipzig, den 14. 03.1917.

11 StA-L; Deutsche Bank, Filiale Leipzig 21017, nr. 258, f. 41.
12 StA-L, Deutsche Bank, Filiale Leipzig 21017, nr. 544. Deutsche Bank, Filialbüro an Direktion der Deutschen Bank Filiale Leipzig, den 14.10.1919.
13 StA-L, Dresdner Bank in Leipzig 21018, nr. 604. Credit-Liste per 31.12.1924.
14 StA-L, Deutsche Bank in Leipzig, 21017, nr. 258. Deutsche Bank Filialbüro an die Direktion der Deutschen Bank Leipzig, 24.04.1922.
15 StA-L, Deutsche Bank, Filiale Leipzig 21017, nr. 544. Kreditakten Theodor Thorer. 16.10.1922. These companies were A. Reichenstein (£10,000), Semi Goldstaub (£10,000), David Dubiner (£15,000), Theodor Thorer (£7,000), and David Biedermann (£20,000).
16 Roberts, *Schroders*, 190.
17 StA-L, Deutsche Bank, Filiale Leipzig, nr. 21017, nr. 550, f. 34. Kreditakte, Leipzig, den 6.07.1927.
18 Youssef Cassis, *City Bankers, 1890–1914*, 37.
19 StA-L, Dresdner Bank in Leipzig 21018, nr. 268. Eitingon Konzern (Vertraulich). 11.11.1929.
20 StA-L, Deutsche Bank, Filiale Leipzig, nr. 21017, nr. 309, Deutsche Bank, Berlin an Deutsche Bank Filiale Leipzig, 7.04.1927.
21 StA-L, Deutsche Bank, Filiale Leipzig, 21017, nr. 386, f. 14. Kölner. Leipzig, den 6.01.1926.
22 StA-L, Deutsche Bank, Filiale Leipzig, 21017, nr. 339, f. 18. Semi Goldstaub Leipzig, den 17.03.1927.
23 StA-L, Deutsche Bank, Filiale Leipzig 21017, nr. 339, f. 25. Semi Goldstaub, Leipzig, den 04.10.1929.
24 StA-L, Deutsche Bank in Leipzig 21017, nr. 309. Filialbüro, an Konsul Eugen Naumann, Direktor der Deutschen Bank Filiale Leipzig, 21.02.1922.
25 Gall, *Die Deutsche Bank, 1870–1995*, 231.
26 Pohl and Raab-Rebentisch, *Die Deutsche Bank in Leipzig*, 52.
27 StA-L, Deutsche Bank, Filiale Leipzig 21017, nr. 309. Eitingon Schild & Co Inc. New York. 11.02.1922.
28 StA-L, Deutsche Bank in Leipzig 21017, nr. 309. Deutsche Bank Filiale Leipzig an Deutsche Bank Filialbüro, Berlin. 05.06.1920.
29 StA-L, Deutsche Bank, Filiale Leipzig 21017, nr. 258, f. 39.
30 StA-L, Dresdner Bank in Leipzig 21018, nr. 44, f. 426. Leopold Apfel, Leipzig, Rauchwaren.
31 StA-L, Dresdner Bank in Leizpig, 21018, nr. 44, f. 447. Ephraim Kirschner, Leipzig.
32 StA-L, Dresdner Bank in Leipzig, 21018, nr. 44, f. 463, Wachtel & Eskreis, Leipzig, Rauchwaren. s.d.
33 StA-L, Dresdner Bank in Leipzig 21018, nr. 44, f. 433. David Chardack, Leipzig Rauchwaren.
34 Sta-L, Deutsche Bank, Filiale Leipzig Leipzig, nr. 207, f. 168. Leipzig, den. 10.08.1927.
35 StAL, Deutsche Bank Filiale Leipzig 21017, nr. 279. Deutsche Bank Berlin an Deutsche Bank, Filiale Leipzig. s;d.
36 BArch, Reichswirtschaftsministerium R 3101, nr. 3638, f. 142.
37 BArch, Reichswirtschaftsministerium R 3101, nr. 3639. Theodor Thorer an das Reichswirtschaftsministerium, 29.12.1921.
38 Pohl, *Die Finanzierung der Russengeschäfte zwischen den beiden Weltkriegen*, 14–15.
39 Rauchwaren: UdSSR Export. Handelsvertretung der UdSSR in Deutschland. Informationsabteilung, Berlin 1927. p. 2.
40 Peter, *Russen in Leipzig*, 66.

41 BArch, Reichswirtschaftsministerium R 3101, nr. 3637. Die deutsche Rauch-warenbranche in Oktober 1921;
42 BArch, Reichswirtschaftsministerium R 3101, nr. 3638, f. 142.
43 Tierhaarverwertung Mucrena AG. Abteilung Rauchwaren, p. 224.
44 StA-L, Dresdner Bank in Leipzig 21018, nr. 305. Zeichnungslist zur Gründung der Rauchwaren Lagerhaus GmbH, s.d. 1923.
45 Ray, *The Canadian Fur Trade in the Industrial Age*, 100.
46 StA-L, Dresdner Bank in Leipzig 21018, nr. 305. Rauchwarenlagerhaus AG, In the Aufsichtsrat of this auction company: Friedrich Erler & Co, M. Bromberg & Co, Eisenbach & Stern, Fein & Co, Gaudig & Blum, and Theodor Thorer.
47 StA-L, Dresdner Bank in Leipzig 21018, nr. 426. Auskunftei W. Schimmelpfeng, Rauchwarenversteigerungs AG, Leipzig, 23.06.1929.
48 StA-L, Dresdner Bank in Leipzig 21018, nr. 426. Dresdner Bank an die Direktion der Dresdner Bank 16.03.1929.
49 Ibid.
50 StA-L, Commerzbank 21016, nr. 411. Betrifft; RAVAG, Berlin. 1.2.1923.
51 Die Kürschnerzeitung, nr. 20, 11.07.1929. pp. 707–8. Eine stille Auktion. Bilder von einer Rauchwarenversteigerung in Leipzig.
52 Ibid.
53 StA-L, Commerzbank in Leipzig 21016, nr. 411 Commerzbank an die Direktion Berlin. 19.1.1923.
54 StA-L, Dresdner Bank in Leipzig, nr. 305. Rauchwarenlagerhaus GmbH, Leipzig, den 27.09.1923. Before 1926 it was known as the Rauchwarenlagerhaus GmbH.
55 Kowalzik, *Jüdisches Erwerbsleben in der inneren Nordvorstadt Leipzigs 1900–1933*, 10.
56 Malbin, *Der internationale rauchwarenhandel vor und nach dem Weltkriege unter besonderer berücksichtigung Leipzigs.*, 28.
57 StA-L, Dresdner Bank in Leipzig 21018, nr. 305. Versteigerung russischer Rauch-waren. 27.09.1923.
58 Die Kürschnerzeitung, nr. 20, 11.07.1929. pp. 707–8. Bilder von einer Rauch-warenversteigerung in Leipzig.
59 StA-L, Commerzbank 21016, nr. 58 and nr. 413: "Geschäftsberichte".
60 StA-L, Dresdner Bank in Leipzig, 21018, nr. 426. Dresdner Bank and die Direk-tion der Dresdner Bank in Leipzig, 14.03.1929.
61 StA-L, Deutsche Bank 21017, nr. 426. Dresdner Bank an die Direktion der Dres-dner Bank, Berlin. 16.03.1929.
62 StA-L, Commerzbank 21016, nr. 411. Generalversammlung RAVAG,16.04.1928.
63 StA-L, Dresdner Bank in Leipzig 21018, nr. 426, Direktion der Dresdner Bank an Dresdner Bank in Leipzig. 18.03.1923.
64 Gross, "Selling Germany in South-Eastern Europe," 29.
65 Leiske, *Leipzig und Mitteldeutschland*, 306.
66 StA-L, Dresdner Bank in Leipzig 21018, nr. 426, Dresdner Bank in Leipzig an die Direktion der Dresdener Bank Berlin. 01.08.1928.
67 StA-L, Commerzbank 21016, RAVAG. 18.07.1928.
68 Fellmann, *Der Leipziger Brühl*, 116.
69 The Times, "Arcos Raided. Offices Seized by the Police. Thorough Search for Documents". 13.05.1927.
70 The Times, "Arcos Raid and Soviet Protest". 14.05.1927.
71 *Vneshnyaya torgovlya CCCP za 1918–1940 gg.* (Statisticheskiy obzor), chast 1, 2, 3.
72 StA-L, Dresdner Bank in Leipzig 21018, nr. 73, f. 2. Kreditantrag Leipzig den 19.10.1926.
73 Niemann, "Die Russengeschäfte in Der Ära Brüning," 154.

74 StA-L, Dresdner Bank in Leipzig, nr. 73, ff. 6–7. Kreditantrag Leipzig den 19.10.1926.
75 Die Kürschnerzeitung, nr. 26, 11.11.1927. p. 940. Die Bedeutung der Leipziger Russen-Auktion.
76 StA-L, Dresdner Bank in Leipzig 21018, Dresdner Bank in Leipzig an die Direktion der Dresdner Bank Berlin, 14.04.1927.
77 StA-L, Dresdner Bank in Leipzig, nr. 75, Die Dresdner Bank in Leizpig an die Direktion der Dresdner Bank, 27.10.1928.
78 StA-L, Dresdner Bank in Leipzig, nr. 73, ff. 6–7. Kreditantrag Leipzig den 19.10.1926. From the National Bank of Comerce, the Dresdner Bank in Leipzig in practice used $68,000; the Dresnder Bank's withdrawal from the credit of the head office never exceeded the sum of $1,560,000.
79 StA-L, Dresdner Bank in Leipzig 21018, nr. 79, Dresdner Bank in Leipzig an Proehl &Gutmann, Amsterdam, 12.10.1928.
80 Kürschnerzeitung, nr. 26, 11.09.1927. Die Bedeutung der Leipziger Russen-Auktion.
81 Sächs. HStA, Aussenministerium 10717, nr. 6772, Abschrift. Reichsverband der Deutschen Rauchwaren-firmen 08.11.1927.
82 StA-L, Dresdner Bank in Leipzig 21018, nr. 79, f. 213. Russische Rauchwarenauktion in Leipzig. Frkt. Zt. 29.3.1929.
83 StA-L, Dresdner Bank in Leipzig 21018, nr. 79, f. 69.
84 Statistisches Jahrbuch Sachsen, issue 1929 (p. 164), issue 1930 (p. 156).
85 StA-L Dresdner Bank in Leipzig 21018, nr. 305.
86 StA-L, Dresdner Bank in Leipzig, nr. 79, f. 93. Auszug Leipziger Neueste Nachrichten, 7.3.1928.
87 Statistisches Jahrbuch für das Deutsches Reich, years: 1924; 1926; 1928; 1930. Teile: Auswärtiger handel.
88 TNA, HBCA (Microfilm Copy). Public Record Office, (BH 3453), A 93.37. Lectures on the Fur Trade. Delivered at the City of London college, p. 93.
89 Die Kürschnerzeitung, 1926, Nr. 9. Leipzig, 21.03.1926. Über die Errichtung von Rauchwarenauktionen in Leningrad.
90 StA-L, Dresdner Bank in Leipzig 21018, Nr. 79, p. 240. Leipziger Neueste Nachrichten, 14.6.1929.
91 Kürschnerzeitung, 1926, nr. 13. Leipzig, 01.05.1926. s. 481.
92 Boch, "The Rise and Decline of Flexible Production: The Cutlery Industry of Solingen since the Eighteenth Century," 176–7.
93 Tavoletti and te Velde, "Cutting Porter's Last Diamond," 308.

References

Balderston, Theo. "German Banking Between the Wars: The Crisis of the Credit Banks." *The Business History Review* 65, no. 3 (1991): 554–605.
Boch, Rudolf. "The Rise and Decline of Flexible Production: The Cutlery Industry of Solingen Since the Eighteenth Century." In *Worlds of possibilities. Flexibility and mass production in western industrialization*, edited by Jonathan Zeitlin and Charles Sabel, 153–88. Cambridge, UK: Cambridge University Press, 1997.
Boelcke, Willi A. *Deutschland als Welthandelsmacht: 1930–1945.* Stuttgart: W. Kohlhammer, 1994.
Cassis, Youssef. *City Bankers, 1890–1914.* Cambridge, UK: Cambridge University Press, 1994.
Fellmann, Walter. *Der Leipziger Brühl: Geschichte und Geschichten des Rauchwarenhandels.* Leipzig: VEB Fachbuchverl., 1989.

———. "Schlaufüchse und Blaufüchse vom Brühl." In *Leipzigs Messen: 1497–1997: Gestaltwandel-Umbrüche-Neubeginn*, edited by Berit Bass, Annett Hietzke, and Hartmut Zwahr, 439–51. Köln: Böhlau Verlag, 1999.

Gall, Lothar, ed. *Die Deutsche Bank, 1870–1995*. München: C. H. Beck, 1995.

Gross, Stephen. "Selling Germany in South-Eastern Europe: Economic Uncertainty, Commercial Information and the Leipzig Trade Fair 1920–40." *Contemporary European History* 21, no. 1 (2012): 19–39.

James, Harold. "The 1931 Central European Banking Crisis Revisited." In *Business in the Age of Extremes: Essays in Modern German and Austrian Economic History*, edited by Hartmut Berghoff, Jürgen Kocka, and Dieter Ziegler, 119–33. Cambridge, UK: Cambridge University Press, 2013.

Kowalzik, Barbara. *Jüdisches Erwerbsleben in der inneren Nordvorstadt Leipzigs 1900–1933*. Leipzig: Leipziger Universitätsverlag, 1999.

Leiske, Walter. *Leipzig und Mitteldeutschland: Denkschrift für Rat und Stadtverordnete zu Leipzig*. Leipzig: Ratsverkehrsamt, 1928.

Malbin, Max. *Der internationale rauchwarenhandel vor und nach dem Weltkriege unter besonderer berücksichtigung Leipzigs*. Oschatz: F. Oldecops erben (C. Morgner), 1927.

Niemann, Hans-Werner. "Die Russengeschäfte in der Ära Brüning." *VSWG: Vierteljahrschrift Für Sozial- Und Wirtschaftsgeschichte* 72, no. 2 (January 1, 1985): 153–74.

Peter, Grażyna-Maria. *Russen in Leipzig: damals, heute*. Leipzig: Europa-Haus, 2003.

Pohl, Manfred. *Die Finanzierung der Russengeschäfte zwischen den beiden Weltkriegen: d. Entwicklung d. 12 grossen Russlandkonsortien*. Frankfurt am Main: Knapp, 1975.

Pohl, Manfred, and Angelika Raab-Rebentisch. *Die Deutsche Bank in Leipzig: 1901–2001*. München: Piper, 2001.

Ray, Arthur J. *The Canadian Fur Trade in the Industrial Age*. Toronto: University of Toronto Press, 1990.

Roberts, Richard. *Schroders: Merchants & Bankers*. Basingstoke: Macmillan, 1992.

Simpson, Christopher, and Germany (Territory under Allied occupation, 1945–1955 : U.S. Zone) Office of Military Government. *War Crimes of the Deutsche Bank and the Dresdner Bank: Office of Military Government (U.S.) Reports*. New York: Holmes & Meier, 2002.

Tavoletti, Ernesto, and Robbin te Velde. "Cutting Porter's Last Diamond: Competitive and Comparative (Dis)advantages in the Dutch Flower Cluster." *Transition Studies Review* 15, no. 2 (2008): 303–19.

9 Promoting the Capital

The Leipzig International Fur Exhibition and Congress in 1930

Introduction

In the long and rainy summer of 1930, the International Fur Trade Exhibition (*Internationale Pelzfach Ausstellung*; IPA hereafter). The IPA was one of the last international trade exhibitions of its kind to be held in Saxony and it specifically aimed to promote the Leipzig fur industry both at home and abroad. It appealed to the broader masses as well as international businessmen and experts. Almost 800,000 visitors headed to the fur exhibition, paying for a 1 RM ticket that allowed them to visit the "educational trade exhibition" and its related festivities. The exhibition was truly international as well: more than 11 exhibit stands of various countries were to be found in the exhibition halls, including ones from fur centres like the United States, Great Britain, and the Soviet Union. Important multinationals like the Hudson's Bay Company had stands at the exhibition. On the sidelines, the International Fur Congress was held, which aimed to set up a federation to regulate the conduct of international business. The IPA was arguably the largest national and international promotion campaign the Leipzig industry ever held.

The IPA was part of the venerable tradition of German, and particularly Saxon, exhibition culture. German exhibition culture centred on organising moderately sized trade exhibitions. Trade exhibitions are either universal, putting the entire regional industry in the spotlight, or specialised, highlighting one particular sector (*Fachausstellung*). Trade exhibitions were popular in Saxony too, the first one being held as early as 1824. Whereas universal exhibitions dominated exhibition culture at first, specialised trade exhibitions in Saxony gradually gained the upper hand. These exhibitions have chiefly been analysed from an 'internal' perspective, as instruments to support Saxony's early industrialisation and as institutions that helped form Saxon particularism on a material level by exhibiting the products and practices that typified the region. Exhibitions were analysed as a stage for "Saxon quality" and "as a form of communication to regional customers by giving a clear overview of the range of products made in Saxony."[1] The role of exhibitions as drivers of regionalised consumption patterns have somewhat overshadowed the international dimension of such events. Hochmuth has acknowledged the importance of the international function of Saxon exhibitions, which originated from "the pressure to defend regional markets with competitive products against imports as well as finding international outlet markets for local products."[2] Kiesewetter noted that exhibitions were necessary instrument for business in Saxony: "The export-oriented industries have to compete on international markets . . . exhibitions were therefore necessary to open new ways for technology transfers and communication."[3] Thus, the international context was an important dimension in staging Saxon exhibitions, both for international marketing and as ways to diffuse new technologies and products.

Furthermore, the exhibitions in Saxony increasingly gained a transregional dimension because of their size. This was an important aspect in the 1897 universal *Thüringisch-sächsische Industrie und Gewerbe Ausstellung* in Leipzig, which assembled 3,500 exhibits and attracted 2,300,000 visitors.[4] The universal exhibition of 1897 served to underline the importance of Leipzig as a mercantile and industrial centre of central Germany.[5] However, this was the last universal exhibition that took place in the city; after this, specialised exhibitions dominated the scene in Leipzig. In 1913, the International Construction Exhibition (IBA or *Internationale Bau-Ausstellung*) took place, assembling the main actors of the German construction industry and attracting an enormous crowd of four million visitors. Industrial districts in Leipzig made use of the specialised trade exhibition for promotional and marketing purposes. In 1914, the BUGRA (*Internationale Ausstellung für Buchgewerbe und Graphik*) represented the book-printing industry, the other major industry clustered in the city of Leipzig; it was organised by the Leipzig Book Printing Assocation (*Buchgewerbe Verein*). Importantly, the book-printing exhibition was used to promote the city of Leipzig as both a national and international centre of the printing industry. Its appeals to internationalism were in the cultural ("book-printing as a binding cultural force") as well as the economic sphere ("by illustrating the importance of Leipzig as leading world centre in book-printing").[6] The pre-war exhibitions set useful examples and a high standard for their neighbours in the fur industry.

The 1930 IPA was thus part of a venerable tradition of Saxon exhibition culture that increasingly shifted from supporting regional economic development to international promotion and self-fashioning. The exhibition will be analysed from local and international perspectives. Firstly, exhibitions allow us to gain a deeper insight into the local social structure that organises them. Alexander Geppert noted that "exhibitions are considered historical gadgets . . . under which it is possible to gain immediate insights into societies as they represent and regard themselves."[7] Due to high investment costs, exhibitions were usually the result of collaborative efforts between local economic agents and the public authorities. Therefore, exhibitions are an important part of my claim that transregional links in the industrial district resulted from local collective action. By analysing the organisation of the IPA, we are provided a window into the organisation of local networks in the industrial district and processes of collective action. Secondly, the exhibition will be analysed as an aspect of translocal connectivity, as a 'pipeline' to the wider world. I will make the case that the IPA suited Leipzig businessmen's strategies 'to restore the position of Leipzig' within the international fur trade. Exhibitions were a useful form of advertising in that regard. Rather than selling and conducting trade, exhibitions had a magnet function, drawing attention to the sector and attracting people from great distances. This magnet function and its usefulness for constructing translocal connections is one of the principal reasons why firms organise exhibitions.[8] In sum, the IPA exhibition allows us to link localised processes of cooperation in the district with the creation of connections to the outside world.

The Origins of the IPA (1926–1929) and Patterns of Local Collaboration

Domestic Origins, International Consequences

The purpose of this section is to situate the initial exposition plans within the social structure of the industrial district. The initial idea to stage a jointly organised exhibition was due to the fact that the Berlin fur industry entertained a similar plan. In October 1926, in a meeting in the city hall of Leipzig it was concluded that "everything must be put in to place in order to counter the plans for a Berlin fur exhibition. The Leipzig plans should illustrate that Leipzig is still the headquarters of the German fur industry. . . ."[9] However, the local fur trade's initial reception of the exhibition plans was lukewarm at best. The furriers and independent retailers in Leipzig, an important part of the district less concerned with internationalisation and whose economic interests differed greatly from the merchant houses on the Brühl, criticised the international concept of the IPA, fearing that it would draw attention to foreign products instead of the German fur industry. Especially galling was the prospect of competing with 'trend-setting' French fur producers.[10] Concern about the promotion of foreign fur production loomed until the beginning of exhibition itself. Only when the organisers finally prohibited selling at the stands and downplayed the commercial dimension of the exposition did the Leipzig furriers more keenly participate in the IPA. Scepticism was not confined to the furriers alone. The German fur trade was equally half-hearted about the IPA, despite the fact that they were arguably the 'objective' allies of the international exhibition. During one of the meetings of the Leipzig Fur Merchants Association in 1927, during which the leaders of the Association discussed the terms of the IPA, a majority of members predicted the failure of the ambitious exhibition.[11]

Despite resistance in the sector, several entrepreneurs were able to push the idea on the fur trading community. Again, the importance of lead firms as facilitators should be stressed. In the early stage of planning, the 'usual suspects' (firms like Theodor Thorer, Friedrich Erler, and Chaim Eitingon AG) played a large role. The lead firms were precisely those that had been involved in other forms of interfirm cooperation, like fur farming and the establishment of auction companies. Members of these firms occupied high positions in the trade associations. Moreover, the organisation of the IPA furthered the ascent of Paul Hollender as the Leipzig fur industry's leading man. Hollender was the president of the Leipzig Fur Merchants Association and was later appointed to be president of the IPA organisation committee. Walter Krausse, a manager of the Friedrich Erler firm, held the position of vice-president.[12] At least in the initial stages, the organisation of the IPA depended on figures in leading firms. However, the organisation expanded quickly. As the idea of the IPA further matured, organisational subcommittees were filled with representatives of the dyeing and dressing industry, furriers, and university scientists (like Hans Nachtsheim).[13] Thus, once a block of lead firms had overcome initial resistance, the IPA organisation came to resemble a microcosm of this local production system.

While domestic concerns and rivalry with Berlin dominated the initial discussions of the IPA's organisation, the ambitions of the organisers soon expanded. It was emphasised that the IPA should not only symbolise Leipzig as the domestic centre of the fur industry, but also support Leipzig's return to the world stage. The IPA committee described the basic rationale underlying the IPA, which stressed the international dimension: "The IPA should not be a vain reflection of our activities, but an advertisement for labour and a support of our world economic interests."[14] The overarching aim was "the propagation of Leipzig as one of the leading European fur metropolises . . . and to regain the position of Leipzig as a centre of the fur trade that was lost after World War I."[15] This aim formed the foundation for local cooperation between economic agents of all segments of the industrial district: the fur trade, the industry, furriers, and experts on fur farming. Since selling was forbidden, it was believed that the exhibition would generate benefits for the local industry in an invisible yet valuable way. Instead of direct commercial gain generated by a traditional trade fair, "a successful exhibition will strengthen the national as well as the world economic position of the fur industry in Leipzig and will reverse the negative post-war trade cycle."[16]

In the pursuit of past glory, the exhibition had to take place on the location that housed the modern trade fairs and the grand pre-war exhibitions, the 'old fair grounds' (*Alte Messegelande*). This urban space between the National Library and the Monument to the Battle of the Nations (*Völkerslachtdenkmal*) was constructed for the occasion of the first large-scale specialised trade exhibition of the IBA, a mass event which welcomed 4,000,000 visitors. The IPA committee and the city council made explicit references to the IBA and BUGRA exhibitions held in this new civic locale.[17] Since 1920, the infrastructure hosted the Leipzig trade fairs, which it continued to do well into the late 1990s. The IPA was to be held at the same location.

In the Pursuit of Past Glory: The IPA and Local Collaboration

The goal of 'international revival' was widely accepted as the underlying aim of the exhibition. Such a goal had been the foundation of earlier projects of local cooperation between firms and other local actors. The exhibition as a 'pipeline' to the wider world became one of the most broadly and clearly supported events in post-war Leipzig. Public figures, both in the city council and the Saxon government, played leading roles in the IPA committee, its organisation, and financial issues. Most important were Walter Leiske in his capacity as head of the Leipzig Traffic Office (*Leipziger Verkehrsamt*) and Dr. Klien, the director of Saxony's Ministry of Economic Affairs (*Sächsisches Wirtschaftsministerium*). Leiske devoted his career to regional economic planning at a time when this discipline was still underdeveloped. After his appointment as director of the Traffic Office in 1926, Leiske developed ideas to redefine the region of Saxony as part of a new economic geography, middle Germany (*Mitteldeutschland*), with Leipzig as the central commercial node.[18] Leiske published his thoughts on propelling the economy of Leipzig in his influential publication series *Leipziger Verkehr und Verkehrspolitik*.[19] In 1928, he released a seminal memorandum entitled "Leipzig and Middle-Germany," in which he proposed to redefine the internal borders of Germany with a strong "Middle-Germany" as its powerhouse. As such, Leiske saw the fur industry as a major regional asset and the IPA suited his scheme for stimulating regional economic activity. He therefore devoted a publication in his series on *Mitteldeutschland* to the IPA and its importance for local economic development at a relatively early stage in the planning.[20]

A more delicate matter was that of finance. The committee hoped to receive contributions from the various political levels in Weimar Germany: the governments in Berlin, Saxony, and the city of Leipzig. This was to be matched by a contribution from local economic agents in Leipzig. These included both the fur sector and the banks, whose involvement in the international business has been underlined before.[21] The first round of fundraising, an important test for the ambitions of the IPA committee, was held in the spring of 1929. Although the federal government refused to finance the exhibition, the IPA enlisted the support of local public authorities and economic actors. The city guaranteed bank loans in the sum of 250,000 RM on behalf of the IPA.[22] This decision was motivated by the following: "In the city's . . . economic policy, there will be close help to facilitate the recovery of the lost pre-war position of the important fur trade in Leipzig, which contributes to the labour market in the city and country, and because the inner forces of the industry have been set in motion during recent years to overcome the catastrophic setback of the war years."[23] In early 1930, when the exhibition committee seemed to have underestimated expenses, the city treasurer gave an additional security of 1,000,000 RM for new bank loans.[24] Following a similar kind of reasoning, the government of Saxony offered a guarantee for about 100,000 RM. This action was noteworthy because the Saxon government had normally refused to support new exhibitions since the early 1920s. Politicians in Dresden were willing to make an exception for "important locally concentrated industries like the book-printing and fur industries in Leipzig."[25] In addition, Klien emphasised the role that the fur trade played in the region's international standing: "The economic goal [of the exhibition] is to strengthen Leipzig's position in the world fur trade . . . because the value of the pre-war trade . . . has almost been reached again."[26]

This picture closely resembled precedents from other local exhibitions. Economic agents and political actors also jointly financed the BUGRA, the 1914 exhibition of the book printers in Leipzig. The contribution of public actors represented 40% of the 1,000,000 marks needed for this exhibition.[27] Local economic actors supplied the rest. In the case of the IPA, the contribution of private actors was slightly smaller than that of the city and the Saxon government. Banks and fur firms raised the sum of 250,000 RM. Participation in the IPA was affordable for all firms, since the amount of contributions apparently corresponded to the size of the business. Contributions never exceeded the sum of 10,000 RM, while smaller firms contributed between 1,000 and 5,000 RM on average. It was clearly intended to allow for as many firms as possible to make a contribution. This intention was realised: 58 firms transferred sums between 1,000 and 10,000 RM to the IPA committee. Judging from the high number of participants, the interest in the IPA had surged in comparison to the indifference in the initial stages of organisation.

Despite the large participation, the actual amount raised by the fur industry was still relatively modest when compared to that of public authorities. Moreover, firms funded only 75% of the 250,000 RM raised by private industry. Large firms adhered to the maximum contribution of 10,000 RM. Only three leading fur firms contributed the maximum sum: David Biedermann, Chaim Eitingon AG, and Thorer. Ariowitsch, one of the wealthiest fur businesses of the Bruhl, provided only 8,000 RM. Despite the presence of their man Krausse on the IPA committee, the company Friedrich Erler contributed a mere 5,000 RM, although its associated dyeing factory Stieglitz & Co paid an equal amount.[28] In contrast, the largest banks made a considerable contribution to the IPA budget of about 61,500 RM—25% of this sum came from the Commerzbank, Deutsche Bank, Darmstädter, and ADCA.[29] The Dresdner Bank donated 7,500 RM and several private banks gave smaller sums. As I have already mentioned, the banks had a large interest in the Leipzig fur trade. The financial makeup of the IPA was thus strongly corporatist and locally entrenched, divided between the state and many embedded economic actors.

The Search for International Partners

Once funding was secured, the collective marketing operation gradually outgrew its domestic dimension and increasingly turned more international.

Like rallying political and financial support locally, the task of assembling an international exhibition was not straightforward. The exhibition committee planned to draw attention to the Leipzig industry abroad, especially from the cities and countries that were the main potential trade partners: Great Britain (London), the US (New York), and the Soviet Union. The promotion campaign would only be effective if leading firms and trade departments in these countries participated at the IPA.

In its international endeavours, the Leipzig fur industry was supported by an important ally: the diplomatic services of the German Foreign Office. Stresemann, the minister of Foreign Affairs, was known for his pragmatic foreign policy: he realised that German economic power could only be restored by re-entering the world market.[30] Apart from supporting the return of German business to the world stage, Stresemann enjoyed good connections with the Saxon industry. Before he learnt the political craft, Stresemann worked for the chocolate manufacturing association in Dresden and was one of the founders of the Saxon Manufacturers Association in 1902 (*Verband Sächischer Industrieller VSI*).[31] In December 1928, Stresemann's Foreign Office listed the IPA as an "exhibition of national importance," which implied that the organisation could expect support from the diplomatic services.[32] In practice, this meant that invitations and information were distributed via diplomatic channels to foreign governments.

The promotion campaign in London, which started in the fall of 1928 when the exhibition plans were still vague, was based on two pillars: attracting attention in the British press and the lobbying of Paul Hollender. The British professional fur trade press played a leading role in introducing the idea of the IPA to London business community. As early as November 1928, the trade journal *The British Fur Trade* published an interview with some eminent managers in Leipzig and the plans of the IPA. The article downplayed the importance of the exhibition for Leipzig whilst highlighting its international dimension: "And let me emphasise this, that it is not a German, or a Saxon or a Leipzig exhibition and Congress which is being prepared and on which we count; it is an international event, in which we hope to see the British Empire, the United States, France, Russia and Austria taking as prominent and credible a part as the German trade itself."[33]

The second reason for the IPA's early successes in Great Britain can be ascribed to the individual lobbying of Paul Hollender. Hollender pursued the agenda of the IPA through 'trade diplomacy,' which involved attending banquets, delivering speeches, and negotiating. In November 1928, he was invited to the banquet of the London Fur Trade Association and delivered a speech illuminating his plans to organise a large-scale international exhibition. The moment was well chosen, as several international guests were present at the autumn fur auctions that preceded the banquet.[34] Although mention was made of the success of Hollender's stay in London, it is difficult to estimate the impact of this kind of diplomacy. To be sure, it did not raise unequivocal support for the IPA. In March 1929, there was resistance among British firm managers convinced that participation in the exhibition would favour their competitors in Saxony.[35] Moreover, the British government refused to accept the official invitation sent by the German ambassador in April 1929. Participation was thereby restricted to the private British fur trade and industry.[36] Fortunately for Hollender, the Hudson's Bay Company decided to participate in the Leipzig exhibition. By January 1930, the HBC had reserved about 900 of the available 3,000 square metres of exhibition space.[37]

The IPA committee largely followed the same set of strategies to lure the Americans to Leipzig: a promotion campaign in the specialised trade press, diplomatic invitations, and a lobbying tour by Hollender, the face of Leipzig's fur industry. A month after his stay in England, Hollender travelled to North America and visited Washington, Chicago, Toronto, and Montreal. He promoted the IPA most intensively in New York by unfolding the detailed plans of the IPA at a luncheon of the Fur Merchants Club.[38] American dyers and wholesalers were particularly interested; they instantly decided to found an American IPA committee. However, American participation was made possible because of the powerful family networks between Leipzig and New York, most notably those embodied by the Eitingon family. Motty Eitingon, leader of the successful Eitingon-Schild Corporation in New York and a regular visitor in Leizpig, was the president of the American IPA section. He promptly reserved 5,000 square metres of the IPA exposition on behalf of the American committee at his own personal risk.[39]

An important difference from Great Britain was the official support of the American government for the IPA. The US Department of Agriculture argued that the IPA offered an unique opportunity to promote the booming American fur business: "The taking of a substantial part of American fur-products by the European market as represented by the valuation of $31,000,000 placed upon our fur exports, is to the advantage of the American farmer and a Government exhibit at the Leipzig exhibition would without question aid in the further development of this export trade."[40] Another motivation for participation could be found in the activities of the Department of Agriculture itself. It heavily supported the growth of fur farming as a new agricultural activity: "The Secretary of Agriculture states further that foreign countries look upon the US Department of Agriculture as a pioneer in the field of investigational work in fur-animal production."[41] The participation of the US Department of Agriculture gave an important impetus to the international dimension of the IPA.

The Soviet Union confirmed its participation in the exposition relatively late, less than a year before the IPA started. Attempts to lure the Soviets to the Leipzig halls looked less persuasive when compared to the diplomatic courtesies extended to representatives in England and North America. Nonetheless, the Soviets responded eagerly and were preparing a section far ahead of other "fur nations."[42] The Soviet zeal in participating at the IPA can be explained from their unfavourable position on the world market.

Firstly, Soviet trade agencies often found themselves excluded from international business agreements. Moreover, Soviet sales representatives were often manifestly distrusted as secret agents of some sort, as was illustrated by the raid of Scotland Yard on ARCOS in May 1927 (see Chapter 8). The Soviet fur trade certainly needed some international advertisement. Secondly, participation in the IPA was necessary because of the strategic importance of furs. Narkomtorg, a Soviet trade secretariat, noted that "the fur trade occupies a vast dimension of our economy and in our international trade. Therefore, expectations for the Soviet section at the exhibition is apparently high . . . and we must be careful that we do not disappoint these expectations: [we must] prepare our exhibition in time and reveal an extensive picture of our fur industry so that we take a prominent and honourable place at the exhibition."[43] Together with the involvement of the US, the Soviet interest expanded the international cachet of the IPA, even though the British and Canadian governments had refused to participate. The goals set by the Germans regarding the international dimensions of the IPA thereby found a sufficient degree of foreign support. It is important to note that many other countries participated as well. Symbolic for the German fur trade, especially for karakul trading, was the participation of mandate South West Africa. Countries like Austria, Poland, Sweden, Denmark, and Finland also confirmed their participation.[44]

Photograph 9.1 The South West African Exhibition at the IPA Next to the Polish Stall (1930). Reproduced with the permission of the Stadtarchiv Leipzig. (Stadtarchiv Leipzig, BA 1986, 20741).

The IPA: Between Specialisation and Universalism

This part of the chapter is devoted to the actual content of the exhibition. The organisation of the IPA was based on two main pillars. On the one hand, it made reference to the successful pre-war exhibitions in Leipzig, the BUGRA and IBA, which had set high standards as prestigious crowd-pullers. On the other hand, the exhibition was essentially international and aimed to promote Leipzig as an international centre in the commerce, production, and distribution of furs. The public of this promotion campaign was traders, experts, and businessmen in Germany and the wider world. Through the connected fur congress held in Leipzig, the IPA committee hoped to institutionalise an international community of fur businessmen that could collectively deal with problems that pertained to the organisation of the trade. The ultimate aim was that the IPA should become a starting point for a stabilised international fur business. The end result was an exhibition that focused both on advertising furs to the broader public and on the educational aims of a specialised trade exhibition. This dualism was noted in one of meetings of the IPA committee in 1929: "Although the IPA has to be tailored for the big masses, the exhibits have to show what is both fine and rare so that the specialised character of the exhibition is preserved."[45]

The IPA as a Crowd-Puller

On 31 May 1930, the IPA officially opened. The 800,000 visitors during the summer found an exhibition space that was divided into five large sections: a general hunting exhibition, the German Hall, the Nation Hall, the Science and Technology Halls, and the Amusement Park. Central to the IPA was the Nation Hall, where exhibits could be seen from 11 foreign countries. Great Britain (900 square metres), France (1,000 square metres), and the USSR (2,000 square metres) ranked amongst the most visible foreign exhibits. The Austrians had created a separate section, the "Wiener Haus."[46] However, this classic exhibition format was held to be insufficient to attract the broader masses. Just as during the universal exhibition of 1897 and the IBA exhibition of 1913 in Leipzig, the IPA also built an 'amusement park,' designed to be a pure crowd-puller. The centre of the amusement park was the swimming pool but it also possessed a wine bar with music and cabaret acts and a genuine Wiener cafe.[47] The IPA also involved other media in order to advertise to the wider public. Notable was the promotion film created by the Leipziger Werk und Werbefilm GmbH. The 72-minute long film was called "Fur's Worldwide Importance" (*"Die weltumspannende Bedeutung des Pelzes"*) and was translated into 12 languages. It formed the backbone of the IPA mass advertising campaign, as it was broadcasted across various European cinemas.[48]

The advertisement of fur work to the broader public not only followed the examples of the preceding local exhibitions as crowd-pullers but also reflected major societal trends. In the first place, mass production in recent decades had co-evolved with patterns of mass consumption. During the First World War, the industry experimented with the production of garments based on 'substandard' fur and new production processes that enabled the imitation of prime furs. These substitutes expanded existing consumption patterns. Whereas previously access to furs was limited to the bourgeoisie, the consumption of fur garments increasingly expanded to lower ranks of society, especially during the second half of the 1920s. The IPA's appeal to the larger public can thus also be read as a consequence of growing fur consumption throughout the 1920s. During the Weimar Republic, the consumer was increasingly identified as a relevant actor and consumerism was recognised as an underlying force both in business and politics.[49] It was this redefinition of luxury consumption and the emergence of Weimar Germany as a consumer society that pushed the fur industry into advertising to a larger public. As the committee noted, "The IPA entails large-scale propaganda for fur. The public, which nowadays can only be convinced by sizeable advertisement, should be drawn to the beauty and importance of fur, thereby causing a massive uplift of consumption."[50]

In general, however, European luxury industries struggled to adjust themselves to such new consumption patterns. Simply put, mass consumption and luxury production were conflicting trends. According to Jean-Claude Daumas, mass consumption patterns offered increased sales opportunities but also put pressure on the status of industries within 'the universe of luxury' that justified higher prices and the use of labour intensive production processes.[51] This trend was all the more complicated for the German fur industry because of the controversial status of luxury products in Weimar Germany. The experience of destitution during World War I and hyperinflation had made German consumers highly sensitive to the availability and price of consumer goods. Consumerism in Weimar Germany was characterised by high expectations and the desire to improve living standards while at the same time the population was traumatised by the fact that basic needs remained unfulfilled.[52] Luxury thus had negative connotations. Politics also increasingly intervened in consumption, making basic needs accessible while at the same time targeting the consumption of luxury goods through taxes. This tension in the promotion of fur consumption is revealed by the fact that the IPA consciously avoided association between the fur industry and luxury: "The goal of the IPA is to explain to the domestic public about fur fashion, which is by no means 'luxurious,' but [consists of] solid, durable, and well-made pelts that are beneficial and economical in the long run."[53]

A Specialised Exhibition?

Having discussed the areas designed for the public spectator, I will now turn to some specialised sections presented for a more select, and international, public. The Nation Hall, the German Hall, and the Halls for Science and

Technology formed the main chunk of the exhibition reserved for those interested in the advancements of the fur industry. These sections were created by a number of specialised committees consisting of industrialists and experts. These reveal some of the developments in the modern fur industry that had defined collective action in the district.[54] The group responsible for the section on fur farming was made up of members of the *Reichszentrale für Pelztier und Rauchwarenforschung*, the research network in Leipzig.[55] The *Deutschlandhalle* demonstrated the organisation of fur farming in Germany and the investigations into it sponsored by the industry.

The science and engineering section in Hall 4 showcased a dressing and dyeing plant in operation and was organised by industrialists and chemists. Covering about 200 square metres, it showcased a production process that turned raw pelts into processed furs ready to be sent to tailors and retailers. While the imitation plant was at the centre of this hall, individual firms from the dressing and dyeing industries occupied stands as well.[56] As the backbone of the industrial district, the fur production process was adequately represented at the exhibition. The German Hall similarly devoted attention to the complicated nature of production. This general overview of production stages not only served to inform the larger public or to glorify the skilfulness of the German dyeing and dressing factories. According to a report of the Hudson's Bay Company, several aspects of this exhibit achieved their educational purpose by anticipating future developments of the international fur trade, especially in terms of reducing the prices of more luxurious furs and garments: "The German fur trade acted wisely in showing their skilfulness in processing furs . . . the much improved imitations may be having an influence in reducing the price of the fine furs, since to the unpractised eye the imitations are so good that the great [price] difference between them and the real article seems unjustifiable."[57] Other exhibits in this hall were staged to glorify the history and future of the German fur industry. The committee had given sufficient space to the German furriers guild to present a somewhat pompous glorification of German craftsmanship (*Meistersaal*, *Kürschnersaal*), exhibiting pieces of art and historical objects related to German fur work.[58]

Although little is known about the substance of the international exhibits, the impressive Soviet stall was an eye-catcher for contemporary observers. It was composed to impress the general public while at the same time portraying the new organisation of foreign fur trade and the advancement of the USSR's dyeing industry. The Soviet section impressed visitors because of architectural experimentation with the stall's setup. Soviet architects made use of 'futuristic' designs, thereby rendering the Soviet section one of the most surprising and intense parts of the exhibition. A German observer noted that "the Soviet exhibition sets the objects as functions of the form. The Soviets are using the exhibition space to the fullest extent, both in terms of height and breadth . . . the stance exhibits many thousands of raw bundled skins to attract attention . . . the Soviets have designed artefacts that extend to the roof."[59] For many attendees, the exhibition also offered a unique opportunity to gain insight into the current situation of the Soviet fur industry. The exhibition allowed the capitalist businessmen to gather information about the system of the state-led fur exploitation in Siberia. The Hudson's Bay Company noted the following: "When carefully examined [the Soviet exhibition] is of great interest, especially as so little is actually known in the outside world of what is going on in Russia . . . if the facts shown are accurate . . . the organisation now in existence for collecting the furs is very much larger and better than before the revolution."[60] The specialised exhibition was thus valued both for the information it provided on new production techniques and for the knowledge given about international markets.

The IPA Congresses and Internationalism

The congresses held in the margins of the IPA were at least as important in promoting international trade as the exhibition itself. The congresses gave the IPA an important transnational dimension. Three congresses were organised: the most important was the general assembly held by international fur businessmen and industrialists, the "World Fur Congress." The Leipzig organisers hoped to construct a more stable international system of

Photograph 9.2 The Exhibition Stall of the USSR at the IPA (1930). Reproduced
with the permission of the Stadtarchiv Leipzig. (Stadtarchiv Leipzig,
BA 1986 20745).

trade by taking advantage of the presence of many foreign delegates and businessmen. There were also meetings of the International Garment Workers' Federation (*Internationale Bekleidungsarbeiter Föderation*) and of the International Rabbit Breeders Congress (*Internationale Käninchenzüchter Kongress*). Debates in the garment workers' congress, held between 15 and 17 June, mainly centred on the stimulation of labour exchange across national markets and the prevention of occupational diseases. Fur workers were often exposed to lungs and skin diseases caused by the chemical substances used in the manufacturing process.[61] The conference of German rabbit breeders, suppliers to the fur industry since World War I, was organised by Hans Nachtsheim. Nachtsheim was an ardent advocate of small-scale animal breeding and co-founder of the National Association of German Rabbit Breeders (*Reichsbund Deutscher Kaninchenzüchter*). The international guests conferred about animal diseases, the economic exploitation of rabbit breeding, and on the diet of rabbits.[62] In contrast to other small livestock keepers, the rabbit breeders had national divisions but lacked an international form of organisation.

The World Fur Congress was undoubtedly the most important conference. It was a historical congress too. Never before had businessmen of the international fur industry conferred together about issues that related to the global fur trade. The World Fur Congress was arguably the culmination point of a spirit of internationalism in the realm of business that surfaced more strongly in the interwar period. In contrast, prior to World War I problems in international trade had caused conflicts between German and British merchants, especially regarding conflicting fairs and auctions. However, there was now support for international coordination.

For example, collisions between events in the industry calendar continued to have an effect on relations between businesses in London and Leipzig. In the plans for the 1928 season, the spring auctions in London and the Easter fur fairs in Leipzig once again largely overlapped. Instead of a boycott and mutual threats, the problem of colliding agendas now led to bilateral negotiations. They took place between the Leipzig Fur Merchants Association and the London Fur Trade Association. Trade associations had gained significance in both cities in the early 1920s. Besides remedying local issues, these institutions were the principal channels for conducting international negotiations. The Leipzig representatives were able to find a compromise that involved postponing the Leipzig fur fairs for a week.[63] However, the compromise was rejected by other Leipzig firms. Despite the failure of international coordination in this specific case, a tradition of international coordination was in the making. It was in this context that the World Fur Congress was held and plans to establish an International Trade Association were forged.

By inviting many international guests, the IPA provided the opportunity for the first World Fur Congress. Key figures of the international fur commerce attended the World Fur Congress along with the representatives of the major national trade associations: Curtis Lampson, manager of the large auction company Lampson & Co and also president of the London Fur Trade Association; Ch. Hanau, president of the French fur trade association Fédération de la Fourrure; and finally J. H. Bleistein of the National Association of the Fur Industry in New York.[64] As in the earlier meetings, the members of the national trade associations played a leading role in the conference. Representatives of the Soviet fur trade were not invited. Similarly, they had been left out of the international business meetings that preceded the World Fur Congress. Coordination was based upon either interfirm relations or trade associations, both of which were absent in the Soviet fur trade.

The conference itself lasted seven days (between 22 and 29 June) and was held in the halls of the Zoological Gardens. It was divided into 12 sections, where no less than 100 papers and speeches were delivered. While a wide variety of issues were addressed, the main thread in the debates concerned removing obstacles to trade. Discussions on how the fur industry could homologate paying conditions and synchronise various culture-bound trade practices resulted in the ambition to set international standards for transactions. In addition, the debates not only touched upon customs and financial issues but also upon matters of standardisation. For instance, discussions took place on reaching an international consensus regarding the nomenclature of fur products.[65] Topics ranged from patenting to the trade press and issues related to retailing and consumption. However, these speeches and discussions were infused with a nostalgia for the international trade prior to World War I. This underlying thought instigated debates on reviving 'old practices' like the system of exchanging young apprentices or merchants between European fur businesses. International exchange was a common practice in family-run German merchant houses and workshops prior to 1914.[66]

In order to facilitate the revival of the pre-war order and to set international standards, the conference ultimately aimed to establish an international fur federation, an overarching institution for the international fur industry. The shape and extent of such an international institution was a matter of debate between the British and German businesses represented by Lampson and Hollander, respectively. Lampson opposed the idea of an international bureau and pleaded for the organisation of annual congresses for representatives of the international fur industry. He promptly proposed that the next session be held during the London auctions. In contrast, Hollender defended the view that the international bureau should form a permanent institution composed of representatives of national associations. The German fur trade won the vote and Hollender himself was elected as the first president of the international fur federation; its bureau was established in Leipzig.

While the establishment of an international bureau was a victory for German intentions, the spirit of cooperation did not last long. It declined as the economic crisis deepened. The follow-up meeting of the International Association, planned for 1932, never took place.[67] Internationalism in the fur industry was thus only short-lived. Nonetheless, it preceded the post-war internationalism and the creation of a more robust institution, the International Fur Federation, in 1949. The effects that the IPA hoped the exhibition would generate were also short. The deepening of the international crisis prevented any benefits from spilling over into the fur industry.

Conclusion

Despite the efforts made by the organising committee, the IPA largely failed to accomplish the ambitious aim of promoting the Leipzig fur industry at home and abroad. Locally, the IPA left a sour taste when it appeared that the exhibition showed a large financial deficit of 720,000 RM.[68] With additional support from the city council and the state of Saxony, the IPA managed to pay off 76.4% of the claims.[69] Obviously, potential economic and commercial benefits were undone by the harmful effects of the economic crisis. In terms of international business relations, the stimulating effects of the exhibition were almost immediately erased by the economic meltdown. The economic protectionism and autarky that came to characterise the 1930s cast a large shadow over the spirit of pan-national cooperation and the plans to revive a pre-war international fur trade. The economic crisis also accounts for the organisational failure of the IPA, although mismanagement also played a role. Disappointing admission revenues deepened the deficit and the budget gap badly affected the local reputation of the industry.

Still, structure and performance should to be separated. The failure of the exhibition does not mean that it was not the result of district processes. In other words, the exhibition should not be defined by its failure but rather as an umbrella institution organised by local actors as a way to act upon the international stage. Exhibitions remain important for marketing in Germany and controversies about their cost effectiveness still overshadow the organisation of exhibitions.[70] Regardless of its efficacy, the organisation of the IPA was the result of collective action to deal with challenges from abroad, namely the changing world market of furs. It was an attempt to collectively improve the wellbeing of the local business system. Similar to fairs and auctions, the IPA was a temporary umbrella institution connecting the district to the wider world. The IPA was not meant to conduct trade; rather, it was hoped that it would produce a 'magnet' effect on the local industry. In debates about 'cost effectiveness,' such considerations gained the upper hand.

The way in which the international fur trade was to be organised in the new international organisation was a projection of local forms of governance in Leipzig and, perhaps, in other fur centres as well. Firstly, it reflected the rise of the Leipzig Fur Merchants Association as the dominant trade association in the city and confirmed the role of Paul Hollender as the leading figure of the industry. After the IPA, Hollender was appointed as president of the first International Fur Federation. Trade associations were to form the core of the bureau and act as coordinating institutions, just as they did locally. Secondly, the IPA and the International Fur Federation was about the construction of the international order in the fur trade: it was to be divided between capitals of the fur industry and based on the institutions that organised fur trading in these centres. The IPA reflected a world fur market that was divided into several major districts: business activity pertained to location. Businesses in Leipzig acted accordingly. Ideas that were spread in the World Fur Congress centred on the regulation of international competition in order to create an international order based on coordination between trade associations in the capitals of the fur industry. Leipzigers saw international coordination largely as a matter of 'cluster-to-cluster' relations and to a large extent tried to maintain this world. Surprisingly, little attention was paid to either integrating resource producers or the delegation from the Soviet Union, despite the importance of such actors for the international fur industry. Trade associations in 'visible fur cities' monopolised the movement of internationalism.

Once more, the importance of the lead firms in the organisation of border-crossing activities has been revealed. A number of firm owners dominated the organisation committee and continued to be at the forefront of the IPA as caretakers of establishing contacts with foreign firms and governments. As mentioned in other chapters throughout this section, lead firms of the Leipzig fur industry integrated local concerns such as 'the international position of Leipzig' into their business and personal activities. While several factions of the local industry were initially opposed to the idea, the lead firms, together with the city administration, managed to convince many other businesses to participate in the IPA. They played the role of facilitators in projects of local collaboration with the aim of improving the status of Leipzig as an international fur centre. The lead firms headed local alliances but were also of seminal importance in constructing international links.

Rather than reviving international trade and stabilising relationships within the international fur industry, the IPA heralded a new international trade system that would be fundamentally dissimilar. The international bureau drowned helplessly in the currents of protectionism and autarky. The plans to create an international bureau that dealt with matters of discordance among the capitals of the fur industry remained a pipe dream. The spirit of cooperation that emerged in the second half of the 1920s did not survive in the 1930s. The disruptive impact of external developments and the new political economy was simply too large to remedy through local collective action. Painfully, the IPA marked the end of the economic order that the organisers had hoped to revive. The Leipzig industrial district entered the different world of the 1930s, one characterised by political and economic instability.

Notes

1 Schramm, *Konsum und regionale Identität in Sachsen 1880–2000*, 24.
2 Hochmuth, *Industrie- und Gewerbeausstellungen in Sachsen 1824–1914*, 125.
3 Kiesewetter, *Die Industrialisierung Sachsens*, 519.

4 Barbier, "Construction d'une capitale: Leipzig et la librairie allemande, 1750–1914," 355.
5 Hochmuth, *Industrie- und Gewerbeausstellungen in Sachsen 1824–1914*, 66.
6 Paar, "Der österreichische Verlagsbuchhandel auf Buchmessen in Leipzig und Wien sowie auf Weltaussellungen von 1850 bis 1930," 89.
7 Geppert, *Fleeting Cities*, 11.
8 Jefkins, *Advertising*, 198.
9 Stadt-Al, Kap. 75 nr. 102, f. 15.
10 Sächs. HStA, Wirtschaftsministerium 11168, nr. 795, f. 122.
11 Stadt-AL, Kap 75 A, nr. 102, f. 177. 13.09.1927.
12 PA AA, Ausstellungswesen, R 117605, The British Fur Trade, November 1928.
13 StA-L, Leipziger Rauchwarenfirmen 20931, Carl Gründling, nr. 231. Fachabteilungen und Fach-Ausschüsse.
14 Kürschnerzeitung 1930, Nr. 4. 01.02.1930. p. 111. Die IPA kommt!
15 Sächs. HStA. Wirtschaftsministerium 11168, nr. 793, ff. 66–70. Drucksache, nr. 367/1929. 11.04.1929.
16 Ibid.
17 Ibid., 67.
18 Leiske, *Leipzig und Mitteldeutschland*, 29. Leiske's Mitteldeutschland encompassed Saxony, Thuringia, Anhalt, Braunschweig and the Province Saxony of Prussia.
19 Lerner, "Walter Leiske."
20 Leiske, "Internationale Pelzfachausstellung Leipzig 1929. Eine Denkschrift."
21 PA AA, Ausstellungswesen, R 117065, IPA an Herrn Reichsaußenministerium Dr. Stresemann, 19.11.1928.
22 Sächs. HStA, Wirtschaftsministerium 11168, nr. 793, f 18.
23 Sächs HStA, Wirtschaftsministerium 11168, nr. 793, ff. 66–70. Drücksache Nr. 367/1929.
24 Sächs. HStA, Wirtschaftsministerium 11168, nr. 794, ff. 165–6.
25 Sächs. HStA, Wirtschaftsministerium 11168, f. 32, Rathaus Besprechung am 19.03.1928.
26 Ibid.
27 Hochmuth, *Industrie- und Gewerbeausstellungen in Sachsen 1824–1914*, 83.
28 Another notable contributor from outside the fur industry was IG Farben.
29 Sächs HStA, Wirtschaftsministerium 11168, nr. 793, f. 107. Garantiefonds Zeichnungen, s.d. The ADCA, Darmstädter und Nationalbank, Deutsche Bank Filiale Leipzig, and Commerz und Privat-bank AG altogether paid 35,000 RM. The Dresdner Bank in Leipzig paid about 7,500 RM.
30 Berghahn, "German Big Business and the Quest for a European Economic Empire in the Twentieth Century," 15.
31 Hirsch, *Gustav Stresemann 1878–1978*.
32 PA AA, Ausstellungswesen, R 117065, Vermerk W 4120, Berlin, 03.12.1928.
33 PA AA, Ausstellungswesen, R 117065, The British Fur Trade, nr. 54. November 1928.
34 PA AA, Ausstellungswesen, R 117065, The Fur World, 03.11.1928.
35 PA AA, Austellungswesen, R 117065, Deutsche Botschaft. London, den 25.03. 1929.
36 PA AA, Ausstellungswesen, R 117065, Foreign Office London, 18.06.1929.
37 PA AA, Ausstellungswesen, R 117067, IPA an das Reichswirtschaftsministerium. Berlin. 16.01.1930.
38 Sächs HStA, Wirtschaftsministerium 11168, nr. 792, Ausschnitte aus der Textil Zeitung, nr. 54. Vom 5.3. 1929.
39 Sächs HStA, Wirtschaftsministerium 11168, nr. 793, ff. 43–7. IPA. Protokoll 30.07.1929.

40 PA AA, Ausstellungswesen R 110766, Document no. 253. Message from the president of the US. 13.01.1930.
41 Ibid.
42 PA AA, Ausstellungswesen, R 110765. IPA an Geheimrat Wiehl.18.10.1929.
43 PA AA, Ausstellungswesen, R 117065, IPA. Leipzig, den 15.10.1929. Abschrift.
44 PA AA, Ausstellungswesen, R 10766, IPA an den Reichskommissar Herrn. Dr. Matthies. 26.11.1930.
45 Sächs. HStA, Wirtschaftsministerium 11168, nr. 792, f. 139.
46 Die Kürschnerzeitung, nr. 14. 11.05.1930, p. 585. Die Eröffnung der IPA.
47 Sächs. HStA, Wirtschaftsministerium 11168, nr. 800, IPA. "Ein grosser Vergnügungspark auf der IPA". 24.04.1930.
48 Sächs. HStA, Wirtschaftsministerium 11168; nr. 795, f. 20.
49 Torp and Haupt, "Einleitung: Die Vielen Wege Der Deutschen Konsumgesellschaft," 14.
50 StA-L, Leipziger Rauchwarenfirmen 20931, Carl Gründig nr. 231, 05.07.1929.
51 Daumas and de Ferrière le Vayer, "Les métamorphoses du luxe vues d'Europe," 14.
52 Torp, "Das Janusgesicht Der Weimarer Konsumpolitik," 257.
53 BArch, Reichsgesundheitsamt R86, nr. 1486. Der Auftakt der IPA. 27.5.1930.
54 StA-L, Leipziger Rauchwarenfirmen 20931, nr. 231 Carl Gründling, Protokoll 7.1.1930.
55 Ibid.
56 Die Kürschnerzeitung, nr. 7, 01.03.1930. p. 199. Wie es steht heute mit der IPA.
57 TNA, HBCA (Microfilm Copy). Public Record Office, BH 2735, A 92.77. 22, f. 94. 18th June, 1930. IPA LEIPZIG 1930. Report from 31st May to 12 June 1930.
58 Die Kürschnerzeitung, Nr. 9. 21.03.1930. p. 276. Der Meistersaal auf der IPA.
59 Die Neue Pelzwarenzeitung, nr. 1029, 7.06.1930. p. 495.Die Eröffnung der IPA in Leipzig.
60 TNA, HBCA (Microfilm Copy). Public Record Office, BH 2735, A 92.77. 22, f. 94.
61 Sächs. HStA, Wirtschaftsministerium 11168, nr. 800, Internationale Bekleidungsarbeiter-Föderation. Internationaler Kongress vom 15. Bis 17 Juni.
62 PA AA, Ausstellungswesen, R 118403, Internationaler Kaninchenzüchterkongress Leipzig, 23–7 August 1930.
63 TNA, HBCA (Microfilm Copy). Public Record Office, BH 2734, A92/77/21, Memorandum with reference to. Fur sales. V. 168. Beaver house, 25.11.1927.
64 Die Kürschnerzeitung, nr. 19, 01.07.1930, p. 689. Der 1. Welt-Pelz-Kongress in Leipzig.
65 Ibid.
66 *Erster Welt-Pelz-Kongress 22.-29. Juni 1930 Tagesordng f. d. Sitzgn = First World-Fur-Congress = Premier Congre`s international de fourrures et pelleteries.* Ausbildung von Rauchwarenhändler und Kürschnern und internationalen Austausch von jungen Rauchwarenhändlern und Kürschnern.
67 TNA, HBCA (Microfilm Copy). Public Record Office, BH 2734, A92/77/22, p. 79.
68 Sächs. HStA, Wirtschaftsministerium 11168, nr. 800, Dresdner Anzeiger, 10.10.1930.
69 Sächs. HStA, Wirtschaftsministerium 11168, nr. 799, Protokoll 6 Oktober 1931.
70 Blythe, *Essentials of Marketing Communications*, 187.

References

Barbier, Frédéric. "Construction d'une capitale: Leipzig et la librairie allemande, 1750–1914." In *Capitales culturelles, capitales symboliques: Paris et les expériences européennes, XVIIIe-XXe siècles*, edited by Christophe Charle and Daniel Roche, 335–61. Paris: Publications de la Sorbonne, 2002.

Berghahn, Volker R. "German Big Business and the Quest for a European Economic Empire in the Twentieth Century." In *Quest for Economic Empire: The European Strategies of German Big Business in the Twentieth Century*, edited by Volker R. Berghahn, 1–35. Providence, RI: Berghahn Books, 1996.

Blythe, Jim. *Essentials of Marketing Communications*. New York: Pearson Education, 2006.

Daumas, Jean-Claude, and Marc de Ferrière le Vayer. "Les métamorphoses du luxe vues d'Europe." *Entreprises et histoire* 46, no. 1 (March 1, 2007): 6–16.

Erster Welt-Pelz-Kongress 22.-29. Juni 1930 Tagesordng f. d. Sitzgn = First World-Fur-Congress = Premier Congre`s international de fourrures et pelleteries. [s. l.]: [s. n.], 1930.

Geppert, Alexander C. T. *Fleeting Cities: Imperial Expositions in Fin-de-Siècle Europe*. New York: Palgrave Macmillan, 2010.

Hirsch, Felix. *Gustav Stresemann 1878–1978*. Bonn: Inter nationes, 1978.

Hochmuth, Enrico. *Industrie- und Gewerbeausstellungen in Sachsen 1824–1914: ihr Beitrag zur kommunalen und regionalen Standortbildung*. Beucha: Sax-Verlag, 2012.

Jefkins, Frank. *Advertising*. New York: Pearson Education, 2000.

Kiesewetter, Hubert. *Die Industrialisierung Sachsens: ein regional-vergleichendes Erklärungsmodell*. Stuttgart: Steiner, 2007.

Leiske, Walter. "Internationale Pelzfachausstellung Leipzig 1929. Eine Denkschrift." In *Leipziger Verkehr Und Verkehrspolitk. Schriftenreihe Des Rats-Verkehramtes Leipzig*, Edited by the city of Leipzig. Leipzig: The city of Leipzig, 1929.

———. *Leipzig und Mitteldeutschland: Denkschrift für Rat und Stadtverordnete zu Leipzig*. Leipzig: Ratsverkehrsamt, 1928.

Lerner, Franz. "Walter Leiske." *Neue Deutsche Biographie*. Accessed September 9, 2013. www.deutsche-biographie.de/sfz50049.html.

Paar, Andrea. "Der österreichische Verlagsbuchhandel auf Buchmessen in Leipzig und Wien sowie auf Weltausstellungen von 1850 bis 1930." Universität Wien, 2000.

Schramm, Manuel. *Konsum und regionale Identität in Sachsen 1880–2000: die Regionalisierung von Konsumgütern im Spannungsfeld von Nationalisierung und Globalisierung*. Stuttgart: Steiner, 2003.

Torp, Claudius. "Das Janusgesicht Der Weimarer Konsumpolitik." In *Die Konsumgesellschaft in Deutschland 1890–1990: Ein Handbuch*, edited by Heinz-Gerhard Haupt and Claudius Torp, 232–50. Frankfurt: Campus Verlag, 2009.

Torp, Claudius, and Heinz-Gerhard Haupt. "Einleitung: Die Vielen Wege Der Deutschen Konsumgesellschaft." In *Die Konsumgesellschaft in Deutschland 1890–1990: Ein Handbuch*, edited by Heinz-Gerhard Haupt and Claudius Torp, 9–27. Frankfurt: Campus Verlag, 2009.

Part IV
Epilogue

10 Economic Depression, Soviet Plan Economy, and Anti-Semitism

The Limits of Collective Action (1931–1939)

Introduction

In the preceding part of the book, the relationship between internationalisation and the local business structure was described as dynamic and interactive. Collective action was brought to the foreground as an important instrument for district participants in the pursuit of re-admission to the world market. In part, local economic institutions and networks were flexible in relation to external challenges stemming from the transformation of the world market in the early 1920s. New forms of interfirm cooperation led to the creation of novel economic institutions like auction companies that replaced obsolete institutions such as the Easter fur fairs. Local identity led to the creation of ambitious projects like the international fur exhibition, a joint venture in international marketing. Similarly, economic actors intensified cooperation, as we saw in the relationship between the local bank system and the fur industry. Furthermore, firm leaders clearly put the 'local' central in their efforts to restore the locality as an international fur market. Individual business activity was designed with the purpose of strengthening the local market—solidarity was a motivating factor. As such, firms and economic actors were surprisingly dynamic in preserving the manufacturing hub amid the changing tides of international commerce in the early 1920s.

Leaving the 'the turbulent and golden twenties' behind us, we have arrived at the 1930s. This is a period when the political and economic developments that disturbed internationalism or transborder business activities could no longer be downplayed or ignored. Three developments will be examined more closely: firstly, the global economic crisis initiated by the Wall Street stock market crash at the end of the 1920s; secondly, the changes in the USSR's foreign trade policy that turned the main trade partner of Leipzig district into an autarkic entity; and finally, the disruptive impact of anti-Semitism in the Third Reich on the social composition of an industrial district based on a balance between Jewish and gentile firms. Whereas all three developments were damaging, it is their interplay that furthered the decline of the Leipzig fur industry.

It should be remembered that the performance and the features of the industrial district should be strictly separated. Economic decline and the contraction of a decentralised business system do not mean that mechanisms for cooperation and sharing disappeared. It could simply indicate that these mechanisms are not working properly or were ineffective against the challenges faced. In this epilogue, I want to reflect on the impact of political and economic crises upon the social structure of the industrial district. How did the district adjust to these turbulent times? What forms did collective action take or was the impact upon social cohesion simply too disturbing for collective action to form? In this sense, this chapter still places emphasis on the mechanisms of the Leipzig fur industry as an industrial district and to what degree the threefold challenges of the early 1930s eroded or reproduced these mechanisms.

The Stock Market Crash in 1929 and the Leipzig Cluster

The Impact of the Crisis

Although it was not the only cause of decline, the years of commercial buoyancy of the Leipzig fur industry ended abruptly in the wake of the stock market crash in November 1929. Many saw the economic backdrop as a temporary interlude, yet matters rapidly worsened. The internationally oriented Saxon economy was badly affected, just as its reputation as the 'storm centre of the trade cycle' would suggest. Between 1926 and 1932, Saxony experienced unusually high levels of bankruptcies: 35.7% of all businesses, much higher than the national level of 25.8%.[1] Between 1930 and 1931 alone, 131 firms in Leipzig were suspended from the trade register.[2] In 1932, the labour market in the city reached rock bottom with 185,392 unemployed workers.[3]

The crisis hit the fur industry hard. In the mid-1920s, the Saxon fur industry had reached its zenith, registering 11,170 workers in 1,091 firms; in the early 1930s, employment levels dropped sharply. By 1933, the number of firms dropped to 888, which coincided with a dramatic reduction in the workforce to 6,119 employees. While the number of fur workers still represented 34.2% of the Reich's total, about half of all such employees lost their jobs and over 200 firms in Saxony's industry had disappeared.[4] The fur industry continued to lose ground at a severe pace. Only one year later, the number of workers decreased again to 5,200. Over the course of five years, the Saxon fur industry lost more than 50% of its workforce.

The crisis had ramifications on the district in a variety of ways. First, as we have seen, the boom in the international fur industry since the late nineteenth century had been largely represented by ascending prices. The international depression caused a stunning deflation in commodity prices. For fur prices, valued dropped to about 40–70%.[5] The economic crisis thus marked the end of the boom that had characterised the international fur trade since the middle of the nineteenth century and had laid the groundwork for the development of the Saxon fur industry. Second, fur contracts traditionally took a long period of time to fulfil and therefore were particularly vulnerable. If they had been agreed upon before the crisis, the value of the raw furs had almost completely vanished by the time they actually reached the world market. This threatened precisely those firms that specialised in commerce with the Soviets, who had a penchant for large contracts and advance credits. Finally, the bankruptcies of larger and smaller firms as well as international insolvencies had an infectious effect on the solvency of the surviving firms in the district. The Fur Merchants Association in Leipzig mentioned that 183 firms went bankrupt in the international fur industry in 1931.[6] Firms contaminated by the defaults of others were unable to respect deals and payment deadlines. Banks and fur firms therefore increasingly called in their debts. More importantly, the defaults also affected the networks and connections that undergirded the social structure of the fur cluster.

The erosion of the social structure because of international insolvencies will be illustrated with the decline of several larger firms in Leipzig: Chaim Eitingon AG, David Biedermann, and the Walter AG. Just as the Eitingon-Schild Co embodied the 1920s boom, the financial problems of this firm came to epitomise the malaise of the international fur industry. Problems in the Eitingon concern had started already in 1929, particularly because of heavy losses booked by the American headquarters, affecting all the company divisions also Leipzig. In 1932, the Eitingon corporation suffered from incredible $5,650,000 deficit.[7] Matters worsened, at least for German creditors, when founding father Chaim Eitingon died in 1932. The Leipzig banks suffered badly from the decline of the group—they had invested a total of 8,415,000 RM in this leading fur business. As the largest creditor with a claim of 4,700,000 RM, the Dresdner Bank was the most badly affected. Next came the DD Bank with 2,377,000 RM and the ADCA with a claim of 1,338,000 RM.[8] The firm finally went into liquidation in 1935, having badly damaged the local banks and other fur firms in the district. Creditors could only exercise limited claims on the assets of the group.

A similar contaminating effect went from the bankruptcy of David Biederman in 1930, due to the sudden death of the owner. The Dresdner Bank claimed 5 million RM of the Biedermann inheritance. However, there was not much to recuperate, as the credit was largely unsecured. Furthermore, the insolvent Biedermann company generally contaminated the Brühl. This was a result of Biedermann's business practice of including smaller firms in large import contracts. In return, these firms had offered bills of exchange that acted as extra securities to convince creditors. The latter now demanded the payment of these securities.[9] Richard Gloeck, a smaller fur merchant on the Brühl, was one of the firms that went into liquidation because of its connection to the Biedermann business.[10]

The crisis not only affected firms active in the commercial sector: the spiral of price decline and lower demand put an end to Walter AG, the largest dyeing factory of the Leipzig district. The employment rate within the factory had plummeted dramatically from 1,400 in 1923 to a mere 250 fur workers in 1932.[11] Given the precarious condition of Walter AG and the downward trend of fur consumption, there was little enthusiasm from the side of the banks to finance a restart of the company after a moratorium. It finally went into liquidation in 1934, after five years of heavy losses.

Despite the avalanche of bankruptcies that eliminated a number of leading concerns, several of the larger firms (Theodor Thorer, Friedrich Erler, and J. Ariowitsch) managed to endure the crisis, even with decreasing trade volumes. Arndt Thorer reported that he was able to avoid considerable losses between 1929 and 1930 because the consumption of Persianer and Astrakhan furs remained relatively stable and deflation in these articles was less dramatic. The business in karakul skins took up 70% of Thorer's business volumes. Moreover, at the end of 1929, Thorer had depreciated its stocks so as to ease the impact of price deflation on his firm. During the subsequent crisis years, Paul Hollender and Arndt Thorer managed to keep their business out of the red. Profits in 1929 amounted to 1,997,000 RM on a business volume of 21,738,000 RM.[12] Business volume dwindled the following year to 16,537,000 RM but profits reached 505,000 RM. The managers of the Thorer concern continued to be active in the Russian business, which provided for their factories and branches inside Germany and abroad at levels that were significantly lower than prior to 1930. While such firms survived the crisis, losses and mistrust caused by the crisis curbed the ability of the surviving firms to take action. In particular, the crisis in the fur industry put an end to the excellent bank-business relations, one of the pillars of foreign relations in the industrial district.

A New Era of Business-Bank Relations?

From what has been set out above, it is clear that the local bank branches had largely ignored the risks concerning their participation in the international fur trade, especially in connecting with the larger firms. Furthermore, credit was given unsecured as a rule. Given their exposure during the fur crisis, local banks now redefined their role in the local economy. The Deutsche Bank in Leipzig lowered its credit portfolio in the fur industry after 1930, which was particularly upsetting to the 'surviving firms.'[13] Early in 1931, Hollender, in his role as president of the German Fur Merchants Association, discussed the impact of the crisis with the banks, in particular the bankruptcy of David Biedermann. Hollender warned that modifications to the lending conditions would injure business and he requested that "the banks should abstain from credit reduction because of the Biedermann affair."[14] Nonetheless, the banks did make their lending conditions more stringent and this affected the firms that had survived the crisis.

Late 1932, the Ariowitsch firm requested credit for the purpose of importing Russian furs. In contrast to previous lending conditions, the Deutsche

Bank in Leipzig now demanded to look into the bookkeeping of the Ariowitsch firm to see whether such credit was justified. Very few businesses allowed banks to pry into their books prior to the crisis. Only after numerous requests did the Ariowitsch firm reluctantly give permission. On studying these documents, which gave finally insight into activities in London and Leipzig, the Deutsche Bank came to the conclusion that Ariowitsch was perfectly capable of operating independently without new bank credit: "The rumours about the Ariowitsch that say that they have $1,200,000 at their disposal are true. They can finance the deal through London."[15] On this basis, the Deutsche Bank refused to offer finance.

Individual firms lost the ability to profit from multiple bank connections and from the advantages derived from friendship and personal networks with bankers. Banks now made collective arrangements in order to reform the credit market. In 1931, for instance, the Dresdner Bank and the Deutsche Bank made a secret agreement to increase the interest rates on acceptance credit for the medium-sized firm Semi Goldstaub. Even though the increase was minimal (0.125%), Goldstaub considered it an insult from his 'friend' Naumann of the Deutsche Bank and a breach in business practice: "For a quarter of a century we have worked together. The personal impression I have of you was the best possible and I have sincerely appreciated you as a true friend of my company. For some time you are no longer the old man I used to know. . . . It seems that you want to break with the good old traditions."[16] The request that Goldstaub should make his accounts transparent was met with similar hostility. Personal networks mattered less and less in bank-business relationships after the economic crisis.

Banks were worried about their participation in the remaining fur firms, even though they survived and operated more carefully than some of their counterparts. As we have seen with the downfall of other major fur firms in Leipzig, the banks had been faced with the problem that securities on the loans were largely insufficient to claim assets from liquidations. Particularly galling to the Dresdner Bank was the structure of the Theodor Thorer firm, the so-called Thorer KG. In a nutshell, the Thorer KG was the overarching holding concern of the Thorer business. But only the trading section, with relatively few assets, belonged directly to the Thorer KG firm. The important factory in Leipzig-Lindenau as well as the branches in London and New York operated relatively independent of the Thorer KG. In other words, the Thorer branches belonged directly to the Thorer family and not to the Thorer KG. As the Dresdner Bank noted, "It is difficult for us to put claims on the valuable fur dyeing factory in Leipzig-Lindenau because our debtor does not possess shares in its individual companies. The control over these firms belongs to the private assets of the associates Paul Hollender and Arndt Thorer. . . . It is therefore doubtful how far the property of the associates can be liquidated to our benefit."[17] Hollender immediately assuaged the worries of the banks and included two new assets as securities for loans. Firstly, the assets of Marie Thorer, his wife and a silent partner in the firm, were forward as security. The new collateral included real estate in Leipzig and its environs. Secondly, Hollender put up the assets of the London subsidiary Raw Furs Ltd as a collateral for the loans.[18] Still, the new security arrangements failed to renew trust. In the summer of 1933, the largest credit providers of the Thorer firm (ADCA, DD Bank, Dresdner Bank, and the Reichskreditgesellschaft) organised a secret meeting, without manager Hollander, in which they collectively agreed upon the fact that Thorer should provide extra guarantees for commercial credit lines. If much to his disliking, Hollander had no choice but to accept the additional security request.

The (secret) coordination on lending conditions marked a landslide in a relationship that used to be characterised by powerful firms on the one hand and competing banks on the other hand. The continuity in personal relationships, a central foundation for the good relationships between banks and businesses, had disappeared as well. Paul Vernickel took over from Eugen Naumann as head of the DD bank in 1930. Although von Klemperer still headed the Dresdner Bank in Leipzig, Alfred Weinkrantz, who had moved from the Danzig branch, was clearly the up-and-coming man since he replaced von Klemperer in that particular meeting.[19] These men personified the new, more stringent, lending policy of the local banks towards the fur industry.

The External Threat Posed by the First Soviet Five-Year Plan

The first Soviet Five-Year Plan in 1928 posed an additional exogenous challenge to the industrial district. In order to understand the impact of the new Stalinist economic policy upon the fur district, we need to separate the general characteristics of the Five-Year Plan, especially its foreign trade dimension, and the particular changes in the Soviet fur trade. In general, Stalin envisioned a self-sufficient industrial economy. The Politburo therefore initiated import substitution in order to decrease dependency upon the import of industrial goods. The Soviet Five-Year Plan was thus accompanied by a surge in industrial production.[20] At the same time, the USSR planned to attain larger trade surpluses by a surge in production and exports of agricultural and other commodities. The new foreign trade policy under the Five-Year Plan was certainly more 'aggressive' in contrast to the flexibility that characterised the NEP.[21] The sudden surge in exports further added to the process of price deflation on the world market, much to the despair of capitalist countries, which saw the practice as "dumping."[22] Indeed, because of the tremendous efforts through collectivisation and forced labour, Soviet-produced commodities grew increasingly detached from world market prices. Although the targets of the Five-Year Plans were never fully achieved, the change in economic policy had profound effects on Soviet society and international commerce.[23]

A Double Threat: Dumping and Soviet Auctions

The Soviet fur trade was part of the Five-Year Plan, but its outcome differed slightly from the general picture. Import substitution in the fur industry was not crucial in the eyes of the planners. Like agricultural commodities, however, furs were central in the surge of exports. The Soviets therefore profoundly transformed fur exporting and its trade parameters. First of all, the Soviets tried to replace the export of raw furs with manufactured furs (dressed and dyed) in order to realise larger added value and incorporate labour-bound processes in the commodity chain into the USSR. In the first stage in 1930, manufactured furs were introduced onto the world market rather aggressively whilst waging a price war. Industrialisation, the more aggressive policy on the world market, and the rolling back of raw material exports obviously jeopardised the Leipzig cluster in its traditional role as a fur market and manufacturing hub.

Initially, the Leipzig community felt only slightly threatened by the surge in industrial fur production in the USSR. German reports on the Soviet fur industry in 1928 described the products being churned out of the new dressing factories as substandard.[24] However, by 1930, the attempts to industrialise fur manufacturing in the Soviet Union were taken more seriously. Upsetting in particular was the Soviet interest in purchasing modern fur dyeing and dressing equipment, often purchased from German factories.[25] Since 1925, Soviet trade agencies indeed systematically increased exports of dressed furs to the world market, a development that reached its climax in 1929. After the launch of the Five-Year Plan and the price deflation in the fur trade, the value of raw fur exports declined rapidly. Exports of manufactured furs and raw ones converged towards 1933. Nonetheless, in the second half of the 1930s, the export value of raw furs continued to rank above manufactured furs, albeit by a much narrower gap than in the 1920s. Figure 10.1 shows the ratio of processed-to-unprocessed furs in the trade between Germany and Russia between 1926 and 1935. Imports of manufactured furs increased in size between 1926 and 1929 but were still dwarfed by the value of raw furs. The ratio between raw and manufactured furs changed drastically after 1931, when manufactured Soviet furs represented almost 50% of the total fur exports to Germany.[26]

Soviet manufacturing proved to be a powerful competitor for the Leipzig fur district since price-cutting was used as a tactic to introduce fur garments on the world market. Indeed, Soviet export commodities ceased to correspond with world market prices during the depression years.[27] The surge in Soviet exports coalesced with the general tendency of falling world market prices. Soviet exports therefore added to declining prices. The term "dumping" was used to describe the sale of agricultural goods on the world market by the Soviets.[28] The same was said of furs. In 1930, the Thorer firm predicted that the Soviets would compensate for the lack of quality by

Soviet fur exports to Germany (1926–1935)

120
100
80
60
40
20
0

1926 1927 1928 1929 1930 1931 1932 1933 1934 1935

▪ raw fur imports   manufactured furs

Figure 10.1 Soviet Fur Imports (Raw Furs versus Manufactured)

systematically undercutting world market prices: "Russian fur products can balance differences in terms of quality by their appropriately cheap pricing."[29] In order to promote the domestic fur industry, Soviet manufactured furs were delivered more cheaply than raw furs, thereby threatening firms on the Brühl, especially those involved in manufacturing. Reports described the arduous efforts of the Soviets to price the Leipzig fur industry out of the market: "Some of the prices for finished furs are so low that they do not even reach the regular prices for raw hides and can be justly called dumping prices: e.g., a squirrel coat made by the Russians is offered for 238RM while German manufacturing cannot sell these for under 800RM. *Peshaniki* [the fur of a suslik] are to be offered for 95RM while the minimum cost price in Germany is 160RM."[30] The arrival of large quantities of manufactured furs meant heavy competition for the crisis-ridden Leipzig fur industry.

The final result of the new foreign trade policies also resulted in changes on the level of international commerce. The Soviets' long-standing wish to gain more systematic control over the trade in furs and reverse dependency on foreign sales markets has been mentioned before; now words were increasingly put into practice. Like in Leipzig, auctions were seen as the instrumental economic institution that would allow control over the organisation of the fur trade. An earthquake struck the international fur trade when the first international fur auction in Leningrad was held in March 1931. In 1932, a second auction took place and was visited by representatives of eight German, six English, four American, and three French firms.[31] The auctions in Leningrad gradually replaced the large Soviet auctions that had been held in Leipzig, affecting the latter's status as an international market. In 1933, the Soviets held two auctions in Leningrad instead of one. It was visited by 50 international firms, 12 of which were German. After 1934, the Leningrad auctions became a permanent institution.[32]

The creation of auctions in the USSR was remarkably similar to the process conducted in Leipzig earlier in the 1920s. The *Soiuspushina* attracted foreign experts to transform the first auctions into an efficient international market institution. It was painfully clear that the intention was to replace the Leipzig auction: the first Leningrad auctions were even held in German.[33] Almost uncanny was the presence of the Leipzig RAVAG auctioneer Büttner, who was now lending his services to the Leningrad auction.[34] Firms in Leipzig that had invested in economic institutions, the system of trade privileges, favouritism, and concessions from the state monopoly were directly exposed to this new form of competition.

Self-Help as Crisis Management: The Limits of Collective Action (1930–1933)

The competition posed by Soviet manufacturing and auctioneering motivated collective action in the Leipzig cluster. Impulses for collective action against this external threat originated from the German Fur Merchants Association and its president Paul Hollender. However, the task at hand was almost impossible. Firstly, the exports of Soviet manufactured furs had to be restricted without disturbing the Soviets. Secondly, and perhaps more importantly, the trade in furs was embedded in fixed bilateral trade relations. Furs were a highly strategic resource both for Berlin and Moscow. Modifications that might disturb the balance of trade could have ramifications for business interests far beyond those of the Brühl. In fact, the interest of the Leipzig fur industry ran directly counter to those of German heavy industry.

In order to explain opposing interests, we need to examine the development of the bilateral German-Soviet trade. In contrast to the period between 1926 and 1929, the deficit of Germany faded and the trade balance was more or less restored in 1930. In 1931, German exports (762.7 million RM) far exceeded Soviet imports (303.5 million RM).[35] Since German exports to the USSR had grown by such large proportions, tipping the balance of trade over in favour of Germany, it was not in the government's direct interest to tolerate import restrictions on fur garments processed in the Soviet Union. Indeed, a drop in imports would curtail the financial abilities of the Soviets to pay for German exports, especially those produced by heavy industry. Here, the fur trade was paramount. Fur imports accounted for roughly 18% (one-third of which were processed furs) of goods imported from the USSR in 1930.[36]

Restricting the flows of furs would automatically disrupt bilateral trade that was already shifting out of balance. A statement from a meeting of the German government in the summer of 1931 illustrates the fear of disturbing the trade balance with the USSR: "German imports will only amount to about 280 million RM. Von Raumer [a prominent member of the *Zentralverband der Deutschen Elektrotechnischen Industrie* (the German

Electro-technical Industry Association)] is worried that this will lead to a standstill in the trade with Russia, since it will no longer be able to pay for its exports . . . One could say that the entire German industry, in particular the electro-mechanical industry, is now living from the trade with Russia."[37] Thus, rather than cutting back, the government ideally wanted to *expand* imports from the USSR by additional 250 million RM. The strategic position of furs in the Soviet foreign trade now turned into a major disadvantage for the Leipzig companies. The Ministry of Economic Affairs (*Reichswirtschaftsministerium*) stated that "sharp restrictions on fur imports will incline the Russians to revise their orders with the German machine industry."[38] In other words, the particular interests of the fur district were at odds with the interests of the more influential heavy industry, particularly those of the powerful German electro-technical industry. The Saxon ambassador in Berlin was well aware that these interests prevented a diplomatic answer to the dumping of manufactured furs on the German market.[39]

With a political solution off the table, the question of importing raw and manufactured furs was increasingly left to businesses and local actors. Hollender, for one, strongly encouraged fur firms in the cluster to follow a strategy of 'self-help.' The policy of self-help was an appeal to individual firms to protect the local industry in their dealings with the Soviets by restricting the proportion of manufactured furs in business dealings. The strategy was of a pragmatic nature. Instead of refusing to import 'substandard' Soviet garments altogether and thereby most likely lose his deals with the Soviets, Hollender tried to negotiate coupling the exports of a small percentage of manufactured furs to a larger percentage of raw furs. He called this practice "allocation" and implemented it in his own business. He explained his strategy in an exposé:

> The way of self-help [*Selbsthilfe*] will be enforced by commanding a large supply contract for raw furs with a corresponding advance on a defined quota of manufactured Soviet products for the European market. In this sense, I believe I will get a detailed insight into *the extent* of exports of manufactured goods and also will be able to contractually limit the efforts of these exports, at least for a time.[40]

It is clear that Hollender believed that the strategy had some specific advantages. In particular, the Thorer concern kept control over the distribution of a quantity of Soviet fur garments on the European markets. However, the execution of the allocation policy was another matter, especially so on the level of the individual firm. In 1931, Hollender accepted a less lucrative deal than he had in mind, 200,000 raw karakuls linked to a corresponding 100,000 dyed karakul skins. This contract nevertheless represented 60% of the total Soviet karakul export (500,000 skins).[41]

Importantly, Hollender tried to apply the principles of the allocation strategy to the collective deals of the district firms: "Because the Foreign

Office and the Ministry of Economic Affairs are, for political reasons, not able to implement quotas in trade negotiations on the quantity of processed fur products in Russia, Leipzig and the Leipzig industry must proceed to help themselves."[42] Collective self-help was put into action once the first auctions in Leningrad were held in March 1931. The auctions in Leningrad were in fact the result of reluctance to accept a larger quantity of manufactured furs for the Leipzig auctions.[43] The Leipzig firms embarked on an independent 'diplomatic' mission to Moscow with representatives of the fur industry. The aim was to establish a limited quota of manufactured furs for sales at the Leipzig auctions. Hollender was joined by Max Ariowitsch, who had good connections in Moscow; consul Schlesinger of the German foreign office; and several bank officials who were closely involved in the auction business. The individual negotiations were a complete fiasco. Moscow easily kept the attempts to fix a quota on imports at bay. In fact, it was able to press its claims against the Leipzigers. The Soviets demanded that the German banks should expand their financing of the import of manufactured furs for the Leipzig auctions. The Soviets played hardball: trade representatives refused any restrictions on the export of manufactured furs and threatened to withdraw the Soviet auctions from Leipzig altogether.[44]

Clearly, Hollender had overestimated the power of the self-help strategy and his own abilities to influence his Moscow contacts in a matter of high strategic importance both for Germany and the USSR. In addition, his approach and his personal single-handed pursuit were increasingly being questioned on the home front. The foreign office heavily criticised Hollender's obstinate behaviour towards the Soviets: ". . . it would have been better if the representatives of Leipzig's fur industry, especially Mr. Hollender, had not embarked on their own in a fight with the Russians and left the whole matter to a question of power of the Russian trade policy."[45] What is more, neighbouring firms also doubted the allocation strategy. In particular, the solidarity of firms specialised in commerce rapidly dwindled after the failed conference with the Soviet trade representatives. Max Ariowitsch, for instance, would no longer run the risk of losing the Russian business altogether. He wrote: "It is better to import processed furs than no furs at all."[46]

In subsequent collective negotiations, the fur firms also accepted larger quotas of manufactured furs.[47] In 1932, the Soviets sold furs for 10 million RM to a consortium in Leipzig, which predominantly consisted of the Jewish trading firms Felsenstein, Ariowitsch, Ehrmann, L & W Fuchs, Mautner & Ahlswede, Gebrüder Neugass, Paul Poser, and Siegried Poser. They were joined by several gentile firms: Theodor Thorer, Robert Ehrmann, and Heinrich Koenigswerther.[48] Leading trade firms owned 80% of the contract: J. Ariowitsch (32%), Theodor Thorer (20%), Robert Ehrmann (16%), and Heinrich Koenigswerther (12%).[49] The contract represented 34% of the total fur exports from the Soviet Union to Germany (which amounted to 18,090,000 RM in raw furs and 15,700,000 RM in manufactured furs in total). This consortium accepted the same ratio as the auction company:

55% of dyed furs against 45% of unprocessed furs, a further indication that the policy of keeping the ratio of raw furs higher than processed furs had largely failed.

Anti-Semitism and the Erosion of the Industrial District (1932–1936)

The economic crisis and the changing parameters of the Soviet fur trade, the emergence of the Third Reich, and its anti-Semitic program in particular, further destabilised the social underpinnings of industrial district. Over the course of the five years between 1933 and 1938, Jewish businessmen in Leipzig were systematically driven out of economic life. Jewish businesses were almost immediately attacked by the new regime and the situation continued to worsen as time went on.[50] On 1 April 1933, a national boycott against Jewish business was held across Germany, which heavily affected the fur business in Leipzig.

News about the hostilities against Jews crossed the German borders rapidly and stirred international sentiment. By the end of March, the English Jewish fur traders decided that the Leipzig trade should be boycotted.[51] In July 1933, the overarching National Council of Fur Trade Organisations in the US boycotted German firms.[52] Since Jewish businessmen held key positions in the international fur industry, gentile businessmen on the Brühl experienced the disruptive impact of anti-Semitic outbursts on international trade. Moreover, the uncertain status of the Jews and their property in Germany discouraged more foreign merchants of Jewish origin from travelling to Leipzig.

The damaging effects on foreign trade initiated a barrage of complaints from stakeholders in the industrial district. One of the first reactions came from the heavily affected Association of German Fur Dyers, an almost exclusively gentile association of industrialists. These industrialists depended upon the supply of raw furs from the Brühl, which was to a large extent organised by Jewish traders. The representatives of the association wrote to chancellor Adolf Hitler, demanding the protection of Jewish individuals and a guarantee of the rights of foreign traders.[53] It was not the only action to protect the Jewish community in Leipzig. Carl Goerdeler, the mayor of Leipzig, was known for his resistance against anti-Semitic policies. According to his own testimony, he crossed SA pickets during the April boycott and went inside Jewish fur businesses trying to avoid plunder and vandalism. Allegedly, Goerdeler also deployed the city police to liberate Jews who had been detained by the SA.[54]

With the Saxon government as mediator, representatives of the fur industry continued to petition to the *Reichskanzlei* to put an end to the excesses against the Jews: "The representatives of the fur trade, under the guidance of Hollender and the mayor Dr. Goerdeler, intend to visit the Reich Chancellery . . . and ask for uniform, clear, and unambiguous guidelines and instructions for lower-ranked party officials, because of the treatment of Jewish fur traders in Leipzig."[55] The Saxon government, sensitive to the problem of regional industrial decline, instructed their ambassador in Berlin to support the delegation. However, the role of the ambassador was carefully limited as it was noted that: "Count Holtzendorff [the Saxon ambassador] should be induced to join only for the purpose to express how important the fur trade is for Saxony's industry. Holtzendorff, however, should not touch upon the political side of things."[56] In sum, gentile businessmen did defend their Jewish colleagues but their reactions were limited to letters of complaint and concealed criticism. An open confrontation with the new regime was clearly not an option.

What is more, several reactions with the aim of helping Jewish colleagues were in fact highly ambiguous and deeply coloured by anti-Semitism. In defending Jewish fur businesses, the Chamber of Commerce in Leipzig divided the Jewish population of the city into a desirable part—the Jews that lived before in Germany since before the War, and an undesirable part—the newly arrived.[57] This reaction of the Chamber of Commerce has to be set in the context of the evolving Nazi policy towards the Jewish population in Germany, which increasingly targeted Jews of Eastern European origin. This culminated in a regulation in the summer of 1933 that enabled the de-naturalisation of recently arrived Jews from Eastern Europe.[58] The regulation particularly affected the Jewish community in Leipzig. One of its characteristics, when compared to other middle-sized Jewish communities in Germany, was the rather high level of foreign-born Jews.[59] In 1925, 68% of the Jews in Leipzig were born abroad. The request of the Chamber of Commerce was intended to protect the older generation of "German-born" Jews. The families that stood at the foundation the Saxon fur industry's success, in the nineteenth century, were seen as more important.

The Chamber of Commerce was not alone in employing such a discourse. Hollender also focused on preserving the rights of the oldest generation at the Brühl. Families like the Eitingons, Felsensteins, and Ariowitschs, all of which were established in Leipzig at the end of the nineteenth century, were arguably the most successful: "The stance of the NSDAP authorities and party members is unchanged . . . however, distinction should be made between the 'long established' Jewish firms and the Jewish merchants from the East who arrived here after 1919."[60] In separating German Jews from Eastern European Jews, businessmen represented reigning anti-Semitic discourses. Although industrialists and traders appropriated a substantial the part of discourse of the new rulers, they were not able to gain protection for even those who they considered the most 'valuable' businessmen.

In early 1934, the devastating impact of the political transition upon the local fur trade and industry had become clear to Hollender. The migration of Jewish entrepreneurs was especially damaging: "There is no question that not only many members of our industry have migrated abroad, but they also took along their customers. The migration of these Jews has strengthened the markets with which Leipzig is competing."[61] London turned into a hotspot for the refugee entrepreneurs. By the summer of 1938, about 8,000 German refugees lived in England, 187 of which persons were classified as refugee entrepreneurs.[62] The British Home Office made attempts to send refugee entrepreneurs to 'declining' areas in Britain, 'special zones,' that were in need of entrepreneurs. However, most of the fur refugees ignored the preferences of the government and settled in London, overwhelmingly so in the case of Leipzig's fur merchants.

A special report about refugees in Great Britain in 1939 singled out the importance of refugee entrepreneurs in the fur industry as one of the most important niches transplanted from Nazi Germany: "One specific example is shown by the fur trade in which there are about sixty refugee firms in Great Britain working as commission agents and brokers which were formerly established in Leipzig or Berlin. In addition, there are some three or four manufacturing furriers now in London employing fifty or sixty workers who previously ran business in Germany. At least one firm exists in London for the dressing and dyeing of furs, many of which were formerly prepared in Leipzig; this firm is managed by a German refugee but gives employment to some 160 British employees."[63] Apart of the refugee entrepreneurs, merchants like J. Ariowitsch & Co moved their headquarters to London, where they had already a branch. What remained of Ariowitsch's business in Leipzig was finally liquidated in 1938.

After damaging Jewish economic life, the next stage involved liquidating Jewish enterprises ("Aryanisation"), which was executed in 1938.[64] However, Jewish business activities had already systematically decreased before this. In 1933, about 100,000 Jewish enterprises were domiciled in Germany; in 1935, numbers plummeted to 75,000–80,000 in 1935 and then 40,000 in April 1938.[65] Many cases demonstrate that German businesses profited from taking over Jewish competitors. However, it has been shown that the debilitating effects on commerce were much higher in Leipzig than the profits gained by such an operation. The Deutsche Bank in Leipzig reported in 1939 that it still had investments of 500,000–600,000 RM in the Jewish part of the Leipzig fur industry. It was stated that: "Discontinuance [of investing in Jewish business], together with the loss of the ancillary business associated with credit (turnover, bill discounting, guarantees, etc.), will also result in a certain diminution of returns."[66] The Aryanisation was therefore unprofitable. More importantly, Jewish merchants had taken their most valuable asset with them: connections. At the end of 1936, 113 fur firms, specialised in foreign trade, had moved their business to London, New York, Paris, Prague, or Milan.[67] Aside from the economic crisis and the Soviet industrial policy, the anti-Semitic policy of the Third Reich heavily disturbed the social structure of the district. All three developments eroded the effectiveness of collective action.

The Decline Leipzig District in the 1930s: Some Concluding Remarks

The abovementioned developments destroyed the equilibrium that existed between the industrial and commercial sectors as well as the harmony between the gentile and Jewish firms. After 1933, the exodus of Jewish firms had a deleterious effect on the value of German fur commerce. Imports and exports shrunk to figures under 50 million RM. After 1935, Germany was no longer the main importer of Russian furs. The export business in raw furs dwindled and imports of raw and processed furs converged—prior to this, the success of the Saxon fur industry was largely based on importing large quantities of raw furs and exporting processed furs abroad. Governmental economic policy equally disturbed the balance in the district. From February 1935, the government put the import of furs under strict control in order to monitor spending in foreign currencies. Firms had to pay on special accounts (*Sondernkonto*) and transfers to the Soviet trade representation only occurred with the permission of the Currency Bureau (*Devisenstelle*).[68] The German Fur Merchants Association in Leipzig noted that this discriminated against the smaller firms in the district: "The new arrangement, as it resulted from payment agreements with Russia, is not to the benefit for the entire sector as it will obstruct the import of furs from Russia for middle and small-sized firms rather to the few larger firms which import from Russia and which have already concluded large deals before 15.02.1935."[69]

Economic exigencies, the migration of the Jews, and the restrictions on the foreign trade eroded the trade in Leipzig to such an extent that it is questionable whether one can still characterise the local fur industry as an

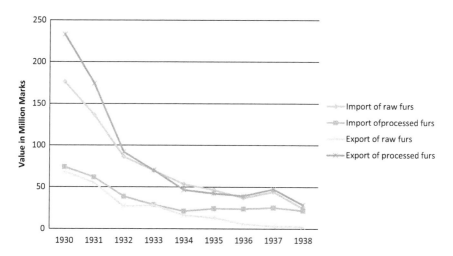

Figure 10.2 Import and Export of Furs (Raw and Manufactured) in Germany (1930–1938)

industrial district. Is it still valid to speak of the fur industry in terms of the defining aspects of the industrial district, like local collaboration, mutual learning, and a balanced size distribution between primarily small and medium-sized firms? It is a question that cannot be unequivocally answered: firms continued to construct collaborative networks but developments in the early 1930s had undoubtedly disrupted size distribution in the district. In terms of the latter, there is little doubt about the fact that Theodor Thorer was now the largest firm and the only one remaining of international importance, whereas the district was previously characterised by few lead firms and an arena of successful smaller businesses. This imbalance eventually led to a countermovement from the smaller firms. In October 1939, several of the smaller firms in Leipzig merged into the RIAG (*Rauchwaren Import Actiengesellschaft*), which was based on a starting capital of 1,000,000 RM. These firms shared the motive of competing at the level of the Thorer firm: "Less pronounced, but therefore not a lesser motive, is a certain unease about the superior position of the company Theodor Thorer on the Brühl. With all due respect to the person of Mr. Hollender and his services to the fur industry, the superiority of his company is uncomfortably felt by all other fur dealers. The deliberation to occasionally form an approximately equal partner is likely to have caused the idea of the merger of several companies into a larger company in the first place."[70]

On the other hand, collective action continued to structure business behaviour in the industrial district, whether carried out by new initiatives or old institutions. Most of these initiatives had however a modest impact. In 1935, the Leipzig Fur Merchants Association closed a deal with Lufthansa, which offered temporary lower rates for airfreight. The Fur Merchants Association hoped that its members would make use of the rapidly expanding airport. After 1935, Lufthansa organised night transports from Russia to Leipzig for use by the fur industry.[71] Another example was the somewhat surprising involvement of several Leipzig firms in the creation of a shipping company, the Nordmeer Studien und Reederei GmbH. The company, with a jointly invested capital base of 160,000 RM, was created in order to organise seal hunting in the North Sea and the Atlantic Ocean. The joint venture consisted of 35 firms in Leipzig, including Theodor Thorer.[72]

It would be easy to conclude that the Second World War, the destruction of the Brühl in 1943, and the collectivisation of the private fur industry by the DDR (*Deutsche Demokratische Republik*, or East Germany) was the end of the story of the Leipzig industrial district. This is true in a literal sense, although some 'fur companies' remained active in Leipzig after collectivisation in the DDR. The "Leipzig model," in which the fur commerce and industry had organically grown through the proximity of firms, inspired post-war reconstruction policy at the local level. A clone of the Brühl was created in Frankfurt am Main. The city attracted many of the German fur traders and industrialists who left the Soviet occupation zone. Frankfurt was also home to former influential members of the industrial district. In 1946, Walter Leiske, the former member of the Leipzig council and one of the masterminds behind the International Fur Exhibition, was appointed president of the Chamber of Commerce in Frankfurt.[73] Leiske, who had nurtured the idea to develop regional economics in central Germany, demonstrated a similarly creative attitude towards the local economy when he subsequently became mayor of Frankfurt. He was successful in luring Leipzig entrepreneurs to his new home. The book-printing and, to a lesser extent, the fur industry were successfully transplanted there. In 1946, Paul Hollender purchased an old leather manufactory in Offenbach, close to Frankfurt, and established a new firm called Thorer and Hollender KG. Other Leipzig firms were said to have established businesses in the Niddastrasse, close to the railway station. With the support of the town hall, the Leipzigers in Frankfurt revived their old trade institutions. One of them was an annual Frankfurt fur fair; as with the Leipzig fair, the new institution took place in the first week after Easter.[74] Moreover, attempts were also made to reconstruct international links. Thorer restored its branches in London, New York, and South Africa. In the summer of 1950, Hollender died in an accident while on a business trip in South Africa and Namibia.

The history of the remarkable transplantation of the Leipzig printing and fur industries, their impact upon the post-war economic recovery, and

Photograph 10.1 The Thorer Company Buildings after the Bombing of Leipzig, December 1943. With permission of the Stadtarchiv Leipzig (BA 1977, nr. 1187).

the extent to which Leipzig arrangements were reconstructed in Frankfurt remains to be written. The same goes for the historical trajectories of decentralised economic activities and the impact they had on future policy makers and a new generation of entrepreneurs in rebuilding the post-war German economy. More generally, the legacy of such historical and organically grown production systems in processes of industrial reconversion remains opens for future research projects that can link history writing with contemporary economics, geography, and politics.

Notes

1 Paulus, *Kommunale Wohlfahrtspolitik in Leipzig 1930 bis 1945*, 24.
2 Ibid., 23–4.
3 Riedel, *Chronik der Stadt Leipzig*, 105.
4 Statistisches Jahrbuch für das Land Sachsen, 1931/34, nr. 34, p. 161. Figures are based on the industrial census held on 16 June 1933.
5 Kindleberger, *The World in Depression, 1929–1939*, 91–4.
6 StA-L, Dresdner Bank in Leipzig 21018, nr. 108, Bericht Reichsverband der Deutschen Rauchwarenfirmen Leipzig E.v. 04.01.1933.
7 Der Rauchwarenmarkt, nr. 30. 15.04.1933. Eitingon Geschäftsverlust für 1932. s.p.
8 StA-L, Dresdner Bank in Leipzig 21018, nr. 269. Dresdner Bank in Leipzig an den Herrn Präsidenten des Landesfinanzamts Leipzig, als Stelle für Devisenbewertung. Leipzig, den 01.12.1932.
9 StA-L, Dresdner Bank in Leipzig 21018, nr. 313. Eitingon schild Co. Inc. Leipzig, 21.10.1931.
10 Sächs. HStA, Wirtschaftsministerium 11168, nr. 799, ff. 62–3. 26.02.1931.
11 BArch, Reichskommissar bei der Berliner Börse, R 3103, nr. 565. Akten betreffend (. . .)Walter AG.
12 Sta-L, Dresdner Bank in Leipzig 21018, nr. 477, f. 31.
13 Pohl and Raab-Rebentisch, *Die Deutsche Bank in Leipzig*, 93.
14 StA-L, Deutsche Bank, Filiale Leipzig 21017, nr. 546, Aktennotiz. 20.02.1931.
15 StA-L, Deutsche Bank, Filiale Leipzig 21017, nr. 209. Betr. J. Ariowitsch, 1.12.1932.
16 StA-L, Deutsche Bank, Filiale Leipzig 21017, nr. 339. Goldstaub, Semi and Eugen Naumann. 04.02.1931.
17 StA-L, Dresdner Bank in Leipzig 21018, nr. 478. Dresdner Bank an die Dresdner Bank in Leipzig. 14.06.1933.
18 StA-L, Deutsche Bank Filiale Leipzig, nr. 549, Kreditakten 1933. Deutsche Bank und Discontogesellschaft an Herrn Oberfinanzpräsident-Devisenstelle, Leipzig. 11.06.1937.
19 Lindenberger, *One Family's Shoah*, 194.
20 Lewis, "Foreign Economic Relations," 206.
21 Dohan, "The Economic Origins of Soviet Autarky 1927/28–1934," 604.
22 Lewis, "Foreign Economic Relations," 209.
23 Gregory, *The Political Economy of Stalinism*, 118–19.
24 Ibid.
25 Sächs. HStA, Aussenministerium 10717, nr. 6772, Abschrift der Eingabe an das Reichswirtschaftministerium 23.08.1930.
26 *Vneshnyaya torgovlya CCCP za 1918–1940 gg.* (Statisticheskiy obzor), chast 2.
27 James, *The End of Globalization*, 159.

28 See in this regard: PA AA, Sonderreferat Wirtschaft R 94389. Auszüge aus: Berliner Börsen Courier, 25.09.1930.
29 Sächs. HStA, Wirtschaftsministerium 11168, nr. 630, f. 26 Abschrift. 19.08.1930.
30 Sächs. HStA, Wirtschaftsministerium 11168, nr. 6772. Beschluss der Vertretung in Berlin 30.06.1932.
31 StadtaL, Kap 66. nr. 18. press clippings: die Ostwirtschaft. Jg. 1932, nr. 4. April 1932, p. 61.
32 StA-L, Dresdner Bank in Leipzig 21018, nr. 75. Durchdruck Leningrader Rauchwarenauktion. 14.03.1933.
33 StA-L, Dresdner Bank in Leipzig, 21018, nr. 82, f. 283.
34 StadtaL, Messeamt Kap. 66. nr. 18., Akten Rauchwarenwirtschaft, Ostwirtschaft. Jg. 1932, nr. 4. April 1932, seite 61.
35 Statistisches Jahrbuch für das Deutsches Reich, 1930, Teil Auswärtiger Handel, p. 233.
36 Ibid.
37 BArch, Akten der Reichskanzlei R 43, Die Kabinette Brüning I und II. Dokumente. Vermerk 29.09.1931.
38 StadtaL, Messeamt Kap.66, nr. 18, Wirtschaftsamt. 6.05.1932.
39 Sächs, HStA, Auswärtiges Amt 10717, nr. 6772. Sächsische Gesandtschaft, Berlin, 14.10.1931.
40 StA-L, Dresdner Bank in Leipzig 21018, nr. 477. Exposé. Leipzig, den 15.2.1930.
41 StA-L, Dresdner Bank in Leipzig, nr. 481, f. 188.
42 Sächs. HStA, Wirtschaftsministerium 11168, nr. 630, f. 199.
43 StadtaL, Messeamt Kap.66, nr. 18. Paul Hollender an OBM: Dr. Goerdeler 12.03.1931.
44 Stadtal, Messeamt Kap 66, nr. 18. Dr. Goerdeler an den Rat der Stadt Leipzig, 13.03.1931.
45 Sächs; HStA, Aussenministerium 10717, nr. 6772. Beschluss der Gesandtschaft Berlin 20.03.1931.
46 Ibid.
47 StadtaL, Messeamt kap 66, nr. 18. Abschrift: im RWM über Reichsfallgarantie am 10.11. 1932.
48 StadtaL, Messeamt kap 66, nr. 18. Wirtschaftsamt. 23.11.1932.
49 StA-L, Dresdner Bank in Leipzig 21018, nr. 220. Leipzig, den 30.01.1933.
50 Riedel, *Chronik der Stadt Leipzig*, 106. The NSDAP also became the largest party in Leipzig, with about 37 % of the votes.
51 StadtaL, Messeamt Kap 66, nr. 18. Leipziger Neueste Nachrichten, 30.03.1933.
52 Ray, *The Canadian Fur Trade in the Industrial Age*, 135.
53 StadtaL, Messeamt Kap 66, Nr. 18, Verband Deutscher Rauchwaren-Zurichtereien und Färbereien, Leipzig an Adolf Hitler, Reichskanzler. 25. 03.1933.
54 Hoffmann, *Carl Goerdeler and the Jewish Question, 1933–1942*, 42; Reich, *Carl Friedrich Goerdeler*, 130.
55 Sächs. HStA. Aussenministerium, 10717, nr. 6772. Nachrichtlich. 28.03.1933.
56 Ibid.
57 Sächs. HStA, Aussenministerium 10717 Nr. 6772. Teilabschrift. 29.4.1933.
58 Hoffmann, *Carl Goerdeler and the Jewish Question, 1933–1942*, 38.
59 Willingham, "Jews In Leipzig: Nationality and Community in the 20th Century," 19. This percentage is much larger when compared to other cities like Frankfurt (19.6%), Konigsberg (8.6%), and Breslau (8.6%).
60 Sta-L, Dresdner Bank in Leipzig, nr. 108, Bericht. 6.02.1934.
61 Ibid.
62 Mosse, *Second Chance*, 22.

63 Simpson, *The Refugee Problem, Report of a Survey*, 142–3.
64 Herbst and Weihe, *Die Commerzbank und die Juden 1933–1945*, 81.
65 Barkai, "Die deutschen Unternehmer und die Judenpolitik im 'Dritten Reich,'" 230.
66 James, *The Nazi Dictatorship and the Deutsche Bank*, 122.
67 Ehler, *Der Leipziger Rauchwarengroßhandel Im Letzten Jahrzehnt*, 148. Ehler estimated that, by 1946, 113 Jewish fur trade firms had moved abroad. These firms represented a business volume of 80 million RM in 1928, 93 million RM in 1929, 57 million RM in 1930, and 60 million RM in 1931.
68 StA-L, Dresdner Bank in Leipzig 21018, nr. 107, Anlage zum Rundschreiben vom 18.02.1935.
69 StA-L, Dresdner Bank in Leipzig 21018, nr. 107. Tätigkeitsbericht Reichsverband Mai 1935.
70 Sta-L, Deutsche Bank in Leipzig 21017, nr. 203. Bericht 14.10.1939.
71 Sta-L, Dresdner Bank in Leipzig 21018, nr. 10, Reichsverband der Deutschen Rauchwarenfirmen. 04.05.1935.
72 StA-L, Deutsche Bank, Filiale Leipzig 21017, nr. 203. Auszug 04.02.1938.
73 Lerner, "Walter Leiske."
74 LAC, RG 25 A 5, volume 1315, file no. T -8–561. Canadian bureau of trade and commerce. 05.05.1953.

References

Barkai, Avraham. "Die deutschen Unternehmer und die Judenpolitik im 'Dritten Reich.'" *Geschichte und Gesellschaft* 15 (1989): 227–47.

Dohan, Michael Repplier. "The Economic Origins of Soviet Autarky 1927/28–1934." *Slavic Review* 35, no. 4 (December 1, 1976): 603–35.

Ehler, Karl-Heinz. *Der Leipziger Rauchwarengroßhandel Im Letzten Jahrzehnt.* Leipzig: Buske, 1938.

Gregory, Paul R. *The Political Economy of Stalinism: Evidence From the Soviet Secret Archives.* Cambridge, UK: Cambridge University Press, 2004.

Herbst, Ludolf, and Thomas Weihe. *Die Commerzbank und die Juden 1933–1945.* München: C. H. Beck, 2004.

Hoffmann, Peter. *Carl Goerdeler and the Jewish Question, 1933–1942.* Cambridge, UK: Cambridge University Press, 2011.

James, Harold. *The End of Globalization: Lessons From the Great Depression.* Cambridge, MA: Harvard University Press, 2001.

———. *The Nazi Dictatorship and the Deutsche Bank.* Cambridge, UK: Cambridge University Press, 2004.

Kindleberger, Charles Poor. *The World in Depression, 1929–1939.* Berkeley: University of California Press, 1986.

Lerner, Franz. "Walter Leiske." *Neue Deutsche Biographie.* Accessed September 9, 2013. www.deutsche-biographie.de/sfz50049.html.

Lewis, Robert. "Foreign Economic Relations." In *The Economic Transformation of the Soviet Union, 1913–1945*, edited by R.W. Davies, Mark Harrison, and S.G. Wheatcroft, 198–216. Cambridge, UK: Cambridge University Press, 1994.

Lindenberger, Herbert. *One Family's Shoah: Victimization, Resistance, Survival in Nazi Europe.* New York: Palgrave Macmillan, 2013.

Mosse, Werner Eugen. *Second Chance: Two Centuries of German-Speaking Jews in the United Kingdom.* Tübingen: J. C. B. Mohr, 1991.

Paulus, Julia. *Kommunale Wohlfahrtspolitik in Leipzig 1930 bis 1945: autoritäres Krisenmanagement zwischen Selbstbehauptung und Vereinnahmung.* Köln: Böhlau, 1998.

Pohl, Manfred, and Angelika Raab-Rebentisch. *Die Deutsche Bank in Leipzig: 1901–2001.* München: Piper, 2001.

Ray, Arthur J. *The Canadian Fur Trade in the Industrial Age.* Toronto: University of Toronto Press, 1990.

Reich, Ines. *Carl Friedrich Goerdeler: ein Oberbürgermeister gegen den NS-Staat.* Köln: Böhlau, 1997.

Riedel, Horst. *Chronik der Stadt Leipzig: 2500 Ereignisse in Wort und Bild.* Gudensberg-Gleichen: Wartberg, 2001.

Simpson, John Hope. *The Refugee Problem, Report of a Survey.* London: Oxford University Press, 1939.

Willingham, Robert Allen. "Jews in Leipzig: Nationality and Community in the 20th Century." The University of Texas, 2005.

11 Conclusion

In this book, I have addressed the apparent paradox of the historical persistence of decentralised economic organisation in Saxony, marked by the concentration of large numbers of small to medium-sized and highly specialised firms, when the region was simultaneously at the forefront of processes of globalisation. In other words, why did a decentralised production system in Saxony prevail despite being the 'storm centre of trade cycles'? This problem was the foundation for the study of the history of the fur industry in Leipzig between 1880 and 1939, as the global centre of the international fur industry was marked by a decentralised business structure. The Leipzig fur capital emerged during the long nineteenth century as an industrial district and it was one of the most open sectors in Saxony. The Leipzig fur industry depended on the organisation of transborder activities for the supply of resources whilst also being open to export markets. I conducted the research in order to remedy the lack of understanding of how regional business systems interact with the outside world. It was argued that historical research has not yet fully taken into account the position of industrial districts within the global economy since industrial districts have usually been discussed within the debate about the history of industrialisation. The research lacuna relates to the internationalisation of the firms in the district on the one hand and the impact of macroeconomic developments on the industrial district on the other.

The International Roots of the Fur Capital

One conclusion to surface in this research is that the assumed mismatch between regional systems and world market openness does not adequately capture the interaction between the industrial district and the outside world. The industrial district in Leipzig did not grow in spite of its transnational connections and world market dependency, but because of it. The life cycle of the district was inextricably connected to the expansion and contraction of the international fur business. The growth and consolidation of the industrial district in Leipzig was to a large extent due to the expansion of international trade in the long nineteenth century whereas its demise was caused by the economic turmoil of the 1930s. The initial growth of the industrial district required little protection from external forces since global manufacturing was in its initial stages. The industrial district managed to emerge in Leipzig because of the city's historical role as a trade centre in furs and its successful entry into a phase where capitalist business came to dominate the global trade. The growth of the district coincided with the boom in world market prices and global competition after 1900. Even after World War I, the firms of the district managed to re-integrate themselves into the flows of world trade. Only in the 1930s did the impact of macro-economic and geopolitical changes prove too disruptive for the district to reproduce itself.

In other words, the importance of transborder activities and transnational connections lay at the very roots of the industrial district. Saxony as a region stood at the forefront of global economic interdependencies that were created by the forceful impact of revolutionary transportation methods, new patterns of human mobility, and the economic boom that typified the long nineteenth century. International railroad networks replaced river shipping and the wandering merchants that had previously joined Saxony to Russia. Human mobility in particular stimulated the formation of the district. Artisans came to Leipzig in the wake of freedom of commerce in 1861, epitomising internal mobility in Germany. The currents of modern mass migration brought entrepreneurs of Jewish origin who connected Leipzig more firmly with the trade in the East. These migration movements helped transform the local fur industry into an industrial cluster.

The phenomenon of national and transnational entrepreneurship was at the root of the industrial district. Whereas first-generation merchants drew on international networks in order to organise the procurement of raw furs, the tremendous possibilities proffered by the conquest of foreign markets lay within the reach of expanding Leipzig fur manufacturing. Transnational entrepreneurship led to the capture of the Brussels and (possibly) the Paris market for processed German furs. In particular, transborder business activities between Leipzig and Brussels were successfully managed through personal connections with members of the immigrant community in Brussels. The organisation of transborder activities through transnational entrepreneurs had a twofold advantage for the firms in Leipzig. Firstly, foreign business adventures were costly affairs and so it made economic sense to consider the option of partnerships with furriers or entrepreneurs on the move. This practice enabled smaller firms to participate in transborder activities. Secondly, this alternative form of transborder business activities kept decentralised activities in the district intact. Entrepreneurs profited from links with foreign markets without having to expand the organisational basis of the firm. By utilising transnational entrepreneurship, the social structure of the district was maintained and patterns of concentration that usually go hand in hand with increases in scale were avoided.

Whereas transnational entrepreneurship signified a viable alternative to firm branching, especially in proximate markets, several district firms did however assume a multinational organisation, in particular the 'lead firms' of Leipzig. However, multinational organisations of Leipzig fur firms were structured through family connections. Branches emerged in important fur centres like New York, London, and Moscow and were usually run by sons and brothers of the firm owner in Leipzig. Through kinship rather than managerial pressure, the link of the firm with Leipzig remained central in the affairs of the business. Even in the 1920s, family multinationals remained organised in such a way that the Leipzig division retained the status as the head office in the family firm network. Only particular circumstances, like the personal and unforeseen ambitions of family members, disturbed the balance in the multinational organisation of the Leipzig businesses. In general, the pursuit of internationalisation through multinational business organisation left local attachment and district participation largely unaffected. In sum, the translocal activities of the industrial district should be conceptualised along lines of scale, even in multinational organisations. Key drivers of transborder connections were individuals, family members, former labourers, or acquaintances.

By emphasising personal connections, this book has added to a growing body of literature that stresses the important yet understudied layers of economic globalisation at the 'micro level,' concealed in a web of transnational ties between a multitude of smaller businesses, brokers, migrants, representatives, and travelling merchants. The organisation of such transnational ties is hard to reconstruct. In unravelling the many links that connected the firms in Leipzig to the outside world, the almost momentary and fragile character of translocal activities should be stressed. Small offices abroad were easily abandoned, partnerships with brokers as easily set up as cancelled. Agents resided in a particular area for as long as it was interesting. The presence of Leipzig firms abroad did not leave an indelible print on the cities in which they settled, in contrast to the presence of multinationals in the early twentieth century. Rather, it was shadowy and ephemeral.

Even though ephemeral, global links and transnational connections were remarkably robust. After World War I, most of the largest Leipzig fur firms were able to restore their presence in foreign fur centres. Unlike larger firms that suffered from sequestration, the physical removal of representation and low-asset branches abroad did not constitute an insurmountable loss. Furthermore, despite the state monopolisation of foreign trade in the USSR, the Siberian trade was characterised by a continuity of personal connections. Some of the Jewish merchants of foreign descent in Leipzig profited from having a nationality other than the German. This is an argument that has been stressed particularly within the context of the Russian trade, where officials of the state agencies were often the same men that ran the tsarist business. Therefore, the scale of translocal connectivity remained situated, to a large extent, on the level of personal connections. In any case, the particular issue of former 'capitalists' in the garb of state officials and their links to foreign business during the early years of the Soviet Union certainly deserves further research.

The Power of Collective Action: Adaptation or Modification?

Aside from the robustness of personal connections in fabricating transnational ties, this research has also put forward the hypothesis that the industrial district built up capacities to deal with exogenous pressures. Economic actors of the industrial district used the same resources that coordinated its internal system of decentralised production, like collective action and collaboration, to adapt to external challenges and to participate in processes of internationalisation. The same local collaborative mechanisms that characterised the success of districts in the industrialising world, the argument ran, shaped the interaction between the district and the outside world.

The capacity to adapt to global competition or macroeconomic challenges was indeed a major source for dynamism in the industrial district. The industrial district did not simply follow the tides of expansion of the international fur business. On the contrary, it managed to adapt at several crucial moments of intensified competition and contraction in international trade. Firstly, the flexibility of the local financial market in Leipzig and the networks between bankers and businessmen in the district allowed the firms to pursue an expansive policy at the turn of the century. At that time, businesses and banks in Leipzig adapted to world market prices that were virtually exploding both in the Siberian and in the North American market segments. After World War I, the nexus between local banks and the fur industry continued on largely the same lines. With a generous credit policy, local bankers allowed the Leipzig fur industry to pursue an expansive international strategy. The banks have therefore been portrayed as economic actors that were closely related to the fur district. Secondly, the Leipzig fur industry adapted to a major modification in the international fur business, namely the establishment of state capitalism in the Soviet Union, most particularly in the case of the foreign trade monopoly. Firms in the district jointly created auction companies, a new sales mechanism especially designed to lubricate deals with the Soviets trade agencies.

What can we learn from the historical trajectories of the industrial district that resulted from external challenges? Firstly, the importance of the 'lead firms' has been stressed. Literature on the industrial district has focused on the individual strategies of lead firms in their creation of links between the industrial district and the outside world. This dimension is certainly true for our case as well. Nevertheless, lead firms were also involved in, and initiated processes of, collaboration and collective action. Secondly, there is an important distinction to be made in the nature of collective action between that which adapts to changes and that which seeks to create alternatives to global problems and the modification of the international system. Certainly, external challenges led to increased collaboration and both categories share the aim to remedy the effects of macroeconomic changes. However, collective action can be adaptive to external challenges in the sense that local institutions are re-modified. The examples given above belong to the latter category. The bank-business nexus adjusted to the financial require-ments for foreign trade and the auction company replaced the Leipzig trade fairs, one of the most important regional institutions. The system of trading on the fairs had become increasingly redundant and therefore firms jointly created new market institutions capable of accommodating changes on the world market.

Collective action can also be the stage for alternatives and the modifica-tion of the supply chain in order to alleviate external pressures. The creation of a new international order in the International Exhibition and Congress in Leipzig was probably the most ambitious form of collective action in the district. The exhibition was not a response to a specific event but rather was designed by Leipzig businessmen to create new mechanisms for inter-national business coordination and to jointly promote the Leipzig business world to a national and international public. New production paradigms featured prominently as alternative projects, entailing the creation of new supply lines that lightened the dependency of the industrial district on the 'capriciousness' of the world market. However, this happened only in extreme circumstances. Processes of resource substitution were introduced during World War I, when the industrial district was separated from the world market. Immediately after the war, when the revival of international trade was still in the distant future, businessmen set their hearts on the cre-ation of fur farming in Germany. Such alternative production paradigms were hard to realise and lost support when firms in the district re-oriented themselves towards the more accessible world market. Moreover, strategies of modification and adaptation could even go hand in hand. Several firms participated in both adaptive and alternative projects. Finally, however, cre-ative collective action is not a guarantee of effectiveness. Certainly, district firms were diligent in creating new projects, but since every single partici-pant could profit from the result of collective actions, participation often failed to reach higher levels.

I would like to formulate some additional remarks with regard to the capacity of the industrial district to deal with external challenges. Firstly, the progressive expansion of collective action had ramifications for the spatial extent of collaborative networks. Evidence has been provided that firms in the district cast a much wider net in terms of collaborative networks. Processes of collaboration were not limited to proximate actors. This was certainly the case in the creation of new production paradigms. Firms in Leipzig created links with the imperial state for the introduction of fur farm-ing in the colonies. In the 1920s, the firms created a research institution in Leipzig that was set up primarily to extract advantages from the creation of fur farming in Germany. Businessmen were able to assemble a strong network that not only profited from the opening of the veterinary faculty of the Leipzig University but also assembled some of the leading agricul-tural experts across Germany's academic landscape. The epicentre of the network was undoubtedly regional, yet it also included the support of leading national scientists.

Secondly, processes of adaptation had ramifications for the local organisation of business. Although solidarity was an important motive, local collaboration forged imbalances or asymmetries within the industrial district. In particular, the growing prominence of the financial sector in the industrial district generated such asymmetries. Banks have an important function in local business entities as the credit market sets the framework for local business growth and strategies. However, the clustering of local banking and fur businesses in Leipzig took on peculiar proportions. Due to the growing financial requirements of the international fur market, the local bank system gradually extended its role as financier of these international operations. The lenient lending market allowed the firms to expand their activities on the international stage before and after the war. The heavy losses incurred by the local banking sector in the wake of the economic meltdown in 1929 demonstrated how unhealthy local clustering of finance and business was. Instead of purifying the district with moderate credit rules and restricting dependency on foreign trade, the leniency of the credit market created a fur industry bubble. Once the international expansion halted, banks corrected lending conditions abruptly, which then disrupted the size distribution of firms in the industrial district. Local bank policy was therefore neither moderate nor consistent, reinforcing upward but also exacerbating downward trends. Due to their involvement in the auction companies, several of the local banks stepped out of their traditional field of financial activities. A few banks became actively involved in fur trading, thereby further expanding bank activities that were dependent upon the international fur market. Furthermore, the growing importance of bankers in the process of wholesale auctioning meant a decline of entrepreneurial power in fur commerce.

An important conclusion seems to be the presence of a common goal as the precondition of collective action. Whereas individual business needs are translated into strategies by the business leader and management, the identification of external threats and their translation into a common goal is largely an invisible matter. It is based upon a sense of local belonging, of being part of a business group in which individual businesses are faced with similar problems. The translation of such a sense of belonging into collective action is to be ascribed to a broad range of institutions, in particular the trade press and collective bodies like trade associations. A number of individuals such as local politicians, prominent businesses, and lead firms also exerted such a function. These actors created a mindset suited for initiating processes of local collaboration. One of the most meaningful mindsets that enabled collective action was the so-called 'comeback' notion, which described the collective desire to reclaim the leading position of the Leipzig industry as an international fur trade and manufacturing centre after World War I. The 're-admission strategy,' or rather strategies, that stemmed from the comeback notion reveals that the industrial district existed in the mindset of contemporaries. The 're-admission strategy' got traction from the end of the war as a concept that was collectively discussed by city officials, businessmen, and other economic actors. The 'restoration discourse,' as vague and incoherent as it often sounded, structured collective action and solidarity mechanisms. The goal of re-admission allowed for businessmen to conceptualise the local as a business strategy within the context of their international activities. This intangible point of departure very much illustrates that the joint ventures, trade consortia, auction companies, and exhibitions are social constructions.

Furthermore, the pursuit of world market re-admission as a common goal highlights the problem of periodisation of economic globalisation from an actor-oriented perspective. Much of the academic debate nowadays centres on the question of whether World War I formed a rupture in terms of world economic integration. Even if there were major differences in economic organisation before and after World War I, I would like to open the debate here on whether pre-war idealisations, or "pressures of continuity," in the post-war period played a much larger role in international business strategies than hitherto assumed. Collective action in the district was strongly inspired by the aim to restore old pre-war connections, especially in regards to the Russian trade. What did such visions mean for other economic actors in between the wars? Did this orient business behaviour throughout Europe or were 'pre-war idealisations' something specifically German? The predisposition of economic actors towards restoring 'the old' may be an aspect in the robustness of global networks, collective action, and post-war business patterns that is perhaps too easily overlooked.

The Construction of the World Market: The Local and the Global

A final question that needs to be addressed here concerns the parts and the whole. In what ways was the small cosmos of entrepreneurs in the industrial district constitutive of the structures of world trade? The way in which the macro and micro levels interact remains a thorny issue. To begin with, this book adheres to the view that markets are, just like industrial districts, social constructions. Generally, the transnational dimension of local business practices and collective action on the macro level has been stressed in this book. Such a transnational view has been put forward by using the concept of the commodity chain. Due to processes of entanglement, the organisation and practices embedded in local structures interacted with the way in which market transactions were organised and strongly influenced the spatial and economic organisation of the international fur trade.

Firstly, on the level of individual businesses, lead firms in the district with their highly mobile personnel were usually lead firms in the governance of the commodity chain as well, especially prior to World War I. To a large extent, the fur merchants in Leipzig set the parameters of trade in the Siberian commodity chain. Individuals, merchants, and businessmen lent trust and shaped market transactions. These merchants had adjusted themselves to Russian credit preferences, possessed great knowledge of the market, and had contacts inside Russia: they were therefore in a position to dominate the internal market. Moreover, the organisation of the international fur trade by individuals was robust and created long-lasting dependencies and ties. The German-Soviet fur trade was initially based on personal contacts between German traders and former tsarist traders. In addition, the Leipzig fur industry was able to coordinate with the early phase of Soviet state capitalism by adjusting its underlying institutions. The importance of fur trading in the economic recovery of the Soviet Union was made possible by the connections, persons, firms, and institutions that had shaped its foreign fur trade. Especially in the second half of the 1920s, the ties between the strategically important Soviet fur trade and the local industry in Leipzig were inextricably close.

Not only did the actions of individuals determine the trade flows but collective action in the district also shaped the geography of the global commodity chain. This was especially the case for fur farming by Leipzig firms. Certainly, the fur industry became less global because of resource substitution through fur farming. Nevertheless, although fur farming was meant to replace global supply chains, it incorporated new geographies and social contexts into the world market of furs. Fur farming as initiated by the Leipzig fur industry brought the arid pastures of South West Africa, colonised by German farmers and Boers, within the structures of world trade. Furthermore, fur farming was responsible for the regionalisation of the fur trade and incorporated farming in old producing areas like North America and 'new' ones like Scandinavia. The construction of new market institutions in Leipzig as joint ventures, such as the auction companies, cemented these spatial developments.

In itself, the concentration of the fur business in the industrial district also contributed to the spatial distribution of the international fur business. The fur trade not only occupied immense frontier spaces but was also at the same time densely concentrated in a limited number of markets in city regions like Leipzig, London, and New York. Subarctic resource frontiers supplied several international centres where trading was connected to manufacturing and from whence distribution links spread across a hinterland. The emergence, regeneration, and decline of trade within city markets determined the structure of the international fur trade and manufacturing. The transformation of cities or city regions into fur capitals was determined to a large extent by their market institutions. Salient were the organisation and modification of large-scale sales event, like fairs and auctions, by local actors. These institutions enabled the temporary concentration of the international trading community, or at least a substantial part of it, and organised the supply of raw material to manufacturers. Tremendous benefits were derived from the fact that a large portion of the international community was brought together in these instances. It made the international fur trade predictable, had an influence on price-setting mechanisms, and generated learning effects in local firms. Thus, Leipzig's market institutions, which were formed regionally and locally by collective action, gave shape to the geography of world trade. It helped maintain the structures of the international fur business, divided into frontiers, hinterlands, and dominant city markets.

Since the political economy of the international fur trade was initially a matter of competition between fur centres, regional politics and local action had a strong influence upon the course of the world market. Global competition existed in the sense that local actors in fur markets actively remodelled institutions. This political economy was pronounced during the interwar period when firms and local administrations more consciously constructed market institutions that reinforced the position of their centres. At this time, awareness about the malleability of market institutions was 'discovered' by local stakeholders throughout the world and also in Leipzig. The intervention of regional and local administration also became more frequent. The city administration in particular favoured the creation of new economic institutions as part of a wider regional economic policy. However, this locally managed political economy in furs was increasingly overrun by state capitalism and modifications to the international political economy, especially in the period between the wars. When Stalin's new economic order replaced the NEP and state-led protectionism gained the upper hand, the regional and local institutions through which the Leipzig firms governed the chain proved ineffective. National and international political considerations came to rule over transnational business practices and exogenous effects could no longer be remedied effectively by local and regional action.

The intrusion of state capitalism that heralded the marginalisation of regional economic policy and the disruptive impact of economic protectionism on the industrial district may be valid lessons as well. In particular, it seems to throw new light on the nature of contemporary exogenous challenges on the industrial district. For instance, contemporary political strategies in the EU, as can be seen in texts like the Regions 2020 or the Small Business Act of 2008, seem to focus on protecting regional business structures from global challenges and stimulating international expansion of small and medium-sized business. However, is this focus correct? To a large extent, historical actors and businesses in industrial districts were able to construct their own mechanisms for internationalisation and capacities to resist exogenous pressures. However, the industrial district seemed unable to cope with the rise of state capitalism, especially after 1930. Whereas the first phase of state capitalism in the USSR, in the garb of the NEP, already brought radical modifications to the industrial district, the political economic developments of the 1930s could not be remedied by local and regional collective action. By no means do I want to draw a literal parallel between the 1930s and the current situation. Nevertheless, many have argued that state capitalism in the contemporary world economy is on the rise again, especially after the economic crisis of 2008 and seems to be given analytical priority over earlier conceptions like the flattening world and economic globalisation.[1] For the last couple of years, Europe and Russia have been waging an escalating trade war, for example, which submerges business interests to political considerations. The main challenge to contemporary industrial districts or regional small businesses in Europe seems to come from the renaissance of state capitalism and the discordance in scale when regional economies deal with international political considerations. The real task for supranational administrations like the European Union is perhaps not so much located in what it defines as 'global competition' but in protecting regional small business from calculated political considerations produced by state capitalism.

Having discussed the interaction between the industrial district and the outside world, I would like to write a few final words on processes of incorporation and the spatial expansions and contractions of the world economy. Incorporation processes are (correctly) often seen through the lens of frontier perspectives and have dealt with the question of how remote entities or non-capitalist structures were integrated into the world economy. However, not only frontier regions are incorporated into global capitalism. It seems important to note that the core was far from a monolithic entity and that 'core structures' like industrial districts or industrial regions in the world economy underwent processes of incorporation and disconnection too. The core of the world economy is marked by heterogeneity, harbouring very dynamic entities that follow a life cycle connected to the expansion and contraction of global commerce. Regions and business communities can be disconnected even though spatially they are located at the 'heart of global capitalism,' and thus become frontiers of capitalism once again. Furthermore, entities in the core of the world economy share with their frontier counterparts aspects of communal agency within processes of incorporation. Small communities in both contexts were constituent of world market integration as well and were able to 'negotiate' their integration in the world market to a certain extent. In addition, incorporation processes are not always to be seen within the dichotomy of frontiers or communities against the system. A commodity chain perspective makes clear that incorporation was not always a process that connected 'a system' and a community but is rather the connection of multiple geographically disparate communities and social systems in frontiers as well as 'core' regions of the world economy. Core entities were relying on new connections too and processes of industrial decline were caused in part by disconnection. Fortunately, the complicated fabric of global capitalism can be unearthed by scrutinizing the creativity of local economic actors.

Note

1 Abdelal, "The Profits of Power."

Reference

Abdelal, Rawi. "The Profits of Power: Commerce and Realpolitik in Eurasia." *Review of International Political Economy* 20, no. 3 (2013): 421–56.

Index

For Product Safety Concerns and Information please contact our EU
representative GPSR@taylorandfrancis.com
Taylor & Francis Verlag GmbH, Kaufingerstraße 24, 80331 München, Germany

www.ingramcontent.com/pod-product-compliance
Ingram Content Group UK Ltd.
Pitfield, Milton Keynes, MK11 3LW, UK
UKHW020939180425
457613UK00019B/475